Modernization Frustrated

The Politics of Industrial Decline in Britain Since 1900

Scott Newton and Dilwyn Porter

Routledge Revivals
Routledge
Taylor & Francis Group

First published in 1988
by Unwin Hyman Ltd

This edition first published in 2026 by Routledge
4 Park Square, Milton Park, Abingdon, Oxon, OX14 4RN

and by Routledge
605 Third Avenue, New York, NY 10158

Routledge is an imprint of the Taylor & Francis Group, an informa business

Publisher's Note
The publisher has gone to great lengths to ensure the quality of this reprint but points out that some imperfections in the original copies may be apparent.

Disclaimer
The publisher has made every effort to trace copyright holders and welcomes correspondence from those they have been unable to contact.

For Product Safety Concerns and Information please contact our EU representative GPSR@taylorandfrancis.com. Taylor & Francis Verlag GmbH, Kaufingerstraße 24, 80331 München, Germany

A Library of Congress record exists under LCCN: 87026555

ISBN: 978-1-041-16987-1 (hbk)
ISBN: 978-1-003-68738-2 (ebk)
ISBN: 978-1-041-16991-8 (pbk)

Book DOI 10.4324/9781003687382

MODERNIZATION FRUSTRATED

The Politics of Industrial Decline in Britain since 1900

Scott Newton
University College, Cardiff
and
Dilwyn Porter
Worcester College of Higher Education

London
UNWIN HYMAN
Boston Sydney Wellington

Published by the Academic Division of
Unwin Hyman Ltd
15/17 Broadwick Street, London W1V 1FP, UK

Allen & Unwin Inc.,
8 Winchester Place, Winchester, Mass. 01890, USA

Allen & Unwin (Australia) Ltd,
8 Napier Street, North Sydney, NSW 2060, Australia

Allen & Unwin (New Zealand) Ltd in association with the
Port Nicholson Press Ltd,
60 Cambridge Terrace, Wellington, New Zealand

First published in 1988

British Library Cataloguing in Publication Data

Newton, Scott
Modernization Frustrated. The Politics of Industrial Decline in Britain since 1900
1. Great Britain—Industries—History—20th century
I. Title II. Porter, Dilwyn
338.0941 HC256.6
ISBN 0-04-322012-6
ISBN 0-04-322013-4 Pbk

Library of Congress Cataloging in Publication Data

Newton, Scott, 1956–
Modernization Frustrated. The Politics of Industrial Decline in Britain since 1900/Scott Newton, Dilwyn Porter.
p. cm.
Bibliography: p.
Includes index.
ISBN 0-04-322012-C (alk. paper). ISBN 0-04-322013-4 (pbk.: alk. paper)
1. Industry and state—Great Britain—History—20th century.
2. Great Britain—Economic conditions—20th century.
3. Great Britain—Politics and government—20th century.
I. Porter, Dilwyn, 1947– . II. Title
HD3616.G72N48 1988
338.941—dc19

Typeset in 10 on 12 point Palatino by Fotographics (Bedford) Ltd
and printed in Great Britain by Billing and Son, London and Worcester

Preface to the Reissue

The question of Britain's 'decline' from great power status in the nineteenth and early twentieth centuries became a topic of lively debate between journalists and politicians of all political colours during the post-World War Two era. In 1945 the country had been one of the victorious 'Big Three' powers, the others being the United States and the Soviet Union. From the mid-1950s, however, Britain suffered a series of setbacks which gradually eroded its elevated international status. First, there was the humiliating outcome of the Suez Crisis (1956). Then came the abandonment of the Blue Streak medium range ballistic missile system, Britain's attempt to build its own independent nuclear deterrent (1960). The British economy, meanwhile, consistently failed to match the achievements of key economic competitors, above all the six members of the European Economic Community established in 1958. British industry's share of global trade contracted. Persistent external deficits led to repeated sterling crises, culminating in the devaluation of the currency in 1967. By the late 1960s it was clear that the UK lacked the means to project its influence on a global scale, and it began a strategic withdrawal from the Far and Middle East, regions once dominated by British power. By the mid-1970s Britain was one of several advanced capitalist states, which now included France, West Germany, and Japan, but it was clear that all of its major competitors had enjoyed consistently higher and smoother levels of annual GDP growth than the UK.

Successive governments after 1959 sought to identify the causes and to find the means to reverse this 'descent from power'[1], with different levels of success (or failure). By the 1980s, historians had joined the argument about decline with their own attempts to explain what some considered a historical process akin to the collapse of ancient Rome or the waning of Imperial Spain. The resulting literature was extensive and of variable quality. It did include, however, the controversial and seminal contributions of

Tom Nairn (*The Break-Up of Britain*), Martin Wiener (*English Culture and the Decline of the Industrial Spirit*), and Correlli Barnett (*The Audit of War*).[2] Although there was no consensus around what had led to Britain's descent, the works of Wiener and Barnett did find favour with Conservative politicians looking to revive what they considered an etiolated entrepreneurial culture.[3]

Modernization Frustrated was written as a contribution to this debate. It was, perhaps, as one reviewer suggested, 'the first study to trace the adverse influence on industrial growth of Britain's distinctive political and financial institutions over an extended period.'[4]

David Edgerton, reflecting on 'declinism' from the vantage point of the late 1990s, categorised *Modernization Frustrated* and David Coates's *The Question of U.K. Decline* (1994) as 'political economies of decline'.[5] Our aim, however, had been to make the distinctive argument that *industrial* Britain had experienced a pronounced decline since the late nineteenth century, though this had been uneven and contested, and even reversed between the late 1930s and the early 1950s. Decline, we contended, had not extended to the entire economy, with the development of the *financial and service sectors* being characterised by expansion and prosperity, although once again, this had been uneven and contested and briefly reversed. We argued, moreover, that the root causes of industrial decline were to be found not so much in policy failures or omissions but much more in the nature, organisation and ethos of the British state itself (in what we could now call its DNA).[6] The book focused on the struggles of Britain's producers, and the political forces supporting them, to break away from this historical legacy and transform the nation into an advanced industrial state. It sought to explain why at certain key moments in the twentieth century, often associated with national weakness and even humiliation, the balance of social and political forces became favourable to the success of this project and why its victories were always fragile and never permanent.

Economic historians have frequently pointed out that over time highly industrialised nations tend to undergo 'change in ... sectoral composition. As a stylised fact, the most prominent such change has been a shift from manufacturing towards services'.[7] The consensus view has long been that this is a natural and usually benevolent process.[8] Our book made no attempt to challenge this general proposition, but its argument did, nevertheless, fly in the face of conventional economic wisdom. In writing it our intention was to produce a history which attempted to explain the occurrence of a specific problem. This was why, over the best part of a century, the British experience of the shift away from manufacturing had been extreme and atypical, going a long way beyond what had happened in comparable countries, with disturbing implications for the nation's long-term social cohesion and stability.

As professional historians we were aware of the risk that a book devoted to such a controversial topic could morph into extended op-ed journalism, and it is arguable that some of the text bears the marks of an approach 'based on contemporary, highly politicized and polemical discourses'.[9] Indeed, there is one section in particular which would be written differently were the book being produced now. This is the chapter dealing with the 1964-79 period, which drew heavily on inadequately informed critiques of the Wilson administrations, mostly from disenchanted left-wing commentators. Neither they nor we had access at that time to the government's own papers from the period, notably those from the Treasury, the Prime Minister's office and key Cabinet Committees. These only became available a decade and more after we were writing. The information they contain, along with the investigations of revisionist writers such as Dorril and Ramsay, point to a much more nuanced picture. It is clear that both the economic achievements of these years - the growth figures look much more respectable now than they did 40 years ago - and the sheer structural difficulties encountered by the Wilson and Callaghan governments in particular, in terms both of external economic constraints and of the resistance from within the State apparatus, were very seriously underestimated.[10]

Despite these deficiencies, we stand by the book's analysis of why sustained industrial modernization has been so problematic in the British context. Its general argument and conclusions were unfashionable when *Modernization Frustrated* made its first appearance in April 1988 at the high point of the Lawson boom and this helped to ensure that it made a limited impact. There was, at the time, much optimistic talk of a British 'economic miracle' and interest in the issue of Britain's 'supposed' decline no longer commanded centre stage. A process of 'mental adjustment' was under way and our contribution to the debate received less attention than it might have done if published a few years earlier.[11]

In subsequent decades, however, the process of deindustrialisation and accompanying societal disintegration noted by *Modernization Frustrated* has continued. The decline of manufacturing has been unrelenting. We noted the acceleration of this process at the start of the 1980s, manufacturing's share of GDP falling from 28 per cent in 1972 to 21 per cent in 1984.[12] Since then it has continued to slide, falling to just under 9 per cent in 2023.[13] For some, especially on the left, this remains a continuing source of frustration. 'We can't just be an association of banks with a country attached any more', a leading trade union official recently argued with some passion. 'We need a real economy', he continued, 'with high-tech manufacturing and infrastructure [and] today you can't rely on the market to deliver that.'[14] The current Labour administration has just launched its own industrial strategy and has from time to time spoken of the need to 'reindustrialise Britain'. Whether that can be achieved in the absence of fundamental changes in the nature of the British state remains an open question.

Scott Newton and Dilwyn Porter, July 2025.

Notes

---

[1] This phrase was used by one historian as a book title: see F. S. Northedge, *Descent from Power: British Foreign Policy 1945-73* (Routledge, 1974).

[2] Tom Nairn, *The Break-Up of Britain* (London: Verso, 1977 and 1981); Martin Wiener *English Culture and the Decline of the Industrial Spirit 1859-1980* (Cambridge: Cambridge University Press, 1981); Corelli Barnett, *The Audit of War* (London: Macmillan, 1986).

[3] In 1981, Sir Keith Joseph, Secretary of State for Industry in Margaret Thatcher's Conservative Government, gave every Cabinet Minister a copy of Wiener's book.

[4] Maurice W. Kirby, 'Institutional Rigidities and Britain's Industrial Decline', *Business History Review*, vol. 63, no.4 (Winter 1989), 934.

[5] David Edgerton, 'The Decline of Declinism', *Business History Review*, vol.71, no.2 (Summer 1997), 201. Edgerton's reference here is to David Coates, *The Question of U.K. Decline: State, Society and Economy* (Hemel Hempstead, Harvester, 1994).

[6] See Scott Newton, 'Historical Notes on Tom Nairn and the British State', *Lobster Magazine*, 85 (2023), https://www.lobster-magazine.co.uk/article/issue/85/historical-notes-on-tom-nairn-and-the-british-state/

[7] Fiona Tregenna, 'A new theoretical analysis of deindustrialisation', *Cambridge Journal of Economics*, Volume 38, Issue 6, November 2014, Pages 1373–1390.

[8] See Robert Rowthorne and Ramana Ramaswamy, 'Deindustrialisation - Its Causes and Implications', *Economic Issues no. 10* (Washington: International Monetary Fund, 1997), for a clear exposition of this argument.

[9] A point made by Jim Tomlinson, 'Thrice Denied: 'Declinism' as a Recurrent Theme in British History in the Long Twentieth Century', *Twentieth Century British History*, vol. 20, no. 2, (January 2009), pp. 227-251. Maurice Kirby observed that the central

argument had 'the undoubted ring of truth', before adding that 'in true polemical fashion the authors overstate their case.' See Kirby, 'Institutional Rigidities and Britain's Industrial Decline', 934-5. See also Kirby's review of *Modernization Frustrated* in the *American Historical Review*, vol. 95, no.3 (June 1990), 829-30.

[10] See Stephen Dorril and Robin Ramsay, *Smear! Wilson and the Secret State* (London: 4th Estate, 1991); Scott Newton, *The Reinvention of Britain* 1960 - 2016 (London: Routledge, 2018), chs. 2 - 4 inclusive.

[11] For this process of 'mental adjustment', see Edgerton, 'The Decline of Declinism', 201-06.

[12] Scott Newton and Dilwyn Porter, *Modernization Frustrated. The Politics of Industrial Decline in Britain since 1900* (London: Unwin Hyman, 1988), p. 197.

[13] Trading Economic (using World Bank data), 25 June 2025, https://tradingeconomics.com/united-kingdom/manufacturing-value-added-percent-of-gdp-wb-date.html

[14] Eddie Dempsey (Rail, Maritime and Transport Workers' Union), interviewed by Jonny Ball, 'Encounter', *New Statesman*, 27 June-3 July 2025, 14.

Contents

Acknowledgements

Thanks are due to Peter Cain, Andy Cooper, Ronnie Kowalski and many friends and colleagues whose critical interest helped us to write this book. We would also like to acknowledge the assistance provided for us during our research by Professor Wynne Godley of the Department of Applied Economics, University of Cambridge.

Dr Porter owes a particular debt to Nuffield College, Oxford, which offered the encouragement of a research visitorship, and to colleagues in the History Division at Worcester College of Higher Education, notably Ted Townley, who offered unfailing support.

Maria Goldoni processed the manuscript and kept her cool while all around were losing theirs. Above all, her personal commitment to the project was a great source of encouragement and inspiration.

Last, but not least, thanks to Charles and Margaret Newton, and to Sandra, Daniel, Philip and Rachel Porter, for their enduring love, tolerance and support. We hope that this book is worthy of all the sacrifices they have made for us over the years.

Introduction

The designation of 1986 as 'Industry Year' was testimony to the weakness of British industry rather than its strength. Trevor Holdsworth, chairman of GKN, one of Britain's major manufacturing companies, has asked: 'What other developed economy could conceive of the necessity for such an event in 1986?' (Holdsworth, 1986, p. 60). But, by the mid 1980s, it was clear that in some important respects Britain was unlike other developed economies. During the long postwar boom which ended with the 1973 oil crisis, growth in the British economy, as measured by most significant indicators, had lagged persistently behind that experienced by Japan, the United States and member countries of the EEC. As it became increasingly apparent that the 'miracle' which had transformed the West German economy in this period was not an isolated phenomenon, the inability to sustain rates of growth which would secure levels of prosperity comparable to those enjoyed by other major industrial nations generated an awareness of the singularity of Britain's performance. In these circumstances, as Sidney Pollard has observed, what required explanation was Britain's failure to experience its own economic 'miracle', its failure to achieve 'what turned out to be possible for others in a competitive, intercommunicating world' (Pollard, 1984, pp. 3–6). Underpinning and compounding this failure was Britain's continuing decline as an industrial producer. By the mid 1980s, Britain, once the world's workshop, was confronted by the prospect of deindustrialization. Its balance of trade in manufactured goods was in the red after 1983 and manufacturing as a proportion of all economic activity had fallen from just under one-third in the early 1960s to little more than one-fifth, lower than any other advanced industrial country. This crisis in the non-oil economy has served to focus attention on Britain's comparative failure in terms of industrial modernization.

The concept of industrial modernization is complex and multi-faceted. It embraces structural change involving the transfer of capital and labour to technologically advanced areas of the productive economy with high growth potential in expanding areas of world trade. At the same time, it embodies a commitment to enhanced industrial efficiency and productive capacity. Thus industrial modernization does not necessarily imply the abandonment of basic industries such as coal and steel but could incorporate their development. It may also include related improvements both in the economic infrastructure, especially in the transport network, and in the social infrastructure through public investment in reforms designed to create a healthy and adaptable workforce. The pursuit of social justice through, for example, measures which broaden the basis of educational opportunity is not incompatible with the pursuit of economic efficiency. Furthermore, commitment on the part of the state to a developmental industrial strategy is required. As Holdsworth argued:

> Britain should have a comprehensive industrial strategy; as we attempt to reverse a long-term decline in our relative economic performance, we need the cohesion and the clear focus that such a strategy could provide, a Government policy consensus under which a mood of creativeness and innovation is fostered. (1986, p. 67)

Recent analysis of industrial policy in twentieth-century Britain suggests that this supportive strategy was notable largely for its absence. British governments seemed reluctant to channel funds into the industrial sector and were generally content to leave the process of rationalization to market forces. 'The experience of other nations, such as France and Japan', as Hall has noted, 'suggests that in order to tackle underlying productivity problems Britain would have needed an industrial policy based less on voluntarism and more on rationalization enforced directly by the state' (1986, p. 278).

Political strategies designed to create that climate conducive to sustained industrial modernization which Holdsworth has idealized have emerged at various crisis points in twentieth-century British history. In his study of Dudley Docker, a Midlands industrialist who consistently advocated such a strategy (albeit in a somewhat extreme form), Richard Davenport-Hines (1984) has reconstructed a series of initiatives in business politics before, during and after the great modernization crisis of the First World War. These initiatives represented a series of challenges to the prevailing drift of economic policy outlined above. Despite the efforts of the Business Leagues based in the Black Country before 1914 and his later work with the Federation of British Industries and the British Commonwealth Union, Docker's essentially corporatist vision of a modernized industrial state did not materialize. In political terms, he failed to engineer that shift in the consensus which was necessary if the interests of producers were to be accorded priority on a permanent basis in the making of state policy. What Davenport-Hines has called Docker's 'anxious resentment' of Britain's industrial decline motivated his political activities as a 'productioneer'. But he was not alone in his anxiety or his resentment. Modernization movements in his own lifetime, focused on national efficiency, tariff reform and postwar reconstruction, tapped the same source of discontent. This book seeks to examine how and why such movements and their more recent variants emerged and why the modernization strategies which they embodied have suffered the recurring fate of marginalization or abandonment.

It has often been argued that the peculiar history of British social development and, in particular, the absence of a comprehensive bourgeois revolution precluded any possibility of a sustained process of industrial modernization. The dominant social partnership between landed and commercial wealth, centred on the City of London, generated a political culture in which the interests of industrial wealth were accommodated or constrained. Forms of wealth creation which could be reconciled with the social position of an English gentleman were assigned a higher status in British society than industrial production. Thus, as Cain and Hopkins (1987, p. 1) have indicated, though the manufacturing sector was important in the nineteenth century, 'it was also less dynamic than is often supposed, and its representatives lacked both prestige and direct access to the "charmed circles" where policy was formulated'. A complementary analysis of social development derived from the nineteenth-century tradition of provincial radicalism is also useful here. Radical commentators from Cobbett to Cobden viewed British society as characterized by a fundamental division of interests separating those who consumed wealth from those who produced it. For Joseph Chamberlain, Birmingham-based screw manufacturer and charismatic late-nineteenth-century radical, this division was articulated in the conflict between the industrial classes, comprising capital and labour, and 'those who toil not neither do they spin', landowners living off agricultural rents and, increasingly, *rentiers* deriving their incomes from overseas investments channelled through the City of London. These interlocking historical perspectives direct attention to the central feature of the political economy of twentieth-century Britain – the dominance of City-based finance capital and the subordination of the interests of production.

In their attempts to account for Britain's decline as an industrial power, economic historians and other commentators have advanced a variety of explanations.[1] As the crisis has deepened the perceived causes have proliferated. British entrepreneurs, content to reap modest profits in traditional sectors, slow to re-equip their plant and reluctant to risk capital in industries with high growth potential, have been criticized for their innate conservatism and lack of drive. Trade union restrictive practices, seeking to preserve jobs in the short term but inimical to new technology and prospects of economic growth in the long term, have also been cited. It has been suggested that British exporters tended to cling too long to captive empire markets, thus forgoing the beneficial impact of efficiency-enhancing competition with modernized rivals, that Britain joined the EEC too late, that the capital market is insufficiently geared to the requirements of manufacturers or, simply, that decline was an inevitable consequence of Britain's 'early start' in industrialization. Though it is acknowledged that these explanations in themselves may each contain an element of truth, it is the contention of this book that they circumvent a fundamental problem. In general, they imply that the decline of the British industrial economy can be remedied by the correct mix of appropriate policies, a judicious touch of planning here or free enterprise there. The key argument advanced here, however, is that the decline of British industry is unlikely to be arrested in this fashion, for the problem arises from the nature of the British state itself.

As Tom Nairn has indicated, the British state, in its economic aspects, has been shaped by the hegemony of finance. Referring to the City of London, he observes that 'the historical configuration of capitalism in Great Britain is such that this one area long ago developed an organic ascendancy over the others – becoming as it were the brain or nervous system of the whole' (Nairn, 1973, p. 18). This ascendancy has been secured by what Geoffrey Ingham has called 'the core institutional nexus' (1984, *passim*), composed of the City, the Bank of England and the Treasury. Both singly and collectively, the institutions which make up this nexus have, in the legitimate pursuit of their own interests, committed the state to a liberal economic orthodoxy which often conflicted with the best interests of British producers. Outside periods of total war, free trade and sound money have consistently been assigned a higher priority in state policy than the maintenance and development of the nation's productive capacity. What has been missing is the essential context in which policies designed to halt Britain's long march into deindustrialization might be successfully applied, one in which the interests of finance and industry are evenly represented and effectively reconciled at the very core of British state institutions.

The thwarted modernization strategies which form a major theme in the ensuing discussion have been modified throughout the twentieth century by prevailing circumstances. Thus, in the late Victorian and Edwardian periods, the strategies proposed by tariff reformers and advocates of national efficiency addressed the particular problem of Britain's relative decline as an industrial power compared to Germany and the United States. During the First World War, the concept of modernization was defined in relation to war aims which included not simply out-producing the enemy but also, for a time, wholesale social and economic reconstruction. Between the wars, the focus shifted to incorporate both industrial rationalization, notably in the merger boom of the late 1920s, and the restructuring of the industrial economy based on expansion of new wave industries such as motor vehicles and electrical goods. The economic imperatives of total war after 1940 dictated the transformation of Britain into a modern industrial state which could be sustained through the transition from war to peace. Erosion of this commitment in the 1950s prompted renewed anxieties about industrial performance relative to other advanced economies as awareness grew that the truly 'miraculous' aspect of postwar economic history was Britain's 'failure to take part in the progress of the rest of the industrialised world' (Pollard, 1984, p. 6). The concern prompted by the failure to sustain growth comparable to the Germans and the Japanese persisted into the 1970s and 1980s and intensified with the onset of absolute decline.

In twentieth-century British politics, strategies designed to achieve industrial modernization have been articulated most forcefully by movements which sought, with varying degrees of success, to unify the interests of all producers. It was a commonplace, for example, amongst tariff reform campaigners after 1903 that those interests which labour and capital had in common were more important than those which divided them. Similarly, Sir Alfred Mond's short-lived initiative in industrial diplomacy in the late 1920s incorporated the same notion of class co-operation. After 1940, the full mobilization of national resources for the war generated unprecedented social solidarity and this was reflected in the industrial policies of the wartime Coalition government and in the programme of the Labour administration which came to power in 1945. In general, however, the aims of producers' alliances have been thwarted by the implementation of state policies characterized by an identification of the City's interests with those of the nation. Moreover, producers' alliances were often handicapped by their own inability to overcome hostility between capital and labour and by the inherent difficulty of developing political formulae through which the conflicting interests of different sectors of industrial capital could be reconciled.

These factors have compounded the problems encountered by modernizing producers in their efforts to modify the political economy of twentieth-century Britain. The structural primacy of commerce, principally City-based finance, over production has been articulated in political terms through the frustration of their strategies for change. Movements for modernization have generally lacked a secure base within the party system. Often they have taken the form of a cross-party or non-party campaign liable to disintegrate under the impact of parliamentary crises when party loyalties become paramount. It may be argued, for example, that the resumption of political normalcy, as the parliamentary basis of the Lloyd George Coalition was eroded and finally destroyed between 1918 and 1922, precluded the successful implementation of the postwar reconstruction programme. In addition, modernization strategies were subject to subversion as political parties shaped them for their own purposes: thus tariff reform was moulded by the Conservative leadership after 1910 to provide a defensive bulwark against Lloyd George's predatory 'socialism', losing, in the process, its radical thrust. It is little wonder that 'productioneer' industrialists, like Docker, held professional politicians in such low esteem (Davenport-Hines, 1984, pp. 71–5). Even when modernization movements were clearly identified with ruling party objectives and sanctioned by the electorate, they were unable to overcome the entrenched authority of the 'core institutional nexus' at the heart of British capitalism. The Labour Party's attempt to build a 'New Britain' after 1964 was aborted because it could not be reconciled with the interests of the financial establishment. The circumstances of total war, however, both reversed the traditional relationship between commerce and production and suspended the normal operation of the party political system. In these circumstances, a context was created in which industrial modernization movements could operate at the centre rather than the margin of the political system, liberated from peacetime constraints. The problem of sustaining the modernizing impulse in the absence of war remains unresolved.

Note: Introduction

1 For a recent and useful critical survey see Warwick, 1985.

CHAPTER ONE

'Wake Up England!': National Efficiency, Tariff Reform and Modernization, 1900–1914

Origins of the Edwardian Crisis

Although Britain emerged from the Boer War (1899–1902) with little glory, there was some consolation in the view that a dangerous complacency had been arrested. For 'a business people', as Kipling's verse reflected, it had been 'no end of a lesson'; the hope was that it would 'do us no end of good'. Shock waves emanating from the battlefields were sufficient to induce a crisis of confidence at the commanding heights of British politics, provoking a debate about the state of the nation which was far-reaching in its scope and its consequences. As intimations of mortality fell like shadows across the empire on which the sun never set, Victorian values and the institutions that embodied them were subject to sceptical re-assessment. By raising a large question mark over the capacity of the British state to organize for war, the South African débâcle brought pre-existing anxieties about social and economic organization to a critical point at which a political movement for modernization was generated. This movement embraced, from 1900, the Fabian–Liberal Imperialist strategy of national efficiency associated with Sidney and Beatrice Webb and Lord Rosebery, and, from 1903, the alternative Liberal Unionist–Conservative strategy of tariff reform, identified principally with Joseph Chamberlain. The rift within the

Edwardian modernization movement tended to reflect the characteristic division of capital in Britain between the commercial and financial interest of the City and the productive interest mainly associated with manufacturing industry. Ensuing political conflict between advocates of the competing modernization strategies signalled the arrival of a decisive phase in the protracted crisis of British capitalism in the late nineteenth and early twentieth centuries.

Opposing factions within the modernization movement shared some common ground. Until May 1903, when Chamberlain's celebrated Birmingham speech forced Edwardian progressives to declare either for or against free trade, this had been tentatively explored at meetings of the Co-efficients, a group convened by the Webbs, which featured both Fabian–Liberal Imperialists and proto-Chamberlainite tariff reformers. Both factions sought reform from above, advocating a more active role for the state. It followed that both self-consciously rejected the predisposition to *laissez-faire* which characterized the nineteenth-century liberal tradition. In this respect Rosebery and Chamberlain were equally anxious to practise the politics of the clean slate. Moreover, the outlook of both groups was conditioned by the ideology of external social Darwinism, whose adherents viewed races, states and empires as the significant participants in the perpetual struggle which led to evolutionary progress. Preoccupation with 'the survival of the fittest' in this sense linked naturally to the theme of imperial decline and fall to which Edwardian modernizers often alluded. The fate of Holland or Spain, great empires reduced to relative impotence in world affairs, struck the appropriate warning note; or, perhaps, Venice, once 'a state scarcely less great than our own, not less commercial, not less naval, not less predominant, which faded away like an empty dream because its rulers took no thought for the future, and did not keep abreast with the time'.[1]

If, as the logic of external social Darwinism suggested, international trade was war carried on by other means, then the campaign brought to an eventually successful conclusion in South Africa was less ominous than the losing battles being fought by British exporters in the markets of the world. The emergence in the late nineteenth century of new industrial powers and the erosion of the liberal world economic order which had underpinned the mid-Victorian boom had sent 'the workshop of the world' into a phase of relative economic decline. Both the modernizing strategies of the Edwardian period aimed to arrest this development through securing conditions which would enable British producers to compete on equal terms with their modernized counterparts, notably in Germany and the United States. Social reform was a feature of both strategies but they differed significantly in their specifically economic aspects. National efficiency invoked state assistance for industry in the form of technical education and sponsored scientific research; consistent throughout with the principles of free trade, modernization was regarded as a precondition of successful competition in an unregulated market. In contrast, tariff reform sought state aid in the form of protective tariffs to secure the home market for British producers, with a system of preferences to encourage imperial trade: regulation of the market was thus regarded as a precondition of successful modernization. Though the modernization movement of the early twentieth century confronted perceived causes of industrial deceleration, it was permanently handicapped by the schism which arose from the ultimately irreconcilable priorities of national efficiency and tariff reform and this contributed to its ultimate failure.

Protectionism, over which Disraeli had pronounced the last rites in the 1860s, revived in the 1880s in response to increasing foreign competition on the home market, a theme later exploited by E. E. Williams's best-seller *Made in Germany* (1896). But, just after the turn of the century, concern about Britain's economic performance reached a new level of intensity. Writing in July 1902, the Webbs noted the existence of 'a state of acute self-consciousness with regard to the organization of industry and commerce, and the influence of financial considerations in national politics' (1902, p. v). This had been prompted, not by any sudden deterioration of the economy, but by the experience of war, especially the national trauma induced by 'Black Week' in December 1899 when a series of military humiliations inflicted by the Boers supplied the circumstances in which disparate criticisms of social and economic policy could be compressed into a forceful, if somewhat incoherent, general critique of British government and its guiding principles. In the encircling mood of deprecation, a connection was assumed between incompetent leadership at all levels, with failure attributed to the same attachment to outmoded methods and policies. Thus British commanders outmanoeuvred in the field by the Boers were paralleled in the burgeoning literature of national efficiency by British consuls outwitted in the market by Germans and Americans. As for 'the influence of financial considerations, in national politics', the war exposed the limitations of the Treasury's conventionally cautious view of public spending and stretched existing sources of revenue to the limit. When Hicks Beach, in his 1902 budget, was forced to resort to a modest duty on imported corn, he raised the spectre of the 'bread tax' and unintentionally provided an opportunity for Chamberlain to re-open the question of free trade or protection.

In a speech in December 1901 which suggested that British exporters should 'wake up' to the progress of foreign rivals in colonial markets, the Prince of Wales caught the authentic mood of 'acute self-consciousness' to which the Webbs later referred. Manufacturing industry, the engine of nineteenth-century material progress, was a particular cause for anxiety. Although industrial output had continued to grow in absolute terms, the rate of growth had slowed from an annual average of 3.1 per cent between 1836–8 and 1872–4 to only 1.8 per cent between 1872–4 and 1900–2. But it was Britain's performance compared to that of more modern industrial states which caused Edwardians the greatest alarm, as production was surpassed first by the United States in the early 1880s and then by Germany around 1905.

Table 1.1 Long-Term Rates of Growth, 1870–1913 (per cent per annum)

	1 Industrial production	2 Industrial productivity	3 Total output[a]	4 Output per head	5 Output per man-hour
UK	2.1	0.6	2.2	1.3	1.5
Germany	4.1	2.6[b]	2.9	1.8	2.1
USA	4.7	1.5	4.3	2.2	2.4

Notes:
[a] GDP at constant prices
[b] Estimated figure
Sources: Columns 1 and 2: Aldcroft, 1968, p. 13, Table II; columns 3, 4, and 5: Crouzet, 1982, p. 377, Table 66.

Measured in terms of industrial production, industrial productivity, total output, total output per head and total output per man-hour, Britain was outpaced in the late nineteenth and early twentieth centuries (see Table 1.1).

As industrialization spread, it was inevitable that Britain's share of world manufacturing production would decline. More serious for a country which required to export manufactures in order to pay for imports of food and raw materials was that its share of the world market for manufactured goods began to decrease rapidly after about 1890. Moreover, British manufactured goods were heavily committed to export trades which were declining, like textiles, rather than those which were expanding, like steel (see Table 1.2). In part, this reflected what was beginning to emerge as a serious structural weakness within Britain's industrial economy which failed to develop on a large scale the new manufacturing products, like chemicals and electrical goods, that were features of the 'second industrial revolution' of the late nineteenth century. Here again comparison with Germany, the United States and even France was unfavourable.[2]

Table 1.2 British Share of World Trade in Manufactured Goods, 1890–1913

	World exports of manufactures	World exports of manufactures: expanding sector	World exports of manufactures: stable sector	World exports of manufactures: declining sector
1890	40.7			
1899	32.5	17.7	18.6	62.9
1913	29.9	21.3	13.3	65.4

Source: Saul, 1965, p. 12, Table V and p. 13, Table VIII.

Though we must take care not to attribute to past generations the wisdom imparted by hindsight, it seems clear that the advocates of national efficiency and tariff reform in the early twentieth century appreciated the general thrust of those trends which economic historians have since quantified. They were capable of drawing their own conclusions. Britain could not have remained for ever in splendid isolation as the world's only industrialized power; moreover, as other nations industrialized they would naturally experience rapid growth. 'All that was obvious', noted Arthur Shadwell in his comparative study of industrial efficiency in England, Germany and the United States.

> But they have done a great deal more than make up for lost time and reduce the start which circumstances gave to this country: they have within the last twenty years or less not only caught up with us in many things in which we were once unrivalled, but have surpassed us in some. They compete successfully not only in neutral markets but in the home market and that with products peculiarly British. (Shadwell, 1905, pp. 647–8)

The implication of this passage, so characteristic of the Edwardian modernization movement, was that while relative economic decline was an unavoidable economic fact of the new world order, the extent of relative decline had been unduly severe and could not be attributed entirely to exogenous factors beyond Britain's control. This led naturally to the conclusion that endogenous factors were responsible for the extent of the relative decline, a view buttressed by evidence of American and German superiority in industrial efficiency, new technology and technical education.

But it is important to place the shortcomings of British industry in this period in a wider perspective and to stress that the prospect was not one of unrelieved gloom. Britain remained a major industrial power, retaining its lead in shipbuilding and as a producer and exporter of cotton textiles. Exploiting the temporary advantages accruing to an old industrial power in a developing industrial world, it dominated world export trade in coal and in textile machinery while achieving a similar predominance in a limited range of new manufactures such as electrical cables, bicyles and sewing machines. One growth area, which economic historians have tended to neglect, was the mass production of cheap convenience foods, tobacco, soap, cosmetics and other items of everyday use, signalling a vigorous response to increased working-class purchasing power after 1870. Expert contributors to a series of lectures at Birmingham University in 1902, reviewing the current state of various sectors of manufacturing industry, indicated a complex pattern of responses, not always unsuccessful, to the more competitive conditions which had emerged. Acknowledging that primacy had been lost and that other countries were making more rapid absolute progress, the iron and steel industry appeared paralysed, unwilling to reconstruct or innovate in the absence of a protected home market. But other reports were more positive. The West Riding woollen and worsted manufacturers, it was suggested, had already woken up. 'No other industry', it was boasted, 'has shown more readiness to throw out obsolete machinery and install new plant in order to meet the ever changing requirements of the day' (Hooper, 1903, p. 119).

Moreover, any discussion of Britain's relative decline as an industrial power has to take into account the performance of other non-industrial sectors of the economy. Here Britain's role as the pivot of international finance and trade is of particular importance. Even at the height of its industrial supremacy, Britain had been a net importer of commodities. In addition to the raw material requirements of manufacturing industry, an expanding urban population was sustained largely through imported food. The resulting visible trade deficit was, however, more than counterbalanced by an invisible trade surplus, reflecting earnings from services like shipping, insurance and banking plus income derived from overseas investments (see Table 1.3).

Table 1.3 Factors in the United Kingdom Balance of Payments, 1886–1913 (quinquennial averages, £m at constant prices)

	Balance of commodity trade	Income from services	Income from dividends and interest
1886–1890	−91.1	94.6	84.2
1891–1895	−130.3	88.4	94.0
1896–1900	−160.6	100.7	100.2
1901–1905	−174.6	110.6	112.9
1906–1910	−142.1	136.5	151.4
1911–1913	−134.3	152.6	187.9

Source: Mathias, 1983, p. 305, Table VII.

For the British economy in this period, comparative advantage lay increasingly with the activities represented by its invisible exports. Thus, while it was in the process of surrendering its role as the world's leading provider of manufactures, it was consolidating its role as a provider of international services. Its merchant fleet retained a lead in the world's carrying trade, insurance premium income derived from abroad increased rapidly and so did the profits accruing to banks from the short-term financing of international trade. Paradoxically, the spread of industrialization which weakened the relative position of Britain's manufacturers contributed substantially to the success of invisible exporters by stimulating world trade expansion (see Crouzet, 1982, pp. 359–70).

The emergence of a powerful, externally oriented service sector with the City of London at its centre had important implications for the industrial economy. Though the interests of shippers, insurers, bankers and brokers were not inevitably opposed to those of manufacturers, they did not coincide with them. This separation was even clearer in the case of the growing sub-class of *rentiers* who derived their income from overseas investment. Capital exports, which the City facilitated with increasing sophistication in the late Victorian period, did not necessarily harm British industry directly; the financing of foreign railway development, for example, may have brought short-term benefits to exporters of rails, locomotives and other capital goods. But the maintenance in the late nineteenth and early twentieth centuries of net capital exports at a level which persistently exceeded gross domestic capital formation suggested that the experience of a Midlands ironmaster struggling to maintain his share of the home market against German imports was more than geographically remote from that of the City of London. As the *Economist* observed: 'London is often more concerned with the course of events in Mexico than what happens in the Midlands, and is more upset by a strike on the Canadian Pacific than by one in the Cambrian Collieries.'[3] In this period, metropolitan financial institutions were not major providers of capital for British industry. Of more than 5,000 securities quoted on the London Stock Exchange in the mid 1900s, fewer than 600 were 'home industrials'. The lack of institutional development which this suggested, however, owed as much to provincial self-reliance as it did to metropolitan indifference, British industrialists tending to re-invest profits or raise short-term personal loans rather than go to the capital market. 'London', continued the *Economist*, 'does not finance new companies in Lancashire and Yorkshire because Lancashire and Yorkshire are "on their own", and take care not to send anything really profitable to London.' It was as if Britain had become the territorial base for two economies which remained relatively independent of each other.

By the start of the twentieth century, therefore, a further aspect of the relative decline of the British industrial economy had become apparent. Decline had been relative not only in terms of previous performance and the faster growth achieved by competitors after 1870, but also in relation to the success of the service sector. The characteristic duality of British capitalism was brought into focus. Capital was not an undifferentiated bloc but was divided into 'fractions', notably the industrial or productive sector and the commercial or service sector dominated by the activities of the City. The absence in Britain of 'finance capital' in the form of a fusion of banking and large-scale production through direct investment reflected the separate development and interests of the two major fractions. In its British manifestation, as Ingham has argued, finance capital had a *commercial* emphasis; its role was to mediate rather than invest. 'The City's profits', he notes, 'have not been primarily in the form of interest, but a deduction from this in the form of brokerage fees or commission – that is, commercial profit from the trading in various forms of investment capital' (1984, pp. 34–5). By channelling funds into undeveloped areas of the globe from the mid nineteenth century, the City had been instrumental in expanding world trade. With its place at the hub of the world financial system secured by free trade and the use of sterling as an international currency, profits were derived from its lion's share of the increasing volume of transactions. Overcommitted to declining sectors of world commodity trade and increasingly aware of free trade as a mixed blessing, the industrial sector was less favourably placed. The effect was to make the duality of British capital more visible by creating a growing awareness of the separate interests of its two major fractions.

But it was not just the existence of two fractions of capital which was brought into sharp relief by the course of late-nineteenth-century economic development; it was the predominance of one fraction over another. The course of English social history is important here. Despite industrialization, no thoroughgoing *bourgeois* revolution had occurred to sweep away the vestiges of aristocratic influence. The agitation preceding the Reform Act

(1832) and the repeal of the Corn Laws (1846) had led, not to revolution, but to an accommodation between the landed gentry and both major fractions of capital. Industrialists gained political parity with the aristocracy, but at a price: in so doing, they rendered themselves liable to containment within what Nairn has called 'the patrician hegemony', a state form which inhibited 'the aggressive development of industrialism' (Nairn, 1981, pp. 24–33). In *English Culture and the Decline of the Industrial Spirit,* Wiener has indicated that containment was achieved mainly through those cultural processes which gentrified the industrialist by superimposing on him inappropriate pre-industrial or non-industrial values (1981, pp. 127–9). In addition, the accommodation of the mid nineteenth century entailed a further check on the progress of industrial capital in that it provided the landed elite with an opportunity to cement their developing relationship with City finance. The 'lord of ten thousand acres' may have made his peace with 'the owner of ten thousand spindles', but he found that the company of the merchant banker was more congenial. Conveniently located in the south of England and blessed with a gentlemanly pedigree which pre-dated the invention of the water frame, the City benefited from a social cachet which industry could not match. Consequently, as the alliance between land and finance was bonded by intermarriage and schooling, the industrial capitalist was progressively disadvantaged in society and politics.

In British society, the links between the City, the Bank of England and the Treasury comprise, in Ingham's phrase, 'the core institutional nexus'. The mutually interactive interests of the separate components of this powerful triple alliance were guaranteed in the late nineteenth and early twentieth centuries by the identification of the state with an essentially liberal view of the economy. This was characterized in political terms by the overriding attachment of both Liberal and Conservative administrations to three policy objectives: the pursuit of free trade, the maintenance of the gold standard and the balancing of the budget at the lowest possible figure. These objectives coincided with the interests of finance capital in its exceptional British form, a reflection in part of the predisposition of governments in which landed wealth remained prominent to turn for economic advice to London rather than to Manchester or Birmingham. For the City, free trade and the existence of a stable mechanism underpinning payments in sterling facilitated its capacity to service the international economy: balanced budgets provided the political surety that these advantages would be maintained. But, by the end of the nineteenth century, the benefits conferred on British industry by this policy framework were less clear. Manchester might still be well served by free trade but Birmingham was dubious. As the quest for national efficiency began in the aftermath of 'Black Week' and awareness of disparities within Britain's overall economic performance were sharpened, the major fractions of capital were drawing apart.

This process was marked by the publication, during the war years, of George Byng's *Protection: the Views of a Manufacturer* (1901). Byng, as chairman of GEC, wrote from the perspective of a producer engaged in a new industry adversely affected by foreign competition on the home market. In order to make a case for tariff protection, he may have exaggerated the extent of its difficulties, but it is clear that the electrical products industry grew relatively slowly in Britain and that the market for more expensive goods was dominated by technologically superior German and American imports. His book, however, went beyond a plea for protection for he was sensitive to the 'due distinction between industry and commerce, between manufacturing and trading, between production and exchange'. Since the adoption of free trade, he observed, merchant bankers had become 'merchant princes'. They constituted the pinnacle of a bloated social pyramid composed of all 'middlemen' deriving income from the service sector, from bankers and shippers to railwaymen, clerks and porters. Concentrating his fire on the upper ranks, he depicted a life-style in which wealth was acquired with comparative ease and spent in the irresponsible pursuit of excessive luxury. In a key passage (pp. 134–63), Byng compared the essentially parasitic middleman unfavourably with the manufacturer whose success, he argued, was dependent on hard work, knowledge, foresight, leadership and a sense of responsibility. Most significantly, he advanced the claim that the national interest would always be better served by manufacturers because, 'leaving the question of abstract patriotism on one side, a successful manufacturer must be a patriot, for the reason that his material interests are bound up in the welfare of the country'. In contrast, the cosmopolitan, commercial interests of the middleman precluded patriotism; he was 'as a matter of fact the enemy of this country'. The purpose of this vigorous, though undeniably crude, assault was to challenge the prevailing economic orthodoxy which identified the interests of the dominant fraction of capital with those of the nation. It was a sign that some producers, at least, were waking up.

Waking Up: (1) National Efficiency

Arising as a direct response to the alarming news from South Africa, the national efficiency movement linked Fabian collectivism with the Liberal Imperialist reaction against the Gladstonian legacy. The most coherent view of its modernization strategy was provided by Sidney Webb's Fabian pamphlet, *A Policy of National Efficiency* (no. 108), published in November 1901. Webb aimed to convert the prevalent 'burning feeling of shame at the "failure" of England' into political action. Convinced that nineteenth-century liberalism was a spent force rendered obsolete by the new competitive world order, he outlined a programme of 'twentieth-century politics', a series of reforms which would raise the efficiency of British society to a level comparable to that of Germany or the United States. The concept of the 'national minimum', a standard of life conducive to personal efficiency below which the state should not allow its citizens to fall, was at the heart of his programme. This standard was to be guaranteed by interventionist measures to secure the abolition of 'sweated' industrial labour, the imposition of minimum standards of housing and sanitation by local authorities and the reform of the poor law. It also embraced 'a large-hearted plan for bringing the whole of our educational machinery up to the standard of any other country'. A few weeks later, Lord Rosebery, the former Liberal prime minister, endorsed Webb's proposals in very general terms, thus placing himself at the head of the national efficiency movement. His Chesterfield speech urged Liberals to abandon their 'fly-blown' Gladstonian principles and to embrace the concept of 'an energetic state' committed to the pursuit of national efficiency through the advancement of technical education and through social reforms designed to combat 'the physical degeneracy of our race'.[4]

The national efficiency movement attacked on a broad front, seeking to undermine those liberal ideas and institutions to which it attributed 'England's failure'. Uncomprisingly technocratic, Webb's proposals amounted to the imposition of Germanic efficiency on British society from above, with Whitehall purged of incompetence and Parliament, reduced to the status of a 'foolometer', processing the recommendations of expert subcommittees. In terms of modernization, the Fabian–Liberal Imperialist strategy was concerned mainly with the machinery of government and the level of social efficiency. It was, of course, anticipated that industrial efficiency would benefit if these were improved, notably from the availability of a healthy and well-educated workforce. Measures were contemplated to counteract 'sweating', for example, through extending existing factory legislation, thus healing what Webb described as 'one open sore by which this industrial parasitism is draining away the vitality of the race'. But though Rosebery privately condemned manufacturers for their 'idiotic' conservatism and Webb berated 'the slackness of our merchants and traders that transfers our commercial superiority to the United States', they showed little inclination towards direct intervention to stimulate Britain's economic performance. As Matthew has noted of the Liberal Imperialists, they 'regarded the free market economy as the best means of industrial progress', seeking only 'to facilitate the working of that economy, not to change it'.[5]

Though it was Chamberlain's tariff reform campaign after 1903 that forced the Fabian–Liberal Imperialist group to spell out its commitment to the free market, national efficiency had from the start represented only a limited departure from prevailing economic orthodoxy. As Fabians, George Bernard Shaw and the Webbs might contemplate direct intervention in the form of public ownership of transport and service industries but, as partners in an alliance, they were constrained by the reluctance of the Liberal Imperialists to sever old party ties. It was the Liberal Party's continuing attachment to Gladstone's Irish home rule policy rather than fundamental differences about social and economic policy which explained the semi-detached status of many of Rosebery's supporters; consequently, the Webbs' 'communistic' agenda made them nervous. When Chamberlain provided them with the opportunity, they were only too glad to prove their Liberal credentials by rallying to the defence of free trade. Their relief was reflected in the propaganda of Rosebery's Liberal League which rivalled that of the Cobden Club and the Free Trade Union in its defence of fiscal orthodoxy. Industrial efficiency, it was argued, would be improved when home producers emulated those techniques which brought foreign rivals success in the open market. The precepts of nineteenth-century liberalism and Edwardian social Darwinism were neatly fused in praise of competition as the key which would unlock the door to progress. It would 'stimulate our manufacturers to greater efficiency in organization and methods, and if it were removed there would be good reason to fear that they would sink into a conservatism that would ultimately be disastrous'.[6]

There were, however, limits to the movement's faith in the free market and some indirect assistance to industry was envisaged. The long-term process of industrial modernization was to be underwritten by the establishment of an appropriate system of state education. Webb's pamphlet had extended the concept of the 'national minimum' to educational provision. Deploring in turn the lack of technical instruction for workhouse children, the absence of a national system of secondary education and the dearth of modern institutions of higher education, he called for a statesman who would 'cut himself loose from official pedantries' and demand the necessary reform, notably the state endowment of 'a dozen perfectly equipped faculties of science, engineering, economics and modern languages'. Rosebery, presumably the statesman whom Webb had in mind, responded positively at Chesterfield to this prompting, but it was Haldane, the architect of the relationship between the Fabians and the Liberal Imperialists, who developed detailed proposals. His scheme for a London 'Charlottenburg', an institution to be modelled on Germany's most prestigious new university, reflected his anxiety to promote scientific research and the teaching of science at the highest level. After its publication in 1903, it was paraded as the national efficiency movement's alternative to the regulation of the market by means of tariffs. 'One good Technical university', it was argued in *Fabianism and the Fiscal Question* (1904), 'is worth ten custom houses.' But the clean lines of the Charlottenburg proposal were not typical of the movement's education policy in general. Its characteristic vagueness and lack of cohesion reflected the Liberal Imperialists' difficulties in reconciling the Fabian predisposition to government by experts with their party's commitment to school boards and other forms of popular control.

For a movement which set its public face against 'muddling through' in all its forms, national efficiency was remarkably attached to *ad hoc* arrangements in the conduct of its own affairs. Its organization embodied two separately constituted elements, the Fabian Society and the Liberal League, linked informally through contacts between the Webbs, Haldane and Rosebery, whose disengaged style of leadership created a persistent climate of uncertainty. There was, moreover, no attempt to build systematically on Webb's original policy statement so that 'national efficiency' as a political concept eluded precise definition. The broad outline remained in itself attractive to an articulate segment of Edwardian opinion which was detached from or disenchanted with the existing party system, but its social base was narrow. Though Rosebery self-consciously embraced the cult of the businessman, suggesting half-seriously that Andrew Carnegie or Sir Thomas Lipton might be invited to test the efficiency of state institutions against the standards achieved by their own firms, the movement represented neither of the major fractions of capital. As a strategy for industrial modernization, national efficiency addressed the issue of technological backwardness which had frequently been identified as a factor in Britain's relative economic decline, but in an oblique fashion which reflected the low priority assigned to the interests of production in its programme of social regeneration. It did provide, however, an indication of a modernization strategy which might be pursued within the context of free trade and imperialism that was not incompatible with the international outlook of the City.

Waking Up: (2) Tariff Reform and Imperial Preference

Though it owed less to the specific stimulus of the Boer War, the origins of the tariff reform movement were located in the same complex of anxieties which had prompted the demand for national efficiency. The movement sprang to life in May 1903 following a speech at Birmingham in which Chamberlain had warned that Britain would have to adapt if it was to survive as a great power in a world of competing empires. Motivated initially by considerations of imperial unity, he argued that free trade should be abandoned and replaced by a tariff system which would allow for fiscal discrimination in favour of imports from the colonies, thus binding the far-flung outposts to the centre 'by relations of interest as well as by relations of sentiment'. Articulating his scheme, at the start, in a piecemeal fashion, he subsequently acknowledged that import duties would provide a measure of protection for farmers and manufacturers exposed to foreign competition on the home market. Stung by Lloyd George, who mischievously suggested that 'Radical Joe' had ditched his long-standing commitment to old age pensions, he then pledged in advance the hypothetical revenue which his proposed tariff would generate. 'Pensions,' he claimed, 'or anything else which cost large sums of money, which have hitherto seemed out of reach, would become practicable if this policy was carried out.' In a speech at Glasgow, a few months later, he announced the prosaic details of the revolution in economic policy which he advocated. He anticipated a 10 per cent duty on foreign manufactures, 5 per cent on foreign meat and dairy produce and two shillings a quarter on foreign grain and flour. Colonial producers were to be granted a substantial preference by allowing their produce free entry to the home market. Without specifically abandoning the link with pensions, he indicated that the revenue accruing from the new duties should be used to offset reductions in existing duties on tea, sugar, cocoa and coffee. The purpose of this modification was to counteract the vehement opposition to 'food taxes' which his first statements had aroused.[7]

Neatly side-stepping Lord Rosebery and the Webbs, Gamble (1985) has argued that the Chamberlainite tariff reform movement was 'the first major political response to Britain's decline, the first major attempt to change the course of British policy' (p. 159). This assessment seems appropriate, particularly if the tariff reformers are compared to their Fabian–Liberal Imperialist contemporaries. Though the rhetoric of national efficiency during and just after the war reflected genuine, widespread public disquiet, the movement's roots were shallow with activists recruited mainly from the ranks of temporarily disaffected Liberal politicians and self-consciously progressive intellectuals. The tariff reform campaign, in contrast, developed some features of a mass movement and could advance a not unrealistic claim to represent major economic interests, such as the iron and steel industry, within the productive sector. In the early twentieth century, ten years after Harcourt's celebrated observation that 'we are all socialists now', the long-term Fabian–Liberal Imperialist commitment to the 'national minimum' did not strike at the heart of economic liberalism in the same way as the Chamberlainite proposal to break with free trade. Rejecting as obsolete the individualist precepts of nineteenth-century liberalism, tariff reformers followed German national political economy in defining the aims of policy in relation to the power of the nation state. Their priority was to foster, maintain and develop its productive capacity. This conflicted with the conventional emphasis on free exchange as a policy objective and challenged the ideological hegemony of economic liberalism and those interests on which it was based.

Chamberlain's campaign forged a link between those who shared his view of tariff reform as a means to imperial consolidation and those who sought protection for hard-pressed farmers and manufacturers. 'Constructive imperialists', like Hewins, the economist who later headed Chamberlain's unofficial Tariff Commission, had been drawn instinctively towards national efficiency in 1901 but had recoiled from its underlying conservatism, especially evident in the movement's attachment to orthodox Cobdenite finance. Rosebery's projected imperial federation, it was argued, would founder on the rock of colonial nationalism in the absence of some economic imperative to unity, and the social reforms necessary to raise efficiency could not be financed without new sources of revenue. Chamberlain's scheme appeared to supply both these deficiencies. Moreover, it blended perfectly with the constructive imperialists' variation on the theme of national political economy which advocated, in Hewins's words, 'the deliberate adoption of the Empire as distinct from the United Kingdom as the basis of public policy and, in particular, the substitution in our economic policy of Imperial interests for the interests of the consumer' (Hewins, 1929, Vol. 1, pp. 50–61). Chamberlain's personal inclination towards this conception of policy and the presence of Hewins, Amery, Garvin and other constructive imperialists at the intellectual core of the movement have led to the classification of tariff reform politics as a species of 'social imperialism'. It has been regarded, not unjustly, as a Bismarckian strategy which sought to protect the interests of capital through the extension of imperial markets while securing the political and social incorporation of labour through popular imperialism, promises of 'work for all' and social reform.

The social imperialists, however, were only one element in the tariff reform alliance. When Chamberlain raised his standard, he also attracted farmers and manufacturers for whom the campaign was primarily a protest arising directly from their particular circumstances within relatively disadvantaged sectors of production. In the late nineteenth and early twentieth centuries, the condition of agriculture appeared to have confirmed some of the worst fears of the diehard protectionists at the time of the repeal of the Corn Laws. Though cattle breeders and dairy farmers serving adjacent markets were sheltered from the depression, arable farmers were hard hit. Prices for wheat and other cereals tumbled as the British market was flooded with imports of American grain rendered competitive by reduced transport costs and the vast economies of scale possible on the prairies. As agricultural rents stagnated or declined, some large landowners responded by switching to more profitable overseas investment, thus reinforcing the connection between landed and commercial wealth at the highest level. Meanwhile, small- and medium-scale arable producers, unable or unwilling to diversify their interests, saw their profit margins diminish or disappear. As the agitation against the removal of the wartime registration duty on imported corn indicated, just prior to the start of Chamberlain's campaign in 1903, they were inclined to the view that their interests had been sacrificed on the altar of free trade. Thus they welcomed even the minimal protection offered by Chamberlain's scheme.

Similarly, the proposed 10 per cent duty on imported foreign manufactures was sufficient to draw support from within industries experiencing the rough edge of relative economic decline. Though allegiance to tariff reform or free trade was not entirely reducible to economic interest, a broad pattern emerged linking Chamberlain's campaign with a complex of heavy industries, often with a strong Midlands base, such as iron and steel; brass, tin and other metal manufacturing trades, some branches of heavy engineering, building materials, chemicals and glass. For such interests, Chamberlain's proposals appeared to offer the advantage of a secure home market, widening opportunities in imperial markets and the possibility that hostile tariffs which excluded them from the home markets of rival industrial nations might be negotiated downwards once Britain had armed itself with powers of fiscal retaliation. For the electrical products industry, established relatively recently, different priorities applied, Byng's protectionism and subsequent support for Chamberlain arising from an appreciation of the particular problems confronting an 'infant industry' in competition with more advanced rivals elsewhere. As the movement snowballed, Chamberlain discovered that the tariff system which he had envisaged primarily as a means of granting preference to the colonies offered the prospect of relief to this significant bloc of industries. He was adopted, in effect, by the less competitive sectors of British manufacturing or, at least, by those sectors where competitiveness was undermined by the unusual circumstances of an open home market.[8]

Arguably, the strength and coherence of tariff reform as a modernizing strategy was impaired by the attachment of backward farming and manufacturing interests which seized on Chamberlain's proposals as an alternative to painful but necessary adjustment and reconstruction. Though the commitment to modernization was implicit rather than explicit, the comprehensive version of the Chamberlainite gospel as preached by the social imperialists embodied more than a commitment to halting relative economic decline: it sought also to correct the pernicious imbalance between the two major fractions of capital, to improve the social efficiency of the nation, and to eradicate internally damaging class conflict. In practice, however, this full gospel was rarely preached, the nature of the political campaign demanding a persistent protectionist emphasis on local or sectional interests. Ashley, an economist sympathetic to the tariff reformers, indicated that they would find it necessary in government to take a broader view, varying rates of duty in different circumstances 'to retain the stimulus and check to our own manufacturers which foreign competition supplies' and abandoning 'certain cheap labour trades and those decaying because of genuine natural disadvantage' (Ashley, 1903, pp. 133–4). Such ideas formed no part of mainstream Tariff Reform League propaganda which stressed defensive rather than reconstructive aspects of 'protection all round'. No preliminary requirements were laid down: industries were offered modest tariff protection without conditions on the assumption that the advantages of a regulated market would provide the necessary incentives to increased industrial efficiency. But while the propensity of the tariff to offer shelter to the relatively inefficient producer should be acknowledged, it might also be indicated that the necessary incentives to enterprise were not always guaranteed by free trade. Pig iron manufacturers, it was noted, replying to critics who suggested that they lacked enterprise and were content with small yields, argued that there was 'no market to rely on that would justify our producers of iron and steel in following American lines' (Jeans, 1903, p. 30).

Underlying the tariff reformers' argument that state intervention, in the form of a tariff, would create 'a market to rely on' and thus provide the spur to industrial efficiency, was the conviction, derived from national political economy, that the first duty of the state was to protect the productive capacity of its citizens. This, in turn, was linked to their view of production as the most important form of economic activity. As Byng's portrait of the virtuous manufacturer had indicated, it was regarded as the parent of all other forms of economic activity and, thereby, innately superior. Within the context of British capitalism in the early twentieth century, however, the interests of production, whether agricultural or industrial, were clearly not superior but subordinate to those of commerce and finance, a relationship underwritten by the commitment of the crucial City–Bank–Treasury nexus to the maintenance of a liberal economy. As a modernizing movement, the ultimate test for tariff reform related to its capacity to modify the relationship between the major fractions of British capital in the interests of production.

Chamberlain's awareness of the structural bias against production was apparent when he confronted a City of London audience at the Guildhall in January 1904. Previous campaign speeches had highlighted, sometimes in a rather melodramatic fashion, the decay of production. In an often quoted passage from a speech made at Greenock a few months previously, he had claimed that: 'Agriculture, as the greatest of all trades and industries of this country, has been practically destroyed. Sugar has gone; silk has gone; iron is threatened; wool is threatened; cotton will go!' Underestimating, perhaps, the extent to which the City had already developed the economic characteristics of an offshore island, the screw manufacturer turned statesman argued that its interests were ultimately underpinned by Britain's imperial role and by the productive capacity of the nation. London, he acknowledged, had become 'the clearing-house of the world', but it could not afford to neglect the workshop. Stressing the parental role of production in economic activity, he suggested that the ubiquitous bill of exchange drawn on London had become the standard currency of world commerce 'because of the productive energy and capacity which is behind it'. The activities of the service sector, in his view, were of secondary importance, being derived from production. Thus, he urged that:

> Banking is not the creator of our prosperity, but the creation of it. It is not the cause of our wealth, but it is the consequence of our wealth; and if the industrial energy and development which has been going on for so many years in this country were to be hindered or relaxed, then finance, and all that finance means, will follow trade to the countries which are more successful than ourselves.

Though Chamberlain was criticized, not without justification, for his failure to grasp the importance of free trade in creating the City's world role, the massive implication of his speech was clear. In demanding a revolution in the fiscal policy of the state, Chamberlain was seeking to re-order its priorities. Under tariff reform, the interests of production would come first.[9]

In this context, Chamberlain's resignation from the Cabinet in September 1903 signified a recognition that this re-ordering of priorities could not be achieved from within. The Treasury had indicated its intention of blocking this route during the winter of 1902–3 when its officials had persuaded Ritchie, the Chancellor of the Exchequer, to repeal the registration duty on corn which Chamberlain had hoped to utilize as the modest cornerstone for a scheme of imperial preference (see Rempel, 1972, pp. 23–7). Tariff reformers, therefore, were forced to pursue their goal by other means, principally by mobilizing sufficient support in the country to exert effective pressure through the normal channels of parliamentary representation. Chamberlain's campaign of speeches and the 'raging, tearing propaganda' of the Tariff Reform League were directed towards this purpose. The strategic objective of tariff reform politics in the Edwardian era was to forge an alliance of producers, a concept which owed much to nineteenth-century Birmingham radicalism with its distinctive emphasis on class co-operation. Whereas Birmingham artisans had once been invited to join their masters in an alliance of 'the industrious classes' against the aristocratic 'old corruption', tariff reform propaganda urged the working man to identify his interest with those of his employer in the contest with foreign trade rivals. A League leaflet (no. 20 in its 'industrial' series), drawing attention to the adverse effects of dumping, typified this approach with its question: 'Are you going to permit the destruction of the British iron and steel trade – the trade that provides your work and wages?' This attempt to promote a producers' alliance through the fusion of the separate classes involved in production did not, of course, preclude the simultaneous effort to construct an alliance between different sectors of production, agricultural and industrial, in the pursuit of tariff reform.

Modernization Marginalized

In its final report, published in 1918, the Balfour of Burleigh Committee on Commercial and Industrial Policy reflected on the conditions prevailing in British trade and industry during the last years of peace. Over-influenced, perhaps, by the boom of 1912–13, the committee's critical comments were prefaced by the observation that industry in the Edwardian period had generally shown 'great vitality and power of extension'. It was noted, however, that these features had been most evident 'in a certain number of long established manufactures of which coal, cotton and the textile trades generally, shipbuilding and some branches of the engineering trades (such as textile machinery) are the most conspicuous'. Significantly, the iron and steel industry was regarded as exceptional in this group, its comparative lack of progress ensuring that it was 'entirely overshadowed' by German and American competition. It was also clear to the committee that in expanding areas of modern industrial production 'the United

Kingdom had taken a very limited share, as is evidenced by our relative weakness in respect of the electrical, chemical and chemico-metallurgical industries; and it is admitted that in a number of smaller trades foreign manufacturers had shown greater enterprise and originality'.[10]

This verdict suggested that those features of Britain's industrial performance which had prompted the impulse towards modernization in the first years of the century were still present on the eve of conflict. With the exception of its reference to iron and steel, the report seriously underestimated the extent to which all Britain's great nineteenth-century industrial staples had become uncompetitive, but there was no doubting the commitment to these long-established sectors of production which accounted for about 50 per cent of industrial output and about 70 per cent of export earnings. The prewar boom, especially marked in exports of coal and cotton, probably served to confirm the bias towards these lumbering giants of low growth potential at the expense of more technologically sophisticated, new wave industries. At the outbreak of war, the comparative absence of a modern industrial sector was dramatically exposed by immediate shortages of synthetic dyes, fine chemicals, magnetos, tungsten and numerous other items 'of great importance as a basis for other manufactures [which] had come to be entirely or very largely under German control'. Here, the committee acknowledged, the enemy had reaped the benefit of 'persistent scientific work and organizing skill'.

There were some improvements in industrial efficiency during the Edwardian period and these were seized on by orthodox political economists to illustrate the benefits of free imports in supplying a healthy stimulus to enterprise. Surveying recent history from the vantage point of the prewar export boom, the *Economist* claimed that British businessmen, who had seemed at the turn of the century 'wedded to traditional and conservative methods', had 'woken up to the situation' and were now emulating their German and American rivals.[11] But though there were some notable successes, such as the manufacture of boots and some specialized machine tools for the bicycle industry, where re-equipped British firms reclaimed the home market from the Americans, major industries remained heavily committed to nineteenth-century methods and organization. The Lancashire cotton industry, for example, was slow to abandon the mule for ring spinning and even slower to take up available new technology for weaving in the form of the Northrop automatic loom. Similarly, though there was a movement towards industrial concentration, particularly evident in the textile finishing industry, the merger wave was weaker than in the United States and thus less capable of delivering the advantages of economies of scale. By itself, the 'great vitality and power of extension' which the Balfour of Burleigh Committee attributed to Britain's industrial economy before 1914 was not sufficient to halt the process of relative decline which had been apparent since the 1880s, or the concomitant shift towards an economy dominated by services.

For tariff reformers, with their predominantly productionist mentality, the continuation of these trends through to 1914 was profoundly disturbing. Convinced that it was more important for Britain to retain its capacity for making iron and steel than to develop its capacity for making mousetraps, they were not consoled by the compensatory progress of industries serving the mass consumer market. An industrial economy based on jam and pickles, favourite objects of Chamberlainite scorn, might accurately reflect the current state of comparative advantage between manfuacturing nations, but it would leave Britain dangerously exposed in the evolutionary struggle between the great powers. Similarly, except where income from overseas investment reflected colonial development, the reformers derived little comfort from the rise of invisible exports. The growing dependence of the national economy on the provision of international services rendered Britain peculiarly liable to damage from external shock induced by factors beyond its control. Moreover, while the interests of the City-dominated service sector defined the parameters of economic policy, the maintenance of the industrial capacity necessary to sustain great power status was precluded. If current trends were not halted, Ashley had warned in 1903, Britain would slide towards de-industrialization while 'great countries . . . manufacture for themselves the staples which they need with assistance from high protective tariffs'. With its major industries ruined in competition with state-aided rivals, decline would begin, culminating in the polarization of British society into two nations, one deriving its income in the form of low wages from services and cheap labour industries, the other living on its overseas investments. Thus, he argued, 'though with some new features – the history of Holland will have been repeated' (Ashley, 1903, pp. 111–13).

The tariff reformers' sense of foreboding was enhanced in the Edwardian period because they were denied the opportunity to apply their corrective strategy of modernization. Unable to formulate policy from a privileged position within the core institutional nexus, they were thrust into the marketplace of electoral politics where tariff reform competed for the attention of the public with Chinese labour, Irish home rule, Welsh disestablishment and other issues of the moment. In such conditions, the development of tariff reform as a crusade for modernization was seriously inhibited. From the start, the Chamberlainites were forced to fight on unfavourable ground chosen by their opponents, who savaged the proposed 'food taxes' on which imperial preference hinged. It was also necessary, in order to maximize support, to emphasize the advantages which a tariff would bring to particular local or sectional interests. As a result, even 'advanced' social imperialist tariff reformers often found themselves defending old-style protectionism rather than advocating a coherent strategy for twentieth-century economic and social transformation.

Moreover, practical politics dictated that tariff reform should be advanced largely through the Conservative Party, an inappropriate vehicle for modernization. While the majority of Conservatives and Liberal Unionists, expecially rank and file party activists in the constituencies, were sympathetic to Chamberlain's proposals, there was resistance from the Balfourite centre and the more extreme 'free fooders' who regarded tariff reform as the antithesis of Conservatism and as likely to damage the essential interests of the party. In particular, it was feared that 'food taxes' would prove unpopular with the electorate and thus impair the ability to defend those historic institutions, such as the House of Lords, to which the Conservative Party was pledged. Similarly, the union with Ireland, to which both Conservatives and Liberal Unionists were committed, might be jeopardized. These formidable barriers obstructed the Chamberlainite campaign to win the Conservative Party over to the new policy, forcing the Tariff Reform League to divert its energies into a war of attrition in the constituencies in an effort to purge the 'free fooders'. The modernizing thrust of the tariff reform policy was obscured in the ensuing welter of factional strife.

Though it appeared after 1908 that their tactics had succeeded in shifting the party leadership towards a pro-tariff position, Arthur Balfour's annexation of Chamberlain's policy was undertaken in a conservative rather than a radical spirit. As both major parties embraced collectivism, the question of revenue became paramount and in these circumstances tariff reform appealed to the Conservative mandarins as a ready-made alternative to the predatory strategy favoured by Lloyd George. If social reform was on the agenda, it seemed preferable to raise the necessary revenue from import duties rather than from increased direct taxation. The modernizing edge of tariff reform, therefore, was dulled as Chamberlain's radical approach was transmuted into 'a conservative policy related primarily to domestic affairs, and even more to the domestic pre-occupations of the propertied classes' (Sykes, 1979, p. 144). When, in 1913, the party's commitment to food taxes seemed likely to prejudice its chances of campaigning successfully against Irish home rule, Chamberlain's policy was put back on the shelf, underlining the essentially subordinate position of tariff reform within mainstream Conservatism.

The limited success of the tariff reform movement within the Conservative party was partly a reflection of its failure to detach British electors from their preference for free trade. This, in turn, reflected its failure to create a producers' alliance of sufficient strength to mount an effective challenge to the hegemony of liberal economics. Despite the efforts of the League's Organized Labour Branch, unkindly – but not unfairly – labelled the 'Organized Laboriously Branch' by free traders, the tariff reformers were generally unsuccessful in countering the insistent suggestion that Chamberlain's scheme would raise the cost of living for the working man and his family. Significantly, they seemed likely to break the attachment of the working-class voter to the 'large loaf' of free trade only in phases of high unemployment, like the winter of 1907–8, when the protectionist argument began to carry weight. This failure was accentuated by the continuing fiscal orthodoxy of the trade unions and the Labour Party. It proved impossible to reproduce on a national scale the class cooperation which sustained Chamberlain in Birmingham. Neither was it feasible to create an effective alliance of all productive sectors. Within the tariff reform movement itself, there was some tension between the interests of agricultural and industrial producers, especially as the commitment to food taxes appeared to reduce the prospects of protection for manufacturers. But most important in this respect were the significant sectors of production which depended on cheap imported raw materials or unrestricted access to the home markets of rival industrialized nations, both of which appeared to be guaranteed by free trade. Coal, cotton, shipbuilding and the food-processing industries were in this position. Industrialists in these sectors turned their backs on tariff reform, ensuring that the movement represented only a fragment of productive capital.

In political terms, it was the Liberal Party which constructed the most effective alliance. The interests of some sectors of production were linked with those of services and finance in defence of free trade, the whole edifice gaining stability from substantial working-class support. In 1906, the 'Liberal landslide' at the polls reflected the solid socio-economic base on which free trade stood. The verdict of the electors also brought into office a number of Liberal Imperialists, such as Asquith, Grey and Haldane, who had campaigned for national efficiency at the start of the century. Though it would be misleading to place too much weight on this link, the policy of the Liberal government, especially after 1908 when Asquith replaced Campbell-Bannerman as prime minister, owed something to the modernization strategy sketched out earlier by Rosebery and the Fabians. There was no attempt to legislate systematically on the lines set out in Webb's pamphlet. The poor law, for example, remained essentially unreformed despite the report of the Royal Commission in 1909. Improvements in technical education were modestly constrained within the limits of the Education Act (1902), though Imperial College of Science and Technology, established in 1907, stood as the monument to Haldane's 'Charlottenburg' scheme. But Lloyd George's trade boards, set up in 1909 to regulate conditions and wages in some 'sweated' industries, and the concern for the welfare of children indicated by the provisions for school meals and medical inspection were not too distantly removed from the Fabian concept of the 'national minimum'. In addition, it might be argued that old age pensions and national insurance, though not reflecting specific policy objectives of the national efficiency movement, were influenced by the desire to emulate the Germanic model of the socially efficient state which Haldane so admired.

Like the modernization strategy which they imperfectly echoed, the Liberal welfare reforms were designed to operate within the context of a free market economy. Industrial policy was similarly constrained. With the exception of marginal interventions, such as the Patent Act (1907), which required foreign patentees to manufacture in Britain, and the Development Act (1909), which set aside modest sums for afforestation, land reclamation and rural industries, the government was prepared to leave the maintenance, promotion and re-structuring of productive capacity to market forces. In practice, the 'New Liberalism' developed freely only within the limits of sound finance and fiscal prudence defined by the City, the Bank and the treasury. The severity of this constraint was especially apparent after 1909 when Lloyd George's 'People's Budget' stretched the conventional boundaries of taxable capacity, thus prompting a significant increase in capital exports as investors deposited securities abroad in order to avoid income tax. It has been argued that these 'Lloyd George investments' restricted the government's room for manoeuvre, depriving it of revenue and impairing its ability to raise more through additional taxation. In consequence, the modest impulse to modernization implicit in the piecemeal reforms of the 'New Liberalism' was thwarted. Social policy remained palliative rather than preventive, the Treasury blocking in 1914 counter-cyclical public works favoured by Lloyd George. Education, regarded as the key to national efficiency, was denied the necessary central government resources to improve the quality or range of schools.[12]

The fate of the modernization movements of the Edwardian era pointed to the presence within the British system of formidable structural constraints which precluded economic development on the lines of other modern industrial states. Of the two movements, national efficiency was the most easily contained because it sought to improve only the social infrastructure through strategic reforms with a view to ensuring in the long term a more competitive performance from British producers on the open market. Lacking a firm base within the two party system, the movement receded after 1903 when Chamberlain's Birmingham speech torpedoed the faint prospect that a centre party might emerge under an all-purpose efficiency umbrella. Committed to the maintenance of unregulated markets, the national efficiency movement was diverted into the campaign to defend free trade. Later, when some national efficiency policies surfaced in the programme of Asquith's government, their development was inhibited by the application of budgetary principles derived from a prevailing orthodoxy in economic policy which the earlier efforts of Liberal Imperialists and Fabians had failed to modify.

Tariff reform represented a much more serious challenge to the liberal economic system. Its productionist sentiment and its demand for regulated home and imperial markets confronted directly the hegemony exerted by the predominant commercial fraction of British capital through the operations of the core institutional nexus in defining the framework of economic policy. The movement's failure to mobilize an effective producers' alliance left it exposed to the vagaries of Conservative politics and led, in 1913, to its exclusion from the electoral agenda. Whether the policy outlined by the tariff reformers would have proved an effective stimulus to industrial modernization remains an open question. As Cain (1979) has argued, in the absence of a 'wider government plan designed to encourage the growth of newer sectors of industry', protection may well have deferred necessary structural change by propping up declining, long-established sectors. Similarly, imperial preference may simply have provided 'bolt holes for traditional industries' (p. 49). But whatever, the hypothetical deficiencies of tariff reform policy, they were politically significant only in so far as they contributed to the triumph of free trade and the decisive affirmation of the domestic ascendancy of the middleman over the manufacturer.

Notes: Chapter 1

1 Rosebery's speech at Chatham, *The Times*, 24 January 1900.
2 Discussion of British economic performance in this section draws heavily on Crouzet, 1982, pp. 359–422. See also R. C. Floud, 'Britain 1860–1914: a Survey', in Floud and McCloskey, 1981, Vol. 2, pp. 1–26; Kirby, 1981, pp. 1–23; Pollard, 1983, pp. 1–19.
3 *Economist*, 20 May 1911, quoted in Kynaston, 1983, p. 7n.
4 Rosebery's speech at Chesterfield, *The Times*, 17 December 1901.

5 Matthew, 1973, p. 250. For national efficiency generally see Scally, 1975, pp. 29–95; Semmel, 1960, pp. 53–82; Searle, 1971, pp. 54–106.

6 *The Benefits of Dumping*, Liberal League Publication no. 69 (1903–5).

7 For Chamberlain's speeches at Birmingham, 15 May 1903, at the House of Commons, 28 May 1903, and at Glasgow, 6 October 1903, see Amery, 1969, Vol. 5, pp. 184–92, 231–5; Vol. 6, pp. 460–7.

8 For an analysis of the components in the tariff reform alliance see Porter, 1978, pp. 2–5. For an account of the difficulties involved in classifying tariff reform and free trade interests see Marrison, 1983, pp. 148–78.

9 For Chamberlain's speeches at Greenock, 7 October 1903, and at the Guildhall, 19 January 1904, see Amery, 1969, Vol. 6, pp. 469–73, 535–40.

10 *Final Report on the Committee on Commercial and Industrial Policy After the War*, Cmnd 9035 (1918), pp. 21–22.

11 *Economist*, 11 January 1913, quoted in Pope and Hoyle, 1985, pp. 44–5.

12 The argument in this paragraph draws heavily on Offer, 1983.

CHAPTER TWO

War, Reconstruction and Normalcy, 1914–1929

The Impact of War

It proved impossible to reconcile the maintenance of a liberal economy with the requirements of total war. At the start, in August 1914, the government envisaged that the British experience of war would be rather less than total and confined largely to the professionals. Military action, it was thought, would be limited to the British Expeditionary Force's supporting role on the left flank of the French army. Meanwhile, with the navy blockading German ports, most shipping lanes would remain open and trade would continue to flow. Some direct intervention in the economy would be necessary in the extraordinary circumstances but, as Winston Churchill assured the City in November, the government was committed to 'business as usual'. When it became clear that the war would not be 'over by Christmas', this position was increasingly difficult to maintain, particularly in view of Kitchener's determination to transform the civilian population into a volunteer 'nation at arms'. By the spring of 1915, 'business as usual' had a complacent, hollow ring. Prices, especially of imported food, had risen rapidly in the first six months of the war, sugar and flour showing dramatic increases of 72 and 75 per cent respectively. The voluntary movement of about a third of the male workforce into either the armed forces or munitions had left in its wake a severely distorted labour market and shortages of skilled manpower. There were also problems of munitions supply, culminating in the 'shell scandal' which precipitated the fall of Asquith's Liberal government in May 1915.

By this stage, the frustrations of increasingly static hostilities in France had been compounded by the distinctly unpromising opening to the Gallipoli campaign. In these circumstances, the shell shortage had a similar effect to the disasters of 'Black Week' in December 1899, raising serious doubts about the capacity of the British state to organize for war. 'Business as usual' had implied faith in free enterprise and confidence that the supply of munitions would expand to meet increased demand. By exposing apparent limitations of the liberal economy, the scandal provided the crisis conditions in which the movement for modernization was regenerated, its characteristic rejection of *laissez-faire* values given new life by the idea that the market mechanism had failed the nation in its hour of need. In 1915, of course, the stakes were much higher than they had been during the Boer War; thus the crisis was more acute and the prospects for modernization more favourable. Having been handicapped in the Edwardian era by the persistence of party strife, Fabians, Liberal Imperialists and tariff reformers welcomed the new fluidity of coalition politics. As liberalism retreated after December 1916 before the inexorable advance of what was widely regarded as Lloyd George's 'great experiment in state socialism', modernizers were heartened not only because the wartime state was intervening directly to promote national efficiency and to regulate the home market in ways which they had advocated before 1914, but also because the government's commitment to 'reconstruction' seemed to indicate that the thrust of these policy developments would be maintained beyond the armistice. They were to be disappointed. Once the transitional phase from war into peace had been negotiated, the conditions essential for sustained reconstruction evaporated. When the postwar boom collapsed in 1920, prewar 'normalcy' (to use the contemporary terminology) was restored. Party politics re-emerged from the shabby wreck of the Lloyd George Coalition and the ideological hegemony of orthodox liberal economics was resumed.

In terms of the structure of the British socio-economic system, 'normalcy' implied a return to the prewar relationship between the two major fractions of capital and the subordination of the interests of production to those of finance. One effect of the war had been to place this relationship in cold storage. The onset of a major conflict between the great powers in 1914 had created conditions in which free trade, the gold standard and the discipline of the balanced budget were inoperative. Thus the City–Bank–Treasury nexus was denied access to those instruments of state policy through which the dominant position of British finance capital within the national economy was normally maintained. Though the long-term survival of this nexus and the relationship which it underpinned was guaranteed by state intervention at the start of the war to ensure that the City could meet any outstanding liabilities,[1] the practical influence of finance was temporarily curtailed. If only because the fight could not go on without munitions and adequate food supplies, the largely unforeseen nature of total war tilted the balance towards production.

This new emphasis, particularly apparent after the establishment of the Ministry of Munitions in June 1915, was reflected in the government's active policy of expanding productive capacity so that the demands of the war effort could be met. An unprecedented sensitivity to the interests of 'the industrious classes', especially labour, was evident and it is significant that Middlemas dates the emergence of 'triangular collaboration' between the government, the employers' associations and the TUC from the period 1917–1920 (Middlemas, 1979, pp. 151–2). Peace cleared the way for the restoration of normal economic priorities, powerfully symbolized by the commitment to return the pound to its prewar rate of exchange with the dollar at the earliest opportunity. Though the 'back to 1914' movement assisted the City, the Bank and the Treasury in their efforts to re-establish prewar spheres of influence, it generated a climate of financial constraint which thwarted the modernizing influence of the Ministry of Reconstruction and handicapped British industry in competition with foreign rivals. In this context, Sir Alfred Mond's attempt in the late 1920s to link capital and labour in an alliance of producers for political action suggests renewed awareness of the peacetime subordination of industrial interests to those of the City.

The State and the Industrial Economy, 1914–1921

There was little indication in the Liberal government's limited measures of economic mobilization in 1914–15 of the massive development of state intervention that was to come. Anticipating that British involvement in the conflict would be marginal and predisposed generally towards economic *laissez-faire*, ministers relied mainly on *ad hoc* extensions of state authority in a variety of forms and justified by reference to specific circumstances. Thus in some instances new bodies were set up with a particular wartime purpose and in others the functions of existing government departments were expanded. At the start of the war, in order to co-ordinate movements of troops and essential supplies, the railways were brought under the direct control of a state Railway Executive, though remaining under company management. Later, in an attempt to direct investment into useful enterprises, the Treasury was required to approve all new share issues on the stock market. And, as the munitions crisis became apparent, reserve powers were granted under the Defence of the Realm Act (1915) permitting state takeovers of factories engaged in war production. Such piecemeal encroachments on the liberal economy left the framework of voluntarism virtually intact but they made a considerable impression at the time. 'One of the things which struck the intelligent working man during the early days of the war', noted Arthur Greenwood, 'was the rapidity with which . . . large measures of state control and action were put successfully into operation' (1914, p. 303). Particularly impressed were those, like Ashley, who had looked to the state in vain before the war as an agency through which market forces might be controlled and productive capacity developed. As early as November 1914, he drew attention to the 'dramatic transformation' of the state's economic role which he believed was taking place.[2]

> Under the pressure of necessity, the government, with the complete support of the nation, instantly abandoned the traditional policy of economic inaction. We now wake up every morning to find government credit extended to some new department of commerce; some branch of trade put under an embargo; some enormous purchase of commodities undertaken . . . ; some extensive new manufactures developed and financial assistance offered to investors, as for the promotion of dye-stuffs.

It seems likely that Ashley, at this early stage of the war, was reading too much into emergency measures such as the ban on exports of benzol, phenol, tuolol and other chemicals required for the manufacture of explosives, and the cheap loans made available to encourage domestic production of such items as chemical dyes and optical instruments which had been supplied exclusively by German imports before 1914. But, in these departures from former practice and especially in 'the stepping of the government into the arena of manufacture', Ashley saw the prospect of national political economy on German or American lines. 'A country', he argued, 'in which government accepts in principle the duty of guaranteeing the permanent production . . . of commodities previously imported from the enemy's country can never be as before.'

What Ashley referred to as 'the traditional policy of economic inaction' was further eroded under the Asquith coalition between May 1915 and December 1916. In this period, Lloyd George's Ministry of Munitions, which was to become the principal engine of wartime state intervention, established its grip on production. It proved almost impossible in the context of the all-consuming war effort to limit the scope of the new ministry's operations; its controls reached out from the munitions industries into the economy as a whole. The emphasis on voluntarism which had constrained the government during the 'business as usual' phase was swiftly abandoned as negotiated agreements with the unions, whereby restrictive practices were suspended and skilled trades diluted with unskilled labour, were given the force of statute law in 20,000 'controlled' establishments. The heavy import duties on motor cars, motor cycles, clocks, watches, musical instruments, films, plate glass and hats introduced in Reginald McKenna's budget of September 1915 marked a further departure from liberal tradition in the interests of expediency. With essential cargo space limited by shipping losses and a foreign exchange crisis looming, the duties were defended by McKenna, a free trader, as necessary for the successful prosecution of the war, though Cobdenite purists detected the thin end of a protectionist wedge. 'If the right of the British maker of kinema films, motor cars and hats to plunder the British consumer be admitted', thundered the free trade *Manchester Guardian* on 22 September, 'what can stand in the way of every other industry getting the same privilege?'

The rapid expansion of state intervention in the economy after December 1916 seemed to vindicate those who had hoped or feared that the pressure of war had initiated an unstoppable process. As Pollard has indicated: 'Some relatively minor control, to deal with an immediate issue, often had repercussions which required government intervention further and further back, until the state found itself directing a major part of the country's industries, and controlling or licensing most of the remainder' (1983, p. 20). Thus, for example, the role of the state as a near-monopoly purchaser of raw wool led to the establishment of a Board of Control to supervise distribution to producers of those supplies not required by military contractors. The Ministry of Munitions, which required a staff of 65,000 civil servants by November 1918, quickly discovered that one regulation led inexorably to another. Under the Lloyd George Coalition, supervision of the strategically important coal and shipping industries was progressively developed until state control was achieved. From the spring of 1917 it was the Coal Controller and the Shipping Controller who made the key decisions, rather than the mine-owner and the ship-owner. The ministry's activities, which included the supervision of production in 250 state-owned factories, mines and quarries, led the government into uncharted territory. By the end of the war, state purchasing accounted for 90 per cent of all imports, and prices, rents and wages were subject to a battery of regulatory orders. To many contemporary observers it seemed that economic liberalism, the orthodoxy which had frustrated the Edwardian modernizers, was dead.

State intervention on this unprecedented scale was sanctioned by the immediate objective of winning the war. In so far as improved efficiency and industrial modernization were promoted, it was primarily to serve that narrow purpose. In these circumstances, the pious wish of the Ministry of Munitions that a re-equipped and more competitive steel industry would emerge from the war tended to give way to short-term priorities, expediency often dictating a policy of extensions to existing, sometimes outmoded, plant and machinery. But, though state intervention did not necessarily lead to enhanced efficiency, and may have enhanced inefficiency in some instances, some long-term benefits were apparent by 1918. The ministry encouraged wider use of arc furnaces, more effective as converters of scrap than the conventional Bessemer process, so that the steel–scrap ratio was raised during the war from 15 to 50 per cent. Standardization was promoted in engineering products, facilitating the widespread introduction of automatic and semi-automatic machinery. Electricity was more generally utilized for industrial purposes, the ministry leading the way in its munitions factories where 95 per cent of machinery was driven by electric power. In addition, there were significant ancillary improvements in cost accounting techniques, labour management and factory welfare provision. While acknowledging that not all wartime advances could be carried over into peacetime production, it was the view of the Balfour of Burleigh Committee that 'the knowledge and experience gained during the war should be a most valuable asset in respect of our post-war trade'.[3]

The enhanced importance of production in the British wartime economy was reflected in the new authority assigned to captains of industry and leaders of organized labour. Before the war, the social alliance of landed and commercial wealth had dominated the command structure of the state: industrial producers, whatever their social class, had generally been unable to gain entry on their own terms. Writing in 1907, 'Artifex' and 'Opifex', two Birmingham gun manufacturers, clearly had this in mind when in *The Causes of Decay in a British Industry* they attributed the decline of their industry to 'the English political climate'. Conscious of their status as provincial outsiders, they noted with regret that the aristocracy seemed less than anxious to incorporate industrial producers into the power structure. 'The Financiers', they complained, 'the minor capitalists, the bankers, the merchants, the international traders, all have been admitted to a direct voice in the government of the country before any of the industrial classes were admitted to its secret councils.' In consequence, they claimed, 'industrial interests, the interests of the humble toiler who produces wealth, have been sacrificed to all other interests' (pp. 269–70). The advent of the Lloyd George Coalition in December 1916 appeared to open the 'secret councils' to some of those who had previously been denied access. In an attempt to invigorate the Whitehall war machine, Allan Smith of the Engineering Employers Federation and Lord Weir of the Federation of British Industries (FBI) were brought in to advise on production; Lord Cowdray, a civil engineering contractor, served as Air Minister and Lord Rhondda, a coal-owner, as Food Controller. The influence of these industrialists in the management of the war economy at the highest level was modestly echoed up and down the country in the District Armaments Committees and other bodies through which manufacturers organized munitions work in the localities. Arthur Henderson, the leader of the Labour Party, joined the War Cabinet, his colleagues George Barnes and John Hodge gaining posts of ministerial rank. Beyond them stretched a small army of official Labour and trade union representatives recruited to various boards, committees and tribunals as the machinery of government expanded. In political terms, it seemed that 'the industrial classes' had arrived.

Having served as Minister of Munitions in 1915–16, Lloyd George had no illusions about the extent to which total war made the state economically dependent on its producers and politically dependent on their representatives. He had learned quickly that there were practical limits to the coercive power of the state. If the ministry was, as he claimed, 'from first to last a businessman's organization', it was partly a reflection of the *de facto* authority of the industrialists on whom it relied to give effect to its directives. Similarly, the Munitions of War Act (1915), which effectively suspended normal industrial relations, was operative on the shop floor only if the agreement of workers was secured, hence the new role for union leaders as 'intermediaries between the government and a labour force whose acceptance of a new industrial discipline was an essential condition of military success' (Miliband, 1972, p. 47). What emerged, in effect, was a social contract binding the industrial classes, both capital and labour, to national service for the duration of the war. By 1916, its basic features were apparent.

> For a short time, under the stress of war, employers and wage-earners have submitted to outside control. The employers, accepting large profits, have done what the Minister of Munitions has commanded. The wage-earners, accepting war bonuses, had given up their restrictive conventions and worked for increased production. (Webb and Freeman, 1916, pp. 56–7)

The composition of Lloyd George's government set the seal of authority on these arrangements. Thereafter, the contract was sustained for the duration by the whole complex of wartime controls and by newly established machinery, like Whitley Councils and the National Industrial Conference, which aimed to promote co-operation between capital and labour.

Once the external pressure of war had been removed in November 1918, the three-way relationship which Lloyd George had fostered between the state, productive capital and industrial labour could not be maintained. Labour left the government in order to establish an independent parliamentary identity and the businessmen who had run the war, effectively as temporary civil servants, returned to their firms. The termination of the wartime contract was signalled by the breakdown of the National Industrial Conference after February 1919. Though it was not the intention of the incoming Conservative-dominated Coalition to make a precipitate bonfire of all economic controls, the absence of Labour weakened their resolve, despite the arguments of Christoper Addison, the Minister of Reconstruction, who viewed the intelligent use of some wartime regulations as essential in ensuring an orderly transition from war to peace. Lloyd George's great experiment, it soon became clear, had not converted the industrialists to collectivism. Freed from their obligations to the state, they were prominent in the headlong charge back to 1914, their faith in economic individualism sometimes strengthened rather than undermined by the experience of state intervention. 'It has been pointed out how enormously production has been increased by state intervention under the Ministry of Munitions', noted a Dumbarton shipbuilder in 1917, 'but all those who are involved know how much this has led to indiscipline, and how terribly wasteful the effort is.' Like many employers, he particularly looked forward to normalization of the labour market and the termination of 'one-sided agreements which would not have been tolerated in less dangerous conditions'.[4] Such sentiments appear to have prevailed in the business community of 1918–19.

Addison, who was anxious not to prejudice the cause of reconstruction by clinging unnecessarily to emergency restrictions began the process of decontrol on the day after the armistice. Within weeks such important commodities as steel and non-ferrous metals had been liberated. Thereafter, the apparatus of the wartime state was dismantled in a piecemeal fasion; there was a surge of deregulation in April 1919 but some food remained on ration until November 1920 and the mines and the railways were not returned to private control until 1921. Perversely, limited licensing hours survived as did the McKenna duties which thus defied the expectation of their reluctant author that 'their failure and consequent removal would be a good object lesson as to the impossibility of tariffs in this country'.[5] But if economic freedom did not quite 'burst out overnight', as A. J. P. Taylor has put it, the general liberalizing thrust of government policy was soon clear. The rapidity with which decontrol proceeded, against the advice of the circumspect but increasingly isolated Addison, reflected the belief that absence of restraint would provide in itself a beneficial stimulus to the economy, restoring prewar levels of activity and guaranteeing employment as the army demobilized. In the context of these very short-term objectives, accelerated decontrol could be justified in that it helped to fuel the boom of 1919–20 which pushed industrial output back to the record level of 1913 and restricted unemployment, measured at 691,000 in December 1920, to only 5.8 per cent of the insured workforce. This boom, however, which had been generated by the peculiar post-war combination of extensive restocking, excessive liquidity and the release of pent-up consumer demand, could not be sustained for any great length of time. As it was, it lasted long enough to provide the government with a useful bridge, carrying it over the political quicksands which attended the immediate transition from war to peace.

In the political conditions pertaining from November 1918 to April 1920, the government's room for manoeuvre was limited. Though the Cunliffe Committee, in its interim report before the end of the war and its final report in December 1919 had recommended a return to the gold standard and a fixed exchange rate of $4.86 to the pound as soon as conditions were favourable, this route back to normalcy was temporarily blocked as Lloyd George's ministers assigned priority to the task of defusing the perceived threat of socialist revolution. In effect, the practice of fixing the value of the pound in terms of gold, thereby fixing its value against other currencies, had been abandoned in 1914 but Britain's departure from this system was not officially signalled until March 1919. The deflationary measures which re-instating the gold standard would have required were ruled out while the potentially explosive combination of military demobilization and industrial unrest remained a political factor. Some measure of the Cabinet's anxiety in this respect was its hasty approval at the end of 1918 for a non-contributory 'out of work donation', payable to all unemployed ex-servicemen and some others. This dole scheme, which conceded at a stroke the radical principle of 'work or maintenance', ran counter to the established actuarial basis of national insurance and cost £66 million by May 1921. The strike organized in Glasgow to support the demand for a forty-hour week in January 1919, broken up by police as the red flag flew over City Hall, seemed especially ominous. It opened a year in which thirty-five million working days were lost to strike action, a figure approaching the peak established during the syndicalist wave of agitation in 1912. Such conditions precluded measures which might increase unemployment or a return to prewar levels of public expenditure.

Allowing the boom to run its course was, for a time, politically expedient but there were dangers attached to this strategy. The boom was characterized not only by increased output and low unemployment but also by rapid inflation as liberated purchasing power chased a supply of goods still subject to constraints while industry adjusted to peacetime requirements. Prices, especially for food and clothing, rose rapidly between 1918 and 1920, compounding the effects of the inflation which had occurred during the war. Earnings reflected the same upward trend, though tending to run ahead of prices at this stage (see Table 2.1). The government, committed to decontrol, progressively denied itself recourse to interventionist measures, such as price fixing or rationing, which might have restrained this inflationary surge and limited its negative impact on British exports. These became

Table 2.1 Indices for Prices and Earnings, 1918–1922 (1913 = 100)

	Consumers' goods and services	Food	Clothing	Average weekly wage earnings
1918	202.5	219.5	300.0	211
1919	222.9	226.7	338.2	241
1920	257.2	265.9	386.6	278
1921	235.0	232.6	285.8	260
1922	202.2	185.5	226.4	209

Source: Feinstein, 1972, Tables 61, 62 and 65.

less competitive as the price differential with American goods widened unfavourably. In addition, the commitment to decontrol left the government relatively powerless to contain the adverse effects of another unfortunate by-product of the boom, raging over-speculation in the shares of cotton, coal and shipbuilding companies.

In April 1920, it became clear that the consequences of rampant inflation had replaced the envisaged threat from the left as the main concern of the Lloyd George Coalition. Though industrial unrest still simmered, the number of working days lost through strikes was declining and the problem of demobilization, which had featured prominently in the Cabinet's pre-revolutionary *scenario* a year earlier, had been successfully negotiated. The government, therefore, was free to re-order its priorities, turning, as Pollard notes, 'from unemployment as a major pre-occupation to callous disregard for it altogether, as soon as the social peace was no longer threatened' (1983, p. 135). Austen Chamberlain's deflationary budget and a rise in the bank rate to 7 per cent in April 1920 slammed on the brakes, simultaneously terminating the postwar boom and signalling a return to the principles of 'sound finance'. Deflationary pressure was maintained throughout 1920 and 1921 with the bank rate remaining at its panic level for almost a year and Chamberlain pursuing a budgetary strategy designed to produce a surplus after six consecutive years of deficits. The Geddes Committee began its review of public expenditure, its infamous 'axe' falling heavily on public health and education. In response, prices and earnings started to fall as rapidly as they had risen (see Table 2.1), but at the cost of a sudden deterioration in output and employment. Total industrial production in 1921 was about 18 per cent lower than in 1920 and, by December, unemployment had risen to 1.9 million, 16.2 per cent of the insured workforce. The government had chosen to deliver a short, sharp shock to the economy. For Britain, it seemed, the route back to normalcy lay via the violent switchback of boom and slump.

The inflation crisis of 1920 and the manner in which it was resolved cleared the way for the implementation of the Cunliffe Committee's recommendations. It had provided the opportunity for the City–Bank–Treasury connection to re-assert over state policy the controlling influence which had been in abeyance since 1914. Cunliffe had suggested that a transitional period of about ten years might be required before normalcy, in the form of the gold standard and the prewar exchange rate, could be achieved. As domestic inflation soared in the postwar boom, this distant prospect appeared to recede as the pound floated downwards, reaching a low point of $3.40 in February 1920. Each institutional component of the crucial financial nexus backed a return to gold. Collectively they formed a powerful lobby for the deflationary policies which would push the pound up towards $4.86. For the City, its essentially commercial interest damaged by the emergence of the United States as the leading creditor nation and the rise of New York as a rival financial centre, government commitment to the gold standard seemed likely to guarantee the future of sterling as an international currency, thereby safeguarding the pivotal role of London markets in the world financial system. The Bank of England also sought to re-establish its prewar position through retrieving the authority over interest rates and domestic money supply which had been usurped by the Treasury during the emergency of 1914–18. As the Cunliffe Committee confirmed, gold standard policies would require both an effective bank rate and a disciplined issue of paper money, thus restoring to the Bank traditional mechanisms of control which had been undermined by the wide circulation of wartime Treasury bills. As for the Treasury, the deflationary prelude required for a return to gold would assist its efforts to reduce the national debt and also supply a compelling pretext for re-asserting its departmental supremacy within the Civil Service as free-spending ministries were brought to heel. For its officials, as Peden has suggested, 'the *means* to restoring the gold standard must have been no less attractive than the end itself'.[6]

What made the interest of finance politically decisive in shaping the government's response to the crisis of 1920 was the emergence of a broad, visible coalition of interests favourably disposed towards deflationary policies. Small savers, people living on fixed incomes and middle-class consumers were especially sensitive to the adverse consequences of price inflation. They formed a receptive audience for the *Daily Mail*'s crusade against 'squandermania' in public expenditure, and a natural constituency for the politics of Northcliffe's Anti-Waste League in 1920–1. Campaigning on the single issue of retrenchment, the League's 'independent Conservative' candidates succeeded in embarrassing the government at several by-elections, though, significantly, they had been absorbed into the official party machine by the end of 1921. In its brief span, the League gave political articulation to a populist chorus which blended supportively with the advice which ministers were receiving from the Bank and the Treasury. Moreover, though many industrial interests condemned the gold standard after it had been re-imposed in April 1925, there was little opposition to its emergence as an over-riding objective of state policy in 1920. The FBI had responded positively to the Cunliffe proposals and, in general, the business community seemed content to leave the technicalities of foreign exchange to the bankers. At this formative juncture in the development of state policy, it did not seem likely that either a return to the gold standard or the measures required to make it possible would expose the latent rift between the two major fractions of capital. Only later did it become apparent that the interests of industry were again to take second place to those of finance.

The triumph of liberal economic orthodoxy in 1920–1 marked the end of a brief period during which it had been possible to define the national interest, in its economic aspect, largely in terms of production. As in peacetime, when the hegemony of British finance capital had been upheld by the collective influence of the City, the Bank and the Treasury over public policy, so, after 1915, the fleeting ascendancy of production had been underpinned by a makeshift institutional nexus embracing leaders of industrial capital and organized labour and new departments of state, principally the Ministry of Munitions. In these conditions, the positive economic impact of the war on industrial production outweighed the negative, at least in the short term. It was noted of the engineering industry in 1918, for example, that 'an enormous quantity of new plant had been installed; existing works had been developed and extended, and a large number of new factories had been built'.[7] Several new manufactures had been established to meet the requirements of wartime import substitution and in key new wave industries, especially the production of aircraft and motor vehicles, military demand induced significant expansion. After 1918, however, the external dimensions of Britain's prewar industrial problem re-appeared in an intensified form. Enhanced export competition from the United States was compounded by extensive Japanese penetration of Asian markets, a development which posed a particular threat to the Lancashire cotton industry. While British manufacturers had been servicing the needs of the war economy, indigenous industrial growth had been stimulated in Australia, Canada, China, India and South America, restricting export opportunities in traditional outlets. Moreover, although war had acted as an agent of industrial modernization, it soon became clear that this process had not gone far enough. In particular, Britain entered the highly competitive postwar overseas markets still burdened with an industrial structure heavily biased towards the nineteenth-century staples, now potentially low growth sectors in terms of output, productivity and exports. During the 1920s, a painful process of adjustment whereby capital and labour shifted to industries with higher growth potential did begin. Simultaneously, finance was re-established as the dominant fraction of British capital, thus terminating the relationship between the state and industry which had served during the war.[8]

The Rise and Fall of Reconstruction, 1916–1922

Though the Edwardian movements for modernization had been marginalized by 1914, war brought them back into the centre of the political arena. In different ways and for different reasons, the prewar advocates of national efficiency and tariff reform had reacted against *laissez-faire* individualism. For Liberal Imperialists and Fabians, the liberal state was deficient in so far as it lacked the apparatus necessary to secure the maximum collective efficiency of its citizens; for Chamberlainites, this inadequacy was evident in the alleged failure under free trade to protect and extend the productive capacity of the nation's industry and agriculture. The underlying social Darwinism which buttressed both Edwardian variations on the theme of modernization ensured that armed conflict would be regarded as the ultimate test of the liberal state and its fitness to survive. When the limitations of 'business as usual' became manifest in 1915, the view was generated that the existing state system had failed the test of war. Writing in 1916, H. G. Wells reflected on this swelling current of opinion. He observed:

> A number of people are saying that this war is to be the end of Individualism. 'Go as you please' has its death-blow. Out of this war, whatever else emerges, there will emerge a more highly organized State than existed before – that is to say, a less individualistic and more socialistic State. And there seems a heavy weight of probability on the side of this view.

In his commentary, Wells indicated that the evident failure of the 'too individualistic British state' to protect its capacity for producing essential war materials, such as the zinc used in the manufacture of cartridge cases, had been especially significant in creating a political climate more favourable to interventionist strategies. 'Individualism', he noted, 'had let zinc refining drift to Belgium and Germany; it was the luck rather than the merit of Great Britain that one or two refineries still existed' (Wells, 1916, pp. 97, 104–5). It was appropriate in these circumstances that the parliamentary machinations which led to the fall of Asquith's Liberal government in the aftermath of the shell shortage scandal should have been initiated by W. A. S. Hewins, a distinguished exponent of national political economy and formerly the secretary of Chamberlain's Tariff Commission. The consensus was shifting in favour of those critics of economic liberalism who were not content to trust to 'Britain's luck'.

These developments opened the way for the emergence of a new policy platform on which most of the prewar advocates of modernization could find a place After May 1915, barriers which had previously divided critics of the liberal system began to collapse. Before the war, in the absence of a Rosebery–Chamberlain centre party on 'co-efficient' lines, the modernization movement had been fragmented by the adherence of individuals to rival elements of the existing party system. Now Coalition government provided a flag of convenience under which Conservatives and Liberals of a like disposition could serve. Moreover, after the introduction of the McKenna duties, it became clear that an accommodation had been reached on the contentious issue of fiscal policy, the great rift valley of Edwardian politics. Though some diehard free traders persisted in their opposition to the duties, most Liberals, even the secretary of the Cobden Club, were prepared to accept this departure from pure Manchester doctrines in the extraordinary circumstances. At the same time, having campaigned unsuccessfully for twelve years, tariff reformers, even unrepentent 'whole hoggers', were in no position to spurn McKenna's modest offering. In this limited sense, there was some substance to their wartime claim that 'we are all tariff reformers now'. Thus, as liberal institutions, like free trade, creaked and gave way under the stress of war, those who sought to modify or transform them discovered an area of common ground. They also found, in the movement for postwar reconstruction, a useful peg on which to hang their ideology of modernization.

The origins of the movement for reconstruction may be traced to the Cabinet committee established by Asquith in March 1916 to advise on the problem of transition which would arise when hostilities ceased. It soon became apparent that this brief had enormous implications, as proposals emerged for resolving anticipated short-term problems which committed the state to long-term intervention on a scale unprecedented in peacetime. Unemployment, housing, even education, were forced on to the agenda, and the report of an agricultural policy sub-committee, outlining a strategy for supporting price levels and guaranteeing a minimum wage for farm labourers, seemed to foreshadow a new relationship between the state and the productive sector. The work of this committee of ministers was important: 'it launched reconstruction; it gave the task a breadth of conception which it never lost'.[9] But the committee, in its original form, did not survive the ascent of Lloyd George and his repudiation of the Asquith legacy after December 1916. The new prime minister appointed his own Reconstruction Committee in the form of a 'think tank' drawing on a range of progressive opinion and Whitehall expertise. This, in turn, was superseded in July 1917 by the Ministry of Reconstruction, the status accorded to the new department reflecting the priority assigned to the task of giving shape to a vision of postwar society which would serve to raise morale and sustain solidarity on national rather than class lines. As a ministry publication indicated in 1918,

> the idea of Reconstruction, of a simple return to pre-war conditions, has gradually been supplanted by the larger and worthier ideal of a better world after the war. The experience through which the country has passed has enlarged its sense of

> what is possible, and at the same time quickened its sense of what is fair and right.[10]

Broadly defined in this fashion, reconstruction appeared to open a new route to modernization, reviving hopes which had been frustrated in the years before the war.

This aspect of reconstruction became increasingly evident after December 1916. Lloyd George's reconstituted Reconstruction Committee and Addison's advisers at the ministry were drawn almost exclusively from overlapping circles of Fabians, advanced tariff reformers – especially those associated with Lord Milner – and unorthodox civil servants with a Munitions background. It was Lloyd George's intention that their aspirations should give shape and detail to the rather amorphous concept of reconstruction, thus 'laying the foundations of a new order'. 'No such opportunity', declared the prime minister when he addressed the first meeting of his chosen few in March 1917, 'had ever been given to any nation before – not even by the French Revolution'. He advised them to begin their great work while the situation was 'malleable', indicating perceptively that these favourable circumstances would continue 'for a short time after the war, but not for long' (Scally, 1975, p. 354).

As the broad agenda of reconstruction developed under Addison, the formative influence of the prewar modernization movements was apparent. The central thrust of the ministry's policy was in the direction of social reform, an emphasis which reflected not only Addison's radical humanitarianism but also the revived and subtly modified nuances of the national efficiency programme, personified by Beatrice Webb, inevitably one of the first appointments to the Reconstruction Committee. The work of a plethora of inquiries, established under the aegis of the ministry, resulted in ambitious proposals to combat the postwar housing shortage by assigning priority to a Treasury-assisted local authority building programme and an outline scheme for a co-ordinated national health service, providing important free facilities for women and children. A parallel development under H. A. L. Fisher at the Board of Education led to the Education Act (1918) which raised the school leaving age to 14. The characteristic Fabian–Liberal Imperialist pre-occupation with administrative efficiency also surfaced, Haldane, appropriately, heading a committee of inquiry into the machinery of government.

These schemes impinged only indirectly on the productive process, except in so far as they formed part of a social imperialist strategy to contain working-class aspirations. More directly, a commitment to improve and extend technical education, the national efficiency movement's stock antidote to relative economic decline, also featured in the reconstruction package, blending with the government's apparent determination to encourage technological progress after 1916 through the work of the Department of Scientific and Industrial Research and its supporting cast of industrial research associations. The familiar, unfavourable comparisons with Germany, commonplaces of the Edwardian 'great debate', re-appeared, given a sharper edge by the experience of war. German superiority in technical education and scientific research, argued a manufacturer in 1916, would ensure that 'when the guns have ceased, our enemies will bring their subtle ingenuity to bear on the trade war, and the brains which invented gas clouds, asphyxiating shells and fire sprays, will invent new trading expedients' (Stewart, 1916, p.15). In these circumstances, reconstructionists were able to intensify the campaign for wholesale educational reform, Sidney Webb advocating not only the raising of the school leaving age to 15 but also a broadening of access to higher education through the establishment of 'town universities', each developing appropriate specialisms related to industry or public administration. Imperial College, Haldane's prewar, 'Charlottenberg', was the model; Oxbridge, suggested Webb, would have to be brought into line. 'Unphilosophical classics', 'forensic exercises in the Union Debating Society' and 'cant about the gothic' would no longer suffice. The new order demanded 'really efficient instruction in the subjects . . . required to fit a man to be a brain-worker in the service of the community' (Webb and Freeman, 1916, p. 76).

As confidence in liberal institutions waned, the tariff reform movement regained its momentum. By September 1915, the Tariff Reform League, unusually silent since the outbreak of hostilities, had resumed its propaganda, issuing *War Notes* to members as fiscal policy was restored to the political agenda in relatively favourable circumstances. It was argued that war had strengthened their case, not least because the government was now impelled to seek new sources of revenue. Shortages of key imported manufactures and pressures on food supply had underlined the advantages of state intervention to protect productive capacity. In addition, a wave of imperial sentiment fostered a renewed interest in preferential tariffs as a means to consolidating the empire as a self-sufficient economic bloc. By 1917, when the reconstruction movement began to gather pace, the tariff reformers appeared to be in a formidable position, capable of moulding postwar trade policy on lines suggested by the Paris Economic Conference of June 1916. The conference resolutions, reluctantly endorsed by Asquith, committed the Allies to mutual economic co-operation on an anti-German basis, extending from war into the period of postwar reconstruction. Protective tariffs to prevent dumping, the means by which the enemy was expected to continue the war after the ceasefire, were thus regarded as merely the prelude to larger measures designed to render the Allies collectively independent of German manufactured goods and raw materials. In response to these developments, the Tariff Reform League modified its original, Chamberlainite programme to encompass the Allied dimension. *War Notes* for March 1917 indicated that the Paris proposals provided 'the only sure basis of victory and defence in the future'. This view, despite the evident difficulties involved in building a permanent edifice of international economic co-operation on the shifting sands of wartime diplomacy, permeated reconstructionist attitudes to trade policy in 1917–18. In particular, it influenced the deliberations of the Balfour of Burleigh Committee, which was instructed to frame its conclusions 'with special reference' to the Paris resolutions, and the work of Edward Carson's Economic Offensive Committee in the last stages of the war (Cline, 1982, pp. 163–74).

Though they suffered some tactical reverses before 1918, those modernizers who invested their hopes in the reconstruction movement were caught unprepared by the postwar reaction. As Wells had implied in 1916, the first premise of reconstruction was that the old system had perished, making it necessary to build anew. The second premise was that it would be possible to utilize the institutional reforms induced by the crisis of total war as the permanent foundation stones of a new social and economic order. For one progressive reconstructionist, the first premise had been satisfied when bankers 'were not able to carry on their business without the help of the State' and then reinforced when 'private enterprise failed to provide us with the guns and munitions we required'. In the conditions pertaining in 1917, the second premise followed naturally.

> We know that the state can do many things in a time of emergency which many people thought it could not do at all without very serious consequences; and there now seems no reason to doubt that, with public opinion behind it, what the state can do in a time of emergency it can do when times are normal. (Sanderson Furniss, 1917, pp. 6–7)

As the state was drawn apparently inexorably along the path which led to Lloyd George's version of 'war socialism', it seemed to reconstructionists that the process was irreversible. Their plans were rooted in this mistaken assumption. They did not anticipate the resurrection of liberalism and a determined effort to turn the clock back to 1914. Between 1918 and the fall of the Coalition in 1922, the limits of what the state could do in normal circumstances were clarified as the reconstruction movement ran aground. Along the broad front of policy, schemes emanating from Addison's ministry and its numerous committees were either curtailed or abandoned. In the absence of an integrated plan, the various policies in the reconstruction portfolio were picked off one by one: they were, it seemed, the first casualties of the peace.

The so-called 'new protectionism', linked to the reconstruction platform through the hopes which tariff reformers invested in the Balfour of Burleigh Committee, was especially vulnerable, for the conditions which underpinned the Paris resolution of 1916 had disappeared by the end of the war. 'We were instructed to consider the resolutions of the Paris Conference', explained Lord Balfour, 'but during the course of our enquiry the circumstances had materially altered.' In particular, the composition of the Allies had been changed substantially through the withdrawal of Russia and the entry of the United States, committed by Woodrow Wilson's 'Fourteen Points' to 'open door' trade policies. Moreover, Germany's sudden economic collapse in 1918, an unanticipated event, tended to nullify the demand for draconian anti-dumping measures, weakening the momentum of the tariff movement. In this fluid situation, the Balfour of Burleigh Committee assiduously steered a middle course. Comment to the effect that the final report would disappoint both free traders and tariff reformers, observed Lord Balfour, 'has given me the most unbounded satisfaction'.[11] Though the report recommended the imposition of a range of duties, there was no commitment to protectionism. Instead 'pivotal' industries were specified and particular circumstances identified where the assistance of a tariff or some other form of state intervention would be justified. This position, which formed the basis of the Dyestuffs Act (1920) and the Safeguarding of Industry Act (1921), served to confirm rather than advance the wartime consensus on fiscal policy with all its attendant constraints. Thus the forward march of tariff reform was temporarily halted.

In terms of Coalition politics, it could be argued that tariff reform was a peculiarly sensitive issue, judiciously assigned a low priority in order to maximize co-operation between Conservatives and Lloyd George Liberals. Moreover, the relationship between protection and industrial modernization was ambiguous: it was by no means certain that tariffs would promote greater efficiency. These considerations did not appear to apply to the question of national electricity supply. The failure of the government's Electricity (Supply) Bill, therefore, provided an unambiguous indication that the postwar consensus was hardening against the modernizing thrust of reconstruction. In its official literature, the Ministry of Reconstruction promoted the view that the beneficial impact of extensive electrification would be comparable to that which followed the adoption of steam power in the early nineteenth century. It would lead to unprecedented economic growth and open a new phase of industrial development. But before this could happen, it was suggested, the decentralized, undercapitalized and poorly equipped supply industry would have to be re-organized and refurbished under the direction of a powerful Electricity Commission. The bill, introduced in May 1919, which embodied these proposals was mutilated beyond recognition on its passage through Parliament, its centralizing principles running counter to the contemporary tide of enthusiasm for decontrol. Condemned as 'extravagant' and 'bureaucratic', it was re-introduced a year later but withdrawn. The emergence of national provision for electricity supply, an essential component of industrial reconstruction, was delayed until after the establishment of the Central Electricity Generating Board in 1926 (Johnson, 1968, pp. 426–30).

This fiasco marked a watershed in the brief history of the reconstruction movement. Thereafter, its momentum slackened. In an attempt to sustain the impetus of synoptic planning, Lloyd George convened a conference of ministers and advisers at Criccieth in July 1919 which considered various radical proposals to stimulate efficiency, innovation and growth in the economy. Two years later, the Gairloch conference, attended by bankers and industrialists, addressed the same agenda but the innovations in industrial policy which stemmed from these initiatives were modest. The most important, the Trade Facilities Act (1921), extended export credit guarantees and empowered the Treasury, subject to a total of £26 million, to underwrite loans for capital projects likely to generate a significant amount of employment (see especially Rodgers, 1986, pp. 105–6). To some extent, social policies associated with reconstruction were insulated from the early wave of postwar reaction which blocked the government's plans for electricity supply. Thus, in 1919, while the political strategy of the Coalition was shaped by the necessity of responding to 'pressure from below', Addison was able to establish a new Ministry of Health, albeit with rather circumscribed powers at local level, and to initiate the drive to build the 'homes fit for heroes' which Lloyd George had promised. The Housing and Town Planning Act (1919), which required local authorities to undertake building programmes funded by loans raised on the capital market and guaranteed by the Treasury, and the Housing Act (1919), which subsidized private contractors, led to the construction of about 200,000 new dwellings by 1922. Though this was a considerable achievement in view of rising costs and shortages of skilled labour, it was not enough to meet a deficiency which, according to the government's own very conservative estimate, stood at 300,000 at the end of the war. The diminished impulse towards reconstruction was especially evident in January 1921 when the housing programme was cut as part of the Coalition's deflation strategy, prompting Addison's resignation as Minister of Health. Building subsidies were ended six months later, sacrificed to the swing of the 'Geddes axe'.

Reconstruction was incompatible with the deflationary measures introduced after mid 1920 as the core institutional nexus recovered its influence over state policy. It embodied a conception of state activity forged in the crisis of 1914–18 when that influence had been diminished. Thus, as they planned in their committees, reconstructionists were not constrained by the view that the 'normal' level of state activity was that which had pertained before the war; similarly, they were not inhibited by pre-1914 notions of 'sound finance'. A Ministry of Reconstruction pamphlet of 1919, referring to the development of technical education, reflected their confident assumptions. 'More active participation of the State is required', it declared, 'through its national institutions, universities and technical schools and considerably larger funds will have to be voted annually to the cultivation and support of research in these places.'[12] Planning on this basis ran into a brick wall in the era of 'dear money'. In this context, the fate of Addison's housing programme was especially instructive for it encountered opposition from the Treasury, the Bank and the City, where the scale of local authority borrowing was said to be distorting the capital market and exerting an upward pressure on interest rates. Addison had been warned in 1918 that the rigid orthodoxy of the Cunliffe Committee 'aimed a serious blow at reconstruction'. It became clear after 1921, as the Treasury cut public expenditure in support of the Bank's policy of returning to the gold standard, that the blow was fatal (see Johnson, 1968, pp. 198–9; also Thane, 1982, pp. 145–6).

In the wake of the rapid price inflation of 1919–20, the political consensus shifted, leaving the reconstruction movement stranded and incapable of mobilizing sufficient support at any level to protect the gains which had been made. Wartime ministries were disbanded – Reconstruction went in June 1919, Munitions in April 1921. While their influence declined and disappeared, the Treasury was reinforced as the government sought to bring public spending under control. Even in those wartime creations which did survive, like the Ministry of Labour, officials lacked the influence and the economic sophistication to formulate credible alternative strategies. Moreover, whereas the Treasury had the implicit support of that section of public opinion which was outraged by 'waste' and re-assured when prices dropped towards 'normal' pre-1914 levels, the reconstruction movement lacked a clearly defined electoral constituency. Wartime organizations, like the Industrial Reconstruction Association, had linked

Addison's theme with the movement for 'co-partnership' between capital and labour, ideally exemplified in the Whitley Councils. A report of the meetings between employers and union representatives convened in the spring of 1918 by Waldorf Astor's Devon and Cornwall Association for Industrial and Commercial Reconstruction indicated that:

> A real desire had been created among the leaders of both sides to unite in the work of reconstructing the country . . . for which men of all classes are laying down their lives. This spirit is strengthened by the growing recognition that human misery, discord and poverty are common foes which all should join in trying to eliminate.[13]

But, as industrial conflict intensified in the immediate postwar period, these sentiments evaporated and it became clear that reconstruction politics could not be sustained on the basis of class co-operation. The British Commonwealth Union, which Docker had hoped would develop on the lines of his prewar Business Leagues, quickly descended into militant anti-Bolshevism. When these 'co-partnership' initiatives faded, reconstruction was deprived of the possibility of organized popular support, a crucial deficiency for a movement with no secure base in the party system.

Normalcy Restored, 1922–1929

As a force for modernization, the reconstruction movement lacked coherence, its motivating ideal eluding contemporary definition beyond that provided by utopian rhetoric. Moreover, its survival was contingent upon the existence of a particular set of political circumstances arising from the wartime emergency. Between 1918 and 1922, these circumstances dissolved as political normalcy was restored in the form of a party system which tended to marginalize coalitionist or cross-party movements. Whatever its deficiencies, reconstruction had unified the disparate elements of the prewar modernization movement, bringing together Fabians, Milnerite tariff reformers and an assortment of bureaucrat-intellectuals. In postwar conditions, the movement fragmented, its separate components becoming isolated from each other as the framework of party politics was reimposed. This development was apparent from the general election of 1918 when Conservative and Liberal Coalitionists, bound by Lloyd George's support for reconstruction, were confronted by the Labour Party campaigning on a manifesto, *Labour and the New Social Order*, which had been drafted by Sidney Webb. This document, committing Labour to the maintenance of state control over the mines and railways, the nationalization of electricity supply and 'the universal enforcement of the national minimum', indicated that socialist transformation could be effected by means of modified reconstructionist policies.[14]

The restoration of normalcy was also evident in the renewed subordination of the interests of productive capital. This was reflected at a political level in the diminished influence of industrialists, both individually and collectively, on the formulation of economic policy. During the war, as Middlemas had suggested, 'the business community reached to the centre of government in an unprecedented fashion'. Industrialists were elevated to cabinet rank and, after 1916, the FBI emerged as a representative institution of employers, staking a claim for parity with the TUC in the management of the war economy.[15] To some extent, the relative weakness of the industrial lobby in the 1920s arose from divisions within industrial capital itself. The FBI's aspirations to represent industry as a whole were severely dented by the persistence within its ranks of a division between protectionists and free traders which inhibited the development of policy: there were also rival institutions, notably the National Confederation of Employers' Organisations (NCEO), founded in 1919. After 1920, FBI membership declined, de-control having removed the contentious regulations which had prompted many industrial interests to affiliate in wartime. The Federation's influence was further reduced by its failure to attract support from the new consumer product industries, the most dynamic growth sector of the industrial economy. In the absence of a unified extra-parliamentary movement, much depended on the parliamentary activities of Allan Smith's Industrial Group which, between 1921 and 1923, 'sought to arm first the Coalition government and then the Conservative government with a programme for dealing with unemployment which would meet the challenge of socialism'

(Rodgers, 1986, p. 118). Advocating public works and state-assisted development, such as an extensive railways electrification, which would relieve unemployment and modernize the industrial infrastructure, Smith's pressure group activity was modestly successful, especially in shaping a package of measures announced by Baldwin's government in November 1923. But, in the restored normalcy of party politics, the Industrial Group was subject to the vagaries of the electorate and its influence was considerably diminished when about half its membership was unseated at the general election which brought Labour to office in December 1923.

Divisions between various industrial interests and the inability to generate a coherent productionist strategy contributed to the triumphant re-assertion of liberal orthodoxy in economic policy which was apparent by the mid 1920s. Free trade, the gold standard and balanced budgets were the policy instruments through which the core institutional nexus sustained the primacy of British finance capital within the domestic economy. In December 1923, the electorate confirmed its attachment to free trade after Baldwin, casting about for a positive response to unemployment standing at 11.7 per cent of the insured workforce, committed the Conservative Party to protection. Though Baldwin was anxious to re-establish a distinctive Conservative platform after the Coalition interlude, it seems unlikely that he intended to precipitate an election with his Plymouth speech in October 1923. The campaign which he unintentionally set in motion caught the Conservatives relatively unprepared, exposing inconsistencies in their protectionist stance. Baldwin, forced to appease the 'free food' lobby, announced that 'essential foods' would be exempt from taxation, thereby alienating agricultural producers whom he then sought to placate with the promise of a subsidy to be funded from the revenue arising from proposed import duties. It was an unconvincing performance, the loss of 107 Conservative seats indicating the extent to which the electorate favoured the time-honoured fiscal certainties offered by Labour and the Liberals. Contemporary analysis of the result suggested that the electoral coalition which could be assembled to defend free trade was as powerful as it had been in 1906. As consumers, electors were inclined to resist a rise in food prices; Baldwin's exemptions, it was noted, did not apply to such popular delicacies as dried fruit and tinned salmon. Moreover, though some trades, notably the motor industry, campaigned for protection, their influence was heavily outweighed by that of the service sector and export-oriented industries, like coal and cotton, which had little or nothing to gain from a protectionist policy. Significantly, the National Federation of Iron and Steel Manufacturers remained silent in 1923, the export markets of its members temporarily secured by the dislocation of German production following the French occupation of the Ruhr. 'There was', noted Francis Hirst of the *Economist*, 'nothing surprising in the victory [of the free traders] except the simplicity of the tariff reformers in thinking they could succeed by a direct appeal to the people.'[16]

Labour's victory at the 1923 election temporarily reversed the modest drift towards import controls which had begun in 1915. The McKenna duties were abandoned and, though they were restored by the Conservatives in 1926, it was clear that tariffs would be erected only in exceptional circumstances or within the constraints of safeguarding. Churchill's appointment as Chancellor of the Exchequer in November 1924 was intended to reassure free traders. His economic orthodoxy, however, was not so rigid as to preclude doubts about the wisdom of returning to the gold standard in April 1925. But, after some hesitation, Churchill was persuaded to follow the line favoured by the City and advocated by the Bank and the Treasury, impelled on this course by the anxiety to protect the international role of sterling as the Dominions threatened independent action to stabilize their currencies in relation to the dollar. The anxious representations of the FBI, according to one recent account, were dismissed, Churchill indicating that it was an 'intolerable presumption' for the Federation to complain about Treasury policy (Davenport-Hines, 1984, p. 87). 'Deafened by the clamorous voices of conventional finance', as Keynes suggested in his celebrated polemic on *The Economic Consequences of Mr Churchill* (1925), the Chancellor thus implemented the recommendation of the Cunliffe Committee, reaching the goal which had shaped financial policy since the abrupt termination of the postwar boom in 1920. More than any other single act of policy, the return to gold at $4.86 signified the triumph of normalcy, the end of the 'long, long trail awinding' into the dreamland of 1914. As the former Treasury official, Sir Basil Blackett, later observed:

> it seemed to many that the goal of normality had been achieved and that it only remained to clear out of the way vexatious problems, such as those of Reparations and Allied debts, and discover a *modus vivendi* by which Britain's restored financial strength could work harmoniously in a world in which London, instead of being the pre-eminent financial centre, had to share the leadership with New York, and to take account of the sudden emergence of the United States as a great world lender. (Blackett, 1935, pp. 2–3)

With free trade reaffirmed and the gold standard reinstated, the holy trinity of liberal financial orthodoxy was completed by the Treasury's sustained pursuit of the balanced budget, though this was not achieved on a consistent annual basis until after 1932.[17]

The restoration of normalcy in the mid 1920s implied the resumption of the prewar relationship between commerce and production. Industrial producers were not seriously consulted about the return to gold: certainly, they lacked influence at the Court of Governors of the Bank of England which was dominated by representatives of overseas banking, insurance and shipping. For the complex of interests encompassed by the City, the advantages of an exchange rate of $4.86 were largely psychological, signalling confidence in its own capacity to fulfil the twin roles of international banker and financial entrepôt on pre-1914 lines. But, as Harold Macmillan indicated, 'making the pound "look the dollar in the face" proved an expensive act of faith' (1966, p. 204). It was soon apparent that sterling was overvalued, in Keynes' estimate by about 10 per cent, thus intensifying competition from foreign imports on the home market and disadvantaging British exporters by making their prices less competitive. During the 1920s, Britain's share of total world exports declined from 17.9 to 10.8 per cent and its share of total world exports of manufactured goods from 29.9 to 23.3 per cent. It seems unlikely that monetary policy was the decisive causal factor in determining these trends, but it did not help. By 1927, Sir Alfred Mond, the progressive colliery owner and chemical manufacturer, was convinced that the over-valued pound had inflicted significant damage on British exporters already burdened with high overheads. The return to the gold standard had administered 'a further check on exports, a further assistance to imports'. He noted that 'some of the countries in South America, where our low exchange rate gave us an advantage over the Americans, have been lost to us again – owing to the action of Mr. Winston Churchill'.

Mond also argued that 'the misdirected zeal to recover our gold basis at the earliest possible moment, rather than the regulation of such policies to keep in step with the industrial position, has been the most fundamental cause of the industrial and political troubles in which we are involved' (1927, p. 7). He was writing in the aftermath of the General Strike of May 1926, a crisis triggered by the breakdown of industrial relations on the coalfields as the colliery owners re-asserted their 'right to manage' and labour sought to resist pay cuts and longer hours of work. For industrial employers, the most important advantage of the deflationary policy which paved the way for the return to gold had been the downward pressure on wage costs. In a period of high unemployment, conditions were favourable for a 'capitalist offensive', especially as wages in many industries were already linked to falling prices through wartime cost-of-living agreements. Rather than modernize plant or submit to rationalization, employers, in these circumstances, often sought to make their exports more competitive by the simple expedient of an attack on wages, a strategy which preserved their rugged independence at the cost of deteriorating industrial relations. The revaluation of sterling in April 1925, by increasing the price of British goods on foreign markets, accentuated the postwar problems of the export industries. For coal mining, which derived no countervailing benefit from cheap imports, the crisis of 1925–6 was especially severe, particularly as German coal production had recently been resumed following the French withdrawal from the Ruhr. Moreover, coalfield industrial relations were highly politicized, the miners having opposed the abandonment of state control in 1921 and committed themselves to nationalization. Thus, it could be argued that organized labour, in showing solidarity with the miners after they had been locked out in May 1926, was signalling its rejection of the macro-economic framework which had been imposed since 1920 and challenging the rationale that had underpinned the decision to return to the gold standard.

Though the strike failed to secure victory for the miners, there were signs in the late 1920s that confidence in normalcy had been eroded. 'It was in the years following 1926', Blackett later recalled, 'that the conviction gradually took shape that the idea of restoring pre-war conditions was misconceived and was becoming a positive impediment to recovery of prosperity' (1935, p. 3). The strike confirmed the view that the maintenance of normalcy on the City's terms was a high risk strategy for industrial capital, requiring a hard line on labour relations which many employers were reluctant to pursue. An increasing number of industrialists, amongst whom Mond was prominent, now looked to rationalization rather than wage cuts as the means by which costs might most effectively be reduced. Industrial concentration developed rapidly in the late 1920s indicated by the unprecedented wave of merger activity which created giant corporations such as ICI, Unilever and Vickers Armstrong. The rise of the corporate economy, usually justified in terms of the economies of scale which could be achieved in production, bulk purchase, marketing and finance, implied a lack of faith in the liberal economy. As these new conglomerates gained monopoly or quasi-monopoly status, they sought actively to stabilize trading conditions by eliminating 'wasteful' competition, thus replacing the controlling influence of market forces with that of the 'visible hand' of scientific management. Rationalization opened up a new route to industrial modernization. In the context of post-1926 industrial relations it also seemed to offer the basis for a reconciliation with labour, the ideologies of rationalization and socialism overlapping to the extent that both denied the economic rationality of the free market. This raised again the possibility that an alliance of producers would emerge to confront the continuing hegemony of finance.[18]

Détente was explored in 1928–9 through the so-called 'Mond–Turner talks', a series of meetings between the TUC representatives led by Ben Turner and a group of employers convened by Mond. Some broad areas of agreement were evident, notably in relation to the establishment of permanent machinery for arbitration and consultation; there was also a commitment to the pursuit of modernization through rationalization, the TUC indicating that it was in the interests of its members to co-operate with employers for the promotion of efficiency. In addition, a general critique of Bank–Treasury orthodoxy was developed and linked to a demand for an official review of financial policy briefed to examine how it might be modified to stimulate industrial expansion. But the limitations of this *rapprochement* were soon apparent. Though the TUC was anxious to re-establish its prestige as a negotiating body after its recent defeat, 'class collaboration' antagonized a strong body of sentiment on the left which held to the view that the rank and file had been 'sold out' by the General Council in 1926. More discouraging, perhaps, was the unrepresentative nature of the Mond group of employers, many of whom had links with ICI and most of whom were drawn from large firms in the most dynamic sectors of the industrial economy such as Austin Motors, Dunlop and GEC. The FBI and the National Confederation of Employers' Organisations stood aside, denying credibility to Mond's initiative in the knowledge that the small and medium-sized firms which comprised the majority of their subscribers were either unwilling or unable to deal with the unions on the basis of the progressive paternalism practised by monopolistic enterprises like ICI. In short, 'Mondism' could not resolve what Ingham has referred to as 'the perennial problem of divisions based upon market situations' (1984, pp. 184–5; see also Gospel, 1979; Middlemas, 1979, pp. 205–9).

Though Mond's unauthorized diplomacy on behalf of the employers faded inconclusively, the attempt to formulate a political agenda in conjunction with organized labour was significant in the context of the late 1920s. It was not only a major contribution to the search for *modus vivendi* in industrial relations following the General Strike, but also a response to the renewed primacy of the interests of British finance capital under the regime of normalcy. As the creator of ICI, Mond was thoroughly committed to industrial modernization through rationalization and, in his view, it was essential that capital and labour should advance in harmony along this route. 'You cannot build an industrial system', he observed, ' . . . unless the captains of industry know they have behind them a willing and contented army' (1927, p. 2). But he was also aware that the consequences of the postwar renaissance of liberal economic orthodoxy, especially the restored gold standard, provided an area of common ground on which the normally antagonistic industrial classes could unite. Throughout the 1920s, the British industrial economy remained in a relatively depressed condition, the persistence of high levels of unemployment reflecting the intensified problems of the traditional export staples and the failure to achieve a rapid transfer of resources into new manufactures with a greater growth potential. Underpinning Mond's embryonic producers' alliance was a rationale which suggested that these conditions were derived from the pursuit of financial policies which favoured bankers and brokers at the expense of manufacturers and workmen, commerce at the expense of production. The failure of the Mond–Turner talks to generate a sustained challenge to the institutional authority of the City, the Bank and the Treasury helped to ensure that British producers entered the 'economic blizzard' in 1929 with their subordinate socio-political status intact.

Notes: Chapter 2

1 See Ingham, 1984, pp. 172–3, 274; also Pollard, 1984, pp. 34–5.
2 Ashley, 1914, pp. 18–19. This pamphlet is the published version of a lecture delivered at Birmingham on 18 November 1914.
3 *Final Report of the Committee on Commercial and Industrial Policy*, p. 23. For the impact of the Ministry of Munitions on industrial efficiency see Wrigley, 1982, pp. 47–52.
4 Sir Archibald Denny's contribution in Carter, 1917, pp. 42–3.
5 Mond to McKenna, 14 October 1915, McKenna MS (Churchill College, Cambridge). According to Mond this was McKenna's private view.
6 Peden, 1985, p. 63. For the attitude of the 'core institutional nexus' see Ingham, 1984, pp. 175–81.
7 Ministry of Reconstruction, *New Fields for British Engineering*, Reconstruction Problems Series No. 5 (1918), p. 1.
8 For the British economy in the immediate postwar period see Kirby, 1981, pp. 24–41; Aldcroft, 1986, pp. 1–10; Pollard, 1983, pp. 135–7.
9 Johnson, p. 31. For general accounts of the reconstruction movement see Marwick, 1965, pp. 239–46; Thane, 1982, pp. 137–55.
10 Ministry of Reconstruction, *The Aims of Reconstruction*, Reconstruction Problems Series No. 1 (1918), p. 4.
11 Lord Balfour to J. M. Robertson, 22 October 1918, Balfour of Burleigh MS (Scottish Record Office), TD 82/21/45. The authors are grateful to Lord Balfour for permission to quote this extract from the Balfour of Burleigh papers.
12 Ministry of Reconstruction, *Industrial Research*, Reconstruction Problems Series no. 36 (1919), p. 26.
13 *Report on the Reconstruction of Industry Prepared after a Conference of Plymouth and Cornish Citizens Who Were Also Employers and Trade Unionists* (Plymouth, The Devon and Cornwall Association for Industrial and Commercial Reconstruction, 1918), p. 3.

14 For a discussion of *Labour and the New Social Order* see Booth and Pack, 1985, pp. 6–12; also Miliband, 1972, pp. 61–3.
15 See Middlemas, 1979, pp. 113–14. For the emergency of the FBI and the NCEO see especially Turner, 1984, pp. 33–49.
16 See Hirst, 1925, pp. 72–88. For Baldwin's decision see Self, 1981, pp. 55–77.
17 For the decision to restore the gold standard see Ingham, 1984, pp. 170–87; also the succinct discussions in Kirby, 1981, pp. 36, 39–43; Peden, 1985, pp 60–7; Pollard, 1983, pp. 136–41; Tomlinson, 1981, pp. 92–105.
18 For the rationalization movement in industry see Hannah, 1983, pp. 27–40.

CHAPTER THREE

The Liberal Consensus Modified, 1929–1940

Towards Orderly Capitalism

When pressed by the Treasury to restore the gold standard, Churchill had indicated that he 'would rather see Finance less proud and industry more content'.[1] Though it could be argued that his capitulation to economic orthodoxy in April 1925 postponed the achievement of this equilibrium, a form of compromise between the two major fractions of British capital had emerged by the mid 1930s. This accommodation was reached through a series of painful adjustments as the world economy slid rapidly into crisis after 1929. Normalcy, which had triumphed in the domestic context by the mid 1920s, was exposed as a fragile illusion as British policy-makers were compelled to come to terms at last with a new world order characterized by economic nationalism. In seeking to restore prewar conditions, as Blackett observed, British policy had been 'of necessity internationally minded'. It had been informed by a conception of a global economic system,

> in which finance and commerce were international, leaping over and all but ignoring, national territorial boundaries – a world which, in spite of the unaccountable refusal of most other nations to adopt the British panacea of Free Trade, welcomed British ships and British goods and British capital everywhere, and, in return found in Britain a ready market for anything they might have to sell and investors ready to supply money for encouraging new enterprise in any part of the world. (Blackett, 1935, p. 4)

This view of pre-1914 conditions may not have corresponded with the experience of those hard-pressed Edwardian manufacturers who had rallied to the cause of tariff reform, but it could be reconciled with the interests of the service sector, particularly finance, as it re-established its organic ascendancy over production in the decade after the war. The abandonment of the gold standard in 1931 and free trade in 1932 signified an awareness that the world economic order which Britain had serviced so profitably in the late nineteenth century had disintegrated. The policy revolution also implied a readjustment of the relationship between finance and industry.

Moreover, as Ingham has observed, the economic catastrophe created conditions conducive to the regeneration of the movement for industrial modernization. 'Policies which had supported the old order had been overturned, and the City itself was much weakened by world recession' (Ingham, 1984, p. 189).

As the political consensus built on liberal economic orthodoxy dissolved, the party system was temporarily destabilized, encouraging the growth of cross-party or non-party pressure groups such as Political and Economic Planning (PEP), established in 1931, and the Next Five Years Group, founded in 1934. The progressive centre, which such organizations embodied, embraced advocates of corporatism and rationalization, like Macmillan and Mond, trade unionist supporters of producer co-operation, like Citrine, and technocratic reformers in the Fabian tradition. All shared the view that reliance on market forces had been discredited and were convinced that the national economy could be managed beneficially by the state, often on lines which were later recognized as distinctively Keynesian. A broad agenda for the reform of British capitalism was developed which went beyond the re-organization of industry on a more efficient basis to include social policies designed to eradicate the damaging environmental legacy of nineteenth-century individualism. Blackett, prominent in these progressive circles despite a career spent in the service of the Treasury and the Bank of England, indicated that modernizers of the early 1930s saw Britain as a country

> crying out for internal reconstruction – for tariffs and quotas to revive agriculture neglected for nearly a century; for protection and rehabilitation of old-established productive industries

> threatened by more up-to-date factories elsewhere . . . a country marred by ugliness and congestion and slums, in need of development expenditure of all kinds and able to absorb much of the annual flow of new capital, which up to the war and in the decade after the war had looked abroad, and not at home, for profitable outlets. (Blackett, 1935, pp. 4–5)

'Orderly and planned reconstruction' on the scale envisaged by PEP and the Next Five Years Group did not materialize in the 1930s, though state policy was modified by the adoption of a number of *ad hoc* strategies which inhibited the free operation of market forces and provided a mildly supportive climate for industrial recovery after 1932. But the core institutional nexus remained sufficiently powerful to deflect more radical strategies for modernization. These tended to become marginalized as the Conservative-dominated National Government established an impressive electoral hegemony and a redefined system of two party politics was restored.

The Crisis of 1929–1932

Although the slump of 1929–32 was less pronounced in Britain than in most industrialized countries, it was sufficiently sharp to administer a severe shock to the national economy. Gross domestic product and industrial output declined rapidly after 1929, returning to pre-slump levels and above only in 1934 (see Table 3.1). Exports proved especially vulnerable, shrinking in volume by 37.5 per cent over three years as demand for manufactured goods contracted in those primary producer markets on which the industrial staples were increasingly dependent. Even before the onset of the global crisis induced by the collapse of the American economy in 1929, it was clear that British export industries were drifting towards recession as an indirect consequence of falling prices for primary products. A worsening visible trade gap combined with reduced earnings from invisible exports to convert a balance of payments surplus of £76 million on current account in 1929 to a deficit of £114 million in 1931, thus fuelling the sterling crisis which drove the pound off gold. Unemployment grew rapidly from about 1.25 million in 1929 to a peak of almost three million in the late summer of 1932, approximately 23 per cent of the insured workforce. Estimates which included uninsured workers have indicated a peak figure for total unemployment of about 3.75 million. Despite the industrial recovery after 1932, pre-1929 levels of employment were not restored until 1937, a reflection of continuing problems in the traditional export staples where the shake-out of labour was especially severe. Industrial areas like Lancashire, the North East, South Wales, Central Scotland and Northern Ireland, which were heavily dependent on cotton, coal, iron and shipbuilding, experienced persistently high levels of unemployment throughout the 1930s. The fate of communities like Jarrow, once the location of busy ironworks and shipyards but by 1934, according to J. B. Priestley, 'an idle and ruined town' with '35,590 inhabitants wondering what is to become of them', provided a continuing and forceful reminder of the limitations of conventional financial wisdom.[2]

Table 3.1 The Impact of the Slump, Gross Domestic Product and Industrial Production, 1929–1934 (1913 = 100)

	GDP at constant factor cost	Industrial production
1929	107.8	125.5
1930	107.0	120.1
1931	101.5	112.3
1932	102.3	111.9
1933	105.5	119.3
1934	112.2	131.3

Source: Feinstein, 1972, Tables 19, 51.

Disenchantment with market forces was increasingly evident in the late 1920s, not least in the movement for industrial rationalization. In the context of party politics, however, 'safety first' attitudes prevailed. Having paid dearly for its attachment to protection in 1923, mainstream Conservatism shrank from the unconventional, the cautious pragmatism of Baldwin's government after 1926 prompting Macmillan and the radical Tory 'YMCA' in *Industry and the State* (1927) to regret the lack of 'some definite industrial policy'. At the general election of 1929, the most coherent strategy on offer was derived from the so-called 'Yellow Book', *Britain's Industrial Future* (1928), the report of the Liberal

Industrial Enquiry initiated by Lloyd George in 1925. The 'Yellow Book' addressed the structural dilemma resulting from the decline of export industries, urging that funds destined for overseas investment should be channelled by a National Investment Board into the development of the domestic economy. This strategy, owing much to Keynes, was modified for electoral consumption, emerging as Lloyd George's 'Orange Book', *We Can Conquer Unemployment*, which outlined an emergency programme of modernizing public works, notably road improvements, designed to create 600,000 jobs. The Treasury, invited by Baldwin to pour cold water on this initiative, responded by arguing that the Development Loan, through which it was proposed to raise the necessary finance, would simply divert funds from private investment, thus hindering the normal process of economic recovery. It was also suggested that the implementation of the Lloyd George scheme would require the renewal of an unacceptable bureaucratic 'dictatorship' akin to that exercised by the Ministry of Munitions in wartime.[3] Insecurely based within a party system which was tending towards polarization on class lines, the Liberals, who won only fifty-nine seats at the general election of May 1929, lacked the political muscle to mount an effective campaign in the face of vehement institutional opposition.

The sudden deterioration in world trade in the autumn of 1929, the collapse of exports and the upsurge in unemployment ensured that the challenge to the hegemony of orthodox political economy implicit in Lloyd George's proto-Keynesian strategy was sustained and enhanced. Early in 1930, it resurfaced in the form of the 'Mosley Memorandum', a policy statement which marked the beginning of a campaign to persuade Ramsay MacDonald's Labour government to detach itself from 'the Treasury view'. *Labour and the Nation*, the manifesto on which MacDonald had appealed successfully to the electorate in May 1929, celebrated the party's attachment to 'tentative, doctrineless socialism', an ideology which inhibited the development of a distinctive economic strategy. *How to Conquer Unemployment*, Labour's timid reply to the 'Orange Book', was strong on rhetoric, invoking in vague terms a vision of industrial modernization, but weak on commitment. 'Everything was there', notes Skidelsky (1967, p. 61), 'but the only definite promise was to set up a committee.' With

Philip Snowden, pillar of Gladstonian rectitude and critic of Lloyd George's 'madcap finance', installed as Chancellor of the Exchequer and a parliamentary majority dependent on Liberal votes, a genuinely socialist response to the crisis of British capitalism was off the agenda. But a memorandum written by Oswald Mosley, then a junior Labour minister, urging the government to bite the bullet of deficit finance in order to reduce unemployment by 800,000, also proved unacceptable. It was rejected by the Cabinet in May 1930, prompting Mosley's resignation. Though he remained popular with the constituency rank and file, he had failed to convert the party hierarchy, the trade union votes swinging the verdict narrowly against him at the party conference in October. This defeat sent Mosley in search of a more appropriate political vehicle for modernization, setting him on a path which led to the British Union of Fascists via the short-lived New Party, a dismal failure at the general election of October 1931.

Mosley's policy incorporated several themes associated with the modernization strategies which had emerged since the turn of the century. Like any orthodox advocate of national efficiency, he sought to reform the machinery of government: the war against unemployment was to be directed by a powerful executive controlled by the prime minister, serviced by various expert bodies including a 'research committee of economists', and linked to a 'development bank'. One of the bank's principal functions would be to arrange the necessary credit facilities of an extensive programme of public works and for schemes of industrial rationalization, viewed by Mosley as an essential precondition of national reconstruction. His short-term expansionist framework for home development was similar to that outlined by Lloyd George: he, too, was influenced by contact with Keynes. But whereas Liberal policy envisaged the continuation of free trade, Mosley was located firmly in the Chamberlainite tradition of modernization, arguing that import controls were required to insulate the national economy from 'the electric shocks of present world conditions'. Later, he was to turn his attention to the development of the empire as a viable economic bloc. Like Joseph Chamberlain, Mosley developed a productionist critique of cosmopolitan finance, confronting the logic of classical political economy which rationalized the operations of the City, the Bank and the Treasury. It did not make sense, he argued in his resignation speech, that

British capital should be exported 'to equip factories to compete against us . . . while it is supposed to shake the whole basis of our financial strength if anyone dares to suggest the raising of money by the Government of this country'. Reflecting on this passage in his autobiography, Mosley noted

> the beginning of the clash between a producers' and a financiers' policy, between my desire to develop a home market based on the purchasing power of our own people, accompanied by the concentration of our resources for the development of this system, and the traditional view that we should lend money abroad and encourage a swollen export trade for the purpose of building a strong position in international finance.[4]

As British capitalism became enmeshed in the global economic catastrophe after 1929, the sinews of the system were exposed. There was an intensified awareness of its characteristic duality and the subordination of production to commerce, especially City-based finance, in the formulation of the national interest. Mosley's politics, categorized by one contemporary critic as 'Birminghamism rampant', articulated powerfully the reaction against the maintenance of an open economy which left British producers vulnerable in an era of high tariffs and low prices. He blended with this the impulse to re-order the priorities which governed state policy by making finance subservient to industry.

Though the extent to which finance was humbled and production exalted should not be exaggerated, it is clear that the slump, as it undermined the foundation of the liberal economy, also destabilized the relationship between the major fractions of British capital. Changes in government policy as the crisis deepened suggested that the ground was shifting. MacDonald's Labour government, with options limited by its commitment to free trade, assumed that the eradication of mass unemployment was contingent on the revival of the traditional export industries on more competitive lines. In order to achieve the enhanced efficiency which was required if lost overseas markets were to be recaptured, the government sought to promote rationalization, through the agency of the Bankers' Industrial Development Corporation (BIDC). With a quarter of its capital subscribed by the Bank of England and the rest, sometimes reluctantly, by other banks and city institutions, the BIDC was started in 1930 to accelerate the process of amalgamation and to eliminate surplus capacity. Firms in a weak financial position (unkind City types labelled the company 'BID: Brought in Dead') were offered new investment for re-equipment but only on condition that they relinquished their independence, compliance often being secured by threatened withdrawal of overdraft facilities. The Lancashire Cotton Corporation, an amalgamation of almost a hundred small firms, and National Shipbuilders' Security, established to purchase and dispose of redundant shipyards, were the most successful products of this initiative. The BIDC appeared to prefigure a closer relationship between the banks and industry without committing the City to 'finance capitalism' in its German or American form. Sound prospects, vetted by the Bank, were to be nursed to the point at which their securities became marketable, thus precluding the permanent fusion of banking and industrial capital. It has been suggested that the Bank initiated this limited operation so as to pre-empt the emergence of more radical proposals (see Hannah, 1983, pp. 64–6; Ingham, 1984, pp. 197–8; Skidelsky, 1967, pp. 151–3).

Similarly, the policy revolution induced by the sterling crisis of 1931, though seeming to indicate that the authority of the institutional nexus at the heart of the British state had been decisively curtailed, signified an adjustment rather than a fundamental shift in the relationship between the industrial and financial sectors. The sharp contraction in world trade after the Wall Street crash, through its adverse impact on Britain's visible and invisible trade balances, reduced the Bank's capacity to defend the gold value of the pound fixed in 1925. An international banking crisis, beginning in the United States and spreading to Europe in mid 1931, stimulated a frantic scramble for liquidity which centred increasingly on London as short-term deposits were withdrawn, depleting the Bank's reserves of gold and foreign currency. It became clear that the overvalued pound had been sustained on the basis of the City's ability to attract 'hot money', thus the outflow of £200 million from London in the summer of 1931 proved fatal to the gold standard. The Labour government's problems were compounded by the reports, published in July, of the Macmillan Committee on Finance and Industry, which drew attention to Britain's weakness as a short-term creditor, and the May

Committee, which controversially estimated a budget deficit of £120 million for 1931–2 and recommended savage economies, including public sector wage cuts and a 20 per cent reduction in unemployment benefit rates. This was more than MacDonald could persuade his Labour Cabinet to swallow and the government fell in August, its willingness to implement the May Committee's strategy having been elevated into a test of confidence on the financial markets. Renewed pressure on Britain's gold reserves in September forced the Conservative-dominated 'National' government, a coalition forged in the political crisis following Labour's collapse, to abandon the gold standard before the international utility of the London money markets was permanently impaired.

For British producers in the late 1920s, the $4.86 pound was a burden. Although the extent to which exports were handicapped may have been exaggerated by those who had opposed the return to gold, it seems clear that the 'dear money' policy required to sustain the pound's value inhibited industrial expansion. After September 1931, the downward float of the pound towards $3.40 made British exports more price competitive, but it was the fall in interest rates which was to have the most significant impact on recovery, notably through the stimulus which cheap mortgages applied to the building industry. Between 1925 and 1929, the nominal bank rate was higher on account of falling prices. After April 1932, when the Treasury began to regulate the influence of gold movements through the operation of the Exchange Equalization Account, the bank rate dipped to 2 per cent, remaining at that level until the outbreak of war in 1939. Thus, for industry, the outcome of the sterling crisis was beneficial. It is necessary to stress, however, that the efforts of the financial community throughout the protracted crisis of 1929–32 sought to avoid the specific eventuality from which industry derived advantage. For the City, the Bank and the Treasury, the preservation of London's role as a centre of international finance was more important than creating conditions in which production might flourish. In accordance with this priority, the Labour government was steered towards a deflationary strategy in 1930–1, Snowden displaying thoughout an unbecoming enthusiasm for the 'drastic and disagreeable measures' which conventional financial opinion deemed necessary to restore market confidence in sterling. The Anomalies Act

(1931), which reduced considerably entitlement to unemployment benefit – especially for married women in depressed areas – was an indication of what was to come. When Labour ministers revolted at the prospect of further cuts as suggested by the May Committee, the National government took over, determined to administer 'in the national interest' the deflationary medicine prescribed by the City (see Ingham, 1984, pp. 187–9; also Miliband, 1972, pp. 169–81; Williamson, 1984).

Even after external pressure forced the pound off gold, the response to the crisis was dictated by financial considerations. MacDonald, now the captive prime minister of the new administration, argued that the commitment to budgetary equilibirium had precluded excessive devaluation and runaway inflation in the aftermath of the capitulation of September 1931. Waving worthless German banknotes, relics of the great inflation of the 1920s, at the electors in October, he claimed that this, in itself, justified 'the purifying fires of deflation' to which the economy was now subjected (Kirby, 1981, p. 63). The abandonment of free trade in 1932, though evidently in conflict with liberal values, could be justified in the same terms. It has been argued that the adoption of protection, ushered in by the Chancellor, Neville Chamberlain, with appropriate deference to the memory of his father, was largely the product of pressure group politics sustained throughout the 1920s by trade organizations, notably the National Federation of Iron and Steel Manufacturers, and after 1924 by the Empire Industries Association (EIA), taking up propaganda work in the tradition of the Tariff Reform League. The slump, according to the EIA's historical account, simply provided the essential context for the successful conclusion of this protracted campaign, bringing about

> the final revelation of the absurdity of *laissez-faire* and the necessity for a co-ordinated Imperial trade policy, with the result that early in 1931 the Import Duties Act was passed which not only protected British home industry but gave an Empire-wide preference to all goods from the Dominions and Colonies.[5]

The political consensus, it seems clear, shifted decisively towards protection during the course of the 1931 crisis which, as one eminent financial journalist indicated, 'restored the country into two bodies of opinion, a small minority, no longer very vocal, who deprecated, whatever the emergency, any departure from the principles of insular free trade, and a large majority in favour of the use of tariffs' (Brooks, 1931, p. 221). Import duties gained credibility as a means of reducing unemployment and as a means of raising revenue. But the decisive arguments, those which counted with the core institutional nexus, stressed the utility of a tariff system in protecting the value of the currency.

When Britain abandoned the gold standard in September 1931, prevailing orthodoxy suggested that a floating exchange rate would eliminate the deficit on external account by a process of automatic adjustment.[6] In the new conditions, as Benham and Robbins urged, 'our balance of trade must balance'. The extent to which the pound would have to fall before this equilibrium was reached soon became an issue of fierce debate in Parliament, in the Treasury and at Cabinet level where a special committee was appointed to consider the balance of trade. Conservative protectionists, a majority in the National government, seized the opportunity to address the anxieties of those whose principal concern was to maintain the value of sterling. It was argued that the side-effects of a downward float to the point at which import–export values would balance was unacceptable. Excessive depreciation would raise the cost of living, generating an inflationary wage–price spiral. Moreover, there was no guarantee that equilibrium could be achieved. Any improvement in visible trade was likely to be offset by a deterioration in invisibles as the cost of repaying war debts contracted in dollars increased and the value of overseas assets denominated in sterling declined. It was acknowledged that protection would raise prices but its overall impact would be to induce stability. Reduced imports would eliminate the trade gap and increased revenue from import duties would enable the Chancellor to balance the budget, allowing foreign confidence in sterling to be maintained. 'Really', observed Chamberlain on introducing the tariff, 'the essential point is the value of sterling.' Thus, following the demise of the gold standard, it became clear that protection, a policy devised with the producer in mind, was, at least in the short term, compatible with the interests of City-based finance, rendered 'less proud' by the catastrophe of 1931. 'This at least must be said', it was noted, 'that the new system could hardly lead to a crisis of more danger than that into which we have passed under the old, and whatever the effects of the change, the morale of the industrial population could hardly grow more depressed and would probably be immediately and greatly strengthened' (Brooks, 1931, p. 262).

Industrial Modernization and State Policy, 1932–1939

As the financial panic receded, a period of economic recovery began, triggered by the onset of a boom in house building towards the end of 1932. This was sustained naturally until early 1937 and artificially thereafter through the beneficial impact of a re-armament programme which created about a million new jobs between 1935 and 1939. In terms of improvements in industrial output and productivity, Britain performed better than either Germany or the United States in the thirties, reversing the pattern of the previous decade. Leading this revival were rapidly expanding new industries such as food canning and processing, household electrical goods and motor manufacturing, located largely in the Midlands and the South, the nationwide supply of electricity having liberated industrial production from the confines of the nineteenth-century coalfields. But though iron and steel shared in the upswing, the relatively slow decline from the high peaks of early 1930s unemployment amongst workers in the old industrial sectors indicated the persistence of slump conditions within a national economy increasingly characterized by gross regional disparities. With 67.8 per cent of the insured workforce in Jarrow and 61.9 per cent in Merthyr on the dole in 1934, it was clear to those who cared to look that the crisis in the liberal economy remained unresolved. The fragility of recovery was apparent after 1937 as an anticipated recession in the United States generated fears that the British economy was on the brink of a further catastrophe to match that of 1929–32. Unemployment levels were rising rapidly in 1938–9 despite re-armament. 'We have already reached a stage', noted Harold Macmillan in *The Middle Way* (1938, p. 9), 'when many observers are beginning to anticipate the next slump.' In this uncertain climate, lack of confidence in the market mechanism and in liberal economic values persisted as 'widespread suffering and distress . . . impelled thoughtful men to review and to question the established theories of society and to formulate what seemed to be common-sense schemes for the better regulation of our economic life' (p.17). The modernization strategies which emerged from this process tended to be motivated by the quest for what Macmillan called 'orderly capitalism'.

In so far as the young member for Stockton-on-Tees and other idealists of the progressive centre were concerned specifically with industrial modernization, they were assisted by a sharpened awareness of the historical divergence of finance and industry and the traditional subordination of the interest of the producer to those of the middleman. The influential report of Lord Macmillan's committee in 1931 had indicated the existence of an investment gap arising from the limited utility of the London money markets in providing funds for small and medium-sized British companies. Though the number of share quotations allocated to 'home industrials' on the London Stock Exchange more than doubled between 1924 and 1929, largely as a consequence of reduced investment opportunities overseas, the City's unsatisfactory relationship with domestic production was frequently identified as a major component in the continuing crisis of the industrial economy. When PEP, the first of the technocratic, reconstructionist movements to surface, established a specialist committee to study the problem of industry, discussion centred so often on the inseparable question of finance that some members pressed for the formulation of a new 'finance group' so that it might receive due consideration. At a popular, middlebrow level, Priestley went further, pinning responsibility for the plight of the 'half-derelict' industrial regions through which he passed on his *English Journey* (1934, 1977) very firmly on the City of London, 'which is always treated', he complained, 'as if it were the beating red heart of England'. If it were, the arteries which carried the life-blood of investment to 'exiled' Lancashire and the north east were blocked. Articulating the productionist sentiment of his native Bradford, he eschewed customary deference to finance, reflecting that the City had done to 'its old ally, the industrial North . . . what the black moustached glossy gentleman in the old melodramas always did to the innocent village maiden' (Priestley, 1977, p. 384). Confronted with this scenario, progressive 'middle opinion' sought to reconcile the 'old allies', promoting schemes through which finance might be linked more closely with production. Finance, in the view of Israel Sieff of Marks and Spencer, the first chairman of PEP, should be 'the handmaid of industry' (see Roskill, 1981, p. 59).

Like previous advocates of modernization in twentieth-century Britain, participants in PEP and the Next Five Years Group sought to regulate capitalism in the interests of national efficiency. Influenced by the state planning initiatives in Italy and the Soviet Union and, after 1933, by the American 'New Deal', they argued that successful reconstruction of the British economy would be achieved only if haphazard and potentially destabilizing market forces were tamed by the highly visible controlling hand of the planner. The origins of PEP as an independent policy institute were rooted in the favourable response to 'A National Plan for Britain', compiled by a journalist, Max Nicholson, and published as a supplement to the *Week-End Review* in February 1931. Nicholson's article attracted the support of a diverse group of intellectuals, such as the biologist Julian Huxley, the educationalist Kenneth Lindsay and the economist Arthur Salter, and also progressive businessmen, like Sieff, all of whom were seeking an appropriate political focus for their anxieties about the drift into decline. In the spirit of what H. G. Wells, in the Edwardian era, had called 'the revolt of the competent', the exclusively white-collar technocrats of PEP recoiled from the confusion to which the liberal state had been reduced by the slump, responding to Nicholson's view that it was 'a Heath Robinson contrivance composed of the clutter of past generations and tied together with rotten bits of string' (1981, p. 6). Its Fabian-style politics of persuasion were intended to convince 'key people' that planning was the appropriate response to the crisis.

Similarly, the Next Five Years Group, which tapped 'middle opinion', more systematically than PEP after 1934, rejected the disposition 'to "muddle through" by successive improvisations as each emergency occurs'. Its programme, outlined in *The Next Five Years: An Essay in Political Agreement* (1935), was designed to be implemented during the course of a single Parliament and sought to rally those who were convinced 'that the community can and must deliberately plan, direct and control – not in detail but in broad outline – the economic development to which innumerable individual activities contribute'.[7] Thus it embraced the whole range of progressive centre views, linking displaced New Liberals, like J. A. Hobson and Seebohm Rowntree, with Clifford Allen, formerly of the Independent Labour Party, and Macmillan's Conservative planners.

Booth and Pack have recently argued that the planning groups of the 1930s tended to fudge policy issues, circumventing fundamental economic problems, such as lack of competitiveness in exports, while drawing up blueprints for administrative reform. Many planners, they have suggested, 'were engaged simply in vacuous exercises in the procedures of decision-making' (1985, p. 190). Though the predilection of the progressive centre for building bureaucratic castles in the air should not be underestimated, this was not necessarily an inappropriate strategy, given their almost total lack of confidence in 'the procedure of decision-making' embodied in a free market economy. Reviewing the performance of Britain's 'highly individualistic economy, confronted by the intricate difficulties at the post-war economic situation', it was Macmillan's view that 'a multitude of individual errors' had led to 'collective ruin'. Bankers, investors, industrialists and workers, he argued, had each pursued their own interests in a legitimate fashion, but they had been unenlightened as to the consequences of their actions in the broad socio-economic context. The confusion and disharmony which had become evident by 1931 reflected the inefficiency of the market mechanism in reconciling beneficially the pursuit of these various interests. He observed:

> It was nobody's business to ask 'What will be the social consequences of the action I propose to take?' . . . There was no national economic policy guiding and co-ordinating the actions and reactions of individuals operating on different sectors of the economic front, for no machinery existed by which that co-ordination and guidance could have been made possible. (1938, p. 190)

This was the rationale which justified proposals for administrative reform emanating from non-socialist 'middle opinion' in the 1930s. With Macmillan's support, the Next Five Years Group promoted an elaborate scheme incorporating, at the highest level, a 'Government Planning Committee', in effect a Cabinet sub-committee, drawing on the expert advice of a permanent 'Economic General Staff'. New institutions in the financial sector were proposed, notably a 'National Investment Board' to regulate the capital market and an 'advisory committee' to keep the Bank of England in touch with economic realities beyond 'the somewhat limited experience of the present court of directors' which, it was noted, 'reflected the point of view of the City, to the exclusion of, and often in contradiction to, the opinions of the country at large'.[8] In the light of Ingham's (1984) analysis of the role of the City, the Bank and the Treasury in maintaining the ascendancy of cosmopolitan finance within the British capitalist system, it may be argued that such proposals seem to confront directly the major institutional constraints on industrial modernization.

The industrial strategy advocated by PEP and the Next Five Years Group drew heavily on the linked themes of corporatism and rationalization which Mond had explored in the late 1920s. Macmillan's *Reconstruction: a Plea for National Unity* (1933) marked the pathway for centre progressives, outlining a proposal for 'National Industrial Councils', essentially quasi-monopolistic, self-governing trade associations underwritten by the state in order to promote the advance of orderly capitalism in each sector of production. This was to be achieved through amalgamation, run-down of surplus capacity, elimination of wasteful competition and development of more efficient facilities for bulk purchasing, marketing and research; in short, through implementing the agenda of rationalization. In 1934–5, Macmillan, assisted by Mond (now Lord Melchett), pursued this objective through the Industrial Reorganization League, a pressure group deriving substantial support from progressive businessmen like Sieff, Sir Herbert Austin of Austin Motors, Lionel Hichens of Cammell Laird and Sir Malcolm Robertson of Spillers. The League sought to organize a body of opinion favourably disposed towards a general enabling bill, drafted by PEP and introduced in the House of Lords by Melchett in November 1934, giving approximate legislative form to the rationalization procedures which Macmillan had outlined in *Reconstruction*. Permissive in character, the bill was intended to strengthen the authority of trade associations in fifteen major industries by granting them access to statutory powers through which agreed programmes of re-organization could be implemented under state supervision. It embodied a strategy for by-passing the recalcitrant individualism of inefficient small producers, a major road-block on the highway to industrial modernization. Though this corporatist initiative gained some Conservative support, the government was less than enthusiastic. Responding to a deputation from the League, the Board of Trade indicated that the proposal was unacceptable because it would jeopardize the interests of consumers and small producers for the sake of big business.

Denied official backing, Melchett's bill was doomed, surviving only as a manifesto commitment in *The Next Five Years*. Its demise was indicative of the constraints on the movement for industrial modernization in the 1930s. Though the prestige of City-based finance capital was significantly reduced after the gold standard and free trade had been abandoned, the interests of producers were insufficiently integrated to generate a decisive political challenge to its hegemony within the British capitalist system. Industrial modernization was forced into the political agenda but the priorities underpinning state policy were not substantially re-ordered. As in the late 1920s, Melchett was able to achieve only a partial mobilization of industrial capital in support of his scheme, the outright opposition of the British Iron and Steel Federation and the British Electrical and Allied Machinery Association preventing any modification in the FBI's circumspect policy of encouraging re-organization on a voluntary basis. As Stephen Blank (1973, pp. 28–30) has observed, though the FBI 'could give its support in theory to re-organization, any actual rationalizing measures would have torn its membership apart' (see also Carpenter, 1976, pp. 13–14). Moreover, the emergence of a modernizing producers' alliance, incorporating both capital and labour, remained an unlikely prospect. Talks between 1929 and 1933 involving the TUC, the NCEO and the FBI had proved largely unproductive, each participant offering a diagnosis of Britain's economic problems fundamentally incompatible with the others. The TUC, as the Mond–Turner episode had suggested, was much influenced by productionist sentiment but its attachment to nationalization, reflecting lack of confidence in existing management rather than commitment to socialist economics, restricted the scope for systematic co-operation with industrial capital (Dintinfass, 1984, pp. 76–92).

In terms of party politics, the movement for industrial modernization was imperfectly represented. There was some substance in Mosley's critique of 'the power of the party machine' which 'crushed all attempts to secure a natural alignment in British politics' (1932, p. 152). Modernizers, though sharing a determination to promote rationalization or to curb market forces, were divided by conflicting party loyalties. As in the Edwardian period, the cross-party characteristics of the movement were a source of weakness rather than strength. Old party watchwords died hard. Though a new consensus on tariff policy emerged after 1932, it did not include the Liberal Party which retained its faith in free trade, signalling its survival as an independent, if declining, political force. Thus, despite a common commitment to Keynesian expanionist policies, it was impossible to sustain co-operation with Conservatives, like Macmillan, for whom a protective tariff was a necessary instrument of state planning. Similarly, though *Labour's Immediate Programme* (1937), a modestly radical five year plan, moved the party into the territory staked out by *The Next Five Years*, there was no prospect of an alliance with the progressive centre. After the débâcle of September 1931, Labour's credibility with its own supporters hinged on maintaining in opposition a distinctive identity as a party of the left. While Labour licked its wounds and cultivated the necessary myth of MacDonald's treachery, re-alignment on a left-centre axis was ruled out, especially as it entailed building bridges for National Labourites, like Allen and Lindsay (see Booth and Pack, 1985, pp. 123–47).

Significantly, the most coherent strategy for modernizing the British economy to emerge from the slump was associated with Oswald Mosley, who had turned his back on conventional party politics after founding the British Union of Fascists (BUF) in October 1932. In *The Greater Britain* (1932), effectively the manifesto of the new movement, Mosley asserted that the existing parties were constitutionally incapable of halting 'the spineless drift to disaster'. 'Potential Fascists', it was claimed, were to be found amongst the younger generation of Conservative, Labour and Liberal activists which had been frustrated by the continuing hegemony of the Baldwin–MacDonald 'old gang'. Mosley's Fascism was self-consciously 'modern' in outlook. The BUF, liberated from the constraints of orthodox parliamentary politics, was to supply the radical modernization movement which Britain lacked: 'the ordered political economy of the Corporate State' was to replace the existing machinery of government, regarded by Mosley as an outmoded legacy of the nineteenth century. New state institutions would spearhead a comprehensive modernization programme, simultaneously addressing the problem of mass unemployment, regarded as a symptom of Britain's failure to transform its economy. It was proposed, for example, that a 'National Investment Board' would divert funds into industry for necessary re-equipment and scientific research, an activity 'not deemed worthy of proper support in this curious muddle of Old Gang politics'. In addition, it would promote essential public works in times of recession, a strategy redolent 'of efficient and virile government in every period of history' which had been stifled in the prevailing climate of liberal economic orthodoxy.

With Ingham's analysis in mind, however, it could be argued that the most revolutionary aspect of the BUF's economic policy was its emphasis on production, which it sought to raise above finance, thus reversing the normal relationship between the two major fractions of capital. Surveying the dismal record of relative economic decline, Mosley contended that 'the great producers' interests on which the strength and stability of our nation must ultimately rest' had been sacrified to the interests of cosmopolitan finance. 'In every struggle between producer and financial interest in recent years', he noted, 'the latter power has been triumphant to the detriment of the national interest.' With an intimation of the anti-semitic sentiment later associated with the BUF's East London campaign, Mosley described the City as a power within the state

> largely controlled by alien elements which arrogates to itself a power above the State, and has used that influence to drive flaccid governments of all political parties along the high road to national disaster. No State can tolerate within its body the irresponsible superiority of such a power, nor the policy inimical to every productive interest which it has pursued. (1932, pp, 115–19)

It was Mosley's intention to seek the voluntary co-operation of the City in financing 'a planned economy of national reconstruction'.

If such co-operation was not forthcoming, drastic state intervention would be necessary to ensure that 'high finance' served the national interest: 'the Gordian knot', he declared, 'must be cut'.

The National government's ambitions were less bold. It sought to promote stability rather than revolution. In so far as there was a retreat from liberal orthodoxy in economic policy in the 1930s, it was piecemeal and within limits prescribed by continuing adherence to the principles of 'sound finance'. As both Snowden and Neville Chamberlain, his successor as Chancellor of the Exchequer, argued, the absence of the gold standard made it more rather than less necessary to balance the budget in order to maintain confidence in sterling. Thus, though more stable external conditions after 1932 would have permitted a modest degree of reflation, the government held to the view that increased public expenditure would reduce the sum available for private investment, hindering the natural forces of recovery. When, in July 1935, Lloyd George updated his 'Orange Book' proposals, demanding an uncompromising 'New Deal' strategy to eliminate unemployment, the official response, published as a pamphlet entitled *A Better Way to Better Times*, suggested that the ideological hegemony of economic liberalism remained intact despite the traumatic events of 1931–2. The ascent from the depths of recession, it was claimed, indicated what could be achieved without resort to compulsion or deficit finance: the government's role was to be confined to 'stimulating or assisting spontaneous development through varying methods fitted to the actual circumstances of each case'.[9] After 1937, this stance was modified by the imperatives of re-armanent, which forced the budget into deficit though, as Middleton has observed, even then the Treasury remained unconvinced by Keynes's advocacy of loan-financed public works expenditure and the pursuit of policies designed specifically to reduce unemployment (1985, pp. 179–80; see also Winch, 1983, pp. 47–65; Aldcroft, 1986, pp. 84–118). Significantly, the commitment to low interest rates, the government's major contribution to industrial recovery, was perfectly compatible with the Treasury's efforts to reduce the burden of the national debt, principally through the downward conversion of the 5 per cent War Loan in 1932.

Seeking only 'to create conditions which would encourage and facilitate improvement in ordinary trade',[10] government strategy precluded intervention on the scale advocated by Keynes, Lloyd George, Macmillan or Mosley. Extensive public works, an integral feature of all non-socialist modernization programmes from the 'Orange Book' to *The Next Five Years*, were ruled out on account of budgetary implications despite the theoretical underpinning supplied by the publication of Keynes's *General Theory* in 1936. Such schemes generated Treasury resistance for the additional reason that they involved the establishment of a new bureaucracy of state planning beyond its immediate control. In the 1920s, government relief works under the supervision of the Unemployment Grants Committee had provided employment for up to 150,000, mainly on road building and improvement. This modest figure was reduced in the 1930s as public expenditure was curtailed, never exceeding 60,000 and falling to a few hundred by 1937. While France, Germany, the United States and Sweden experimented with deficit finance and contra-cyclical public works, British policy remained within the self-imposed constraints of orthodox finance. Modernizing the ecomomic infrastructure was assigned a low priority and ambitious projects canvassed since the early 1920s, such as complete main line railway electrification, remained on ice.

Regional policy, intended to counter the impact of the slump in the old industrial areas, was similarly inhibited by the government's reluctance to abandon the base-line of liberal economic orthodoxy. Though the official recognition of 'special' areas had major implications for the future of industrial policy, it was also a palliative designed to contain at a manageable level protest arising from continuing high levels of unemployment.[11] Initiatives generated by the Special Areas (Development and Improvement) Act (1934), which appointed commissioners to promote industrial development in the north-east, West Cumberland, Central Scotland and South Wales, were hampered from the start by inadequate funding and a narrow brief. At first, the commissioners sought to breathe life into old industries, but the emphasis shifted after the Special Areas Reconstruction (Agreements) Act (1936) and an attempt was made to attract new industries into the 'special areas' by offering subsidies in the form of rebates on rent, rates and taxes. The scope of regional policy failed to match the size of the problem. By the beginning of 1939, the commissioners had spent less than £10 million of which only about £3 million had been used to start new businesses. Fifty thousand new jobs were created, many on new industrial estates such as Team Valley and Treforest, but this achievement made little impression on the high levels of unemployment which persisted until the outbreak of war in areas dominated by the declining export staples. Despite the inducements, firms were reluctant to leave the more prosperous south; a survey of 5,800 businesses undertaken in 1935 discovered that only eight were even prepared to consider moving to a 'special area'. As one contemporary critic observed:

> To provide new work for wages in South Wales is impossible. The Special Commissioner, equipped with millions of money, in sight or on call, has found out this far-reaching truth if nothing else . . . No employer is going to plant a factory in an area where the purchasing power of the public is low and the striking power of labour is high. No expert adviser of an expanding business will voluntarily recommend a site in South Wales.

Lacking powers of compulsion, the commissioners were unable to correct the pernicious regional imbalance which increasingly characterized the British economy or to achieve major diversification of the industrial structure in the areas under their supervision. The best hope for the Rhondda, argued the semi-serious pamphleteer, was 'to declare the area open as a Museum or Exhibition to illustrate the Industrial Revolution of the Nineteenth Century'.[12]

Reluctance to breach the voluntary principle was evident in connection with industrial rationalization where the government's strategy was significantly more cautious than that which had been embodied in Melchett's enabling bill. In agriculture, which experienced severely competitive market conditions in the interwar period as world primary product prices slumped, government co-operated with producers to stabilize domestic conditions, notably through the establishment of marketing boards for milk, potatoes, pigs and hops. Though these initiatives, especially when operated in conjunction with import quota restrictions, were successful in protecting the interests of most producers, the government remained reluctant to involve itself directly in rationalization schemes for industry, perhaps intimidated by the scale of intervention which would have been required. In particular, it showed only a modest inclination to use the tariff as a lever of industrial policy. It was not unknown for the Import Duties Advisory Committee, the body which administered the tariff after 1932, to sanction 'exceptional treatment' for an industry only on condition that it puts its house in order. The steel industry, recognized as being 'in a notoriously bad way', was granted substantial assistance in the form of a 33.3 per cent import duty in 1932, temporarily raised to 50 per cent in 1935 so as to facilitate negotiations with European producers. Linked to this assistance was the requirement that rationalization should be effected under the direction of the British Iron and Steel Federation. Of the traditional export staples, steel staged the most impressive recovery in the 1930s, Britain's share of world output rising from 7.6 per cent in 1931 to 9.7 per cent in 1937. But as one of the 'tariff makers' later recalled, sustained pressure for industrial modernization was the exception rather than the rule. 'Save in the case of iron and steel', he noted, 'the Committee's interest was occasional only and incidental to its tariff function' (Hutchinson, 1965, pp. 131–2, 158; see also Pollard, 1983, pp. 69–70).

Writing in 1935, Sir Basil Blackett of PEP acknowledged that liberal ideology remained sufficiently entrenched in Britain to impose significant constraints on modernization from above. It acted as a brake, slowing the movement towards a managed or planned economy. 'British planning', he observed, 'will at all costs be made to conform with British ideals of freedom.' Thus the National government was reluctant even 'to talk about planning, or to speak of planned reconstruction', mainly because the concept of a planned economy was inevitably associated with compulsion (Blackett, 1935, p. 18). Though the government established machinery to manage the exchange rate and kept interest rates low, state intervention in the productive sector was on an *ad hoc* basis: there was no self-conscious modernization strategy on the lines of *The Greater Britain, Reconstruction* or *The Next Five Years*. State policy after 1932 was sufficiently flexible to sustain recovery but insufficiently interventionist to control the predominant influence of market forces in shaping the emerging economic structure. In so far as industrial modernization entailed resolving structural problems through internal rationalization and the transfer of resources from declining export trades to consumer goods industries with high growth potential, there was progress, but it seems likely that this was checked by the government's reluctance to impose re-organization on manufacturers or to stimulate demand. There was a shift away from the nineteenth-century staples. Whereas they had accounted for 37 per cent of net industrial production in 1924, their share had dropped to about 28 per cent by 1935. Over the same period, the contribution of 'new' industries, comprising electrical engineering, vehicle manufacture, non-ferrous metals, rayon, paper, printing and publishing, grew from 14 to 21 per cent. Significantly for the future relationship between the two major fractions of capital, the service sector expanded. While numbers employed in mining and manufacturing declined in the interwar years, substantial increases were recorded for banking, insurance, distribution and a range of miscellaneous services, including tourism,[13] generating speculation that Britain's ultimate role in the international division of labour 'will be that of a playground and park and museum to exercise the youth and soothe the declining years of the strenuous industrial leaders on either side of the Pacific Ocean'.[14] There were few indications in the industrial policy of the National government that this fate would be resisted.

For British industry in the 1930s, recovery was not synonymous with reconstruction. Though the ascendancy of the City, the Bank and the Treasury was shaken by the crisis of 1929–32, it had not been destroyed. Thus it was possible to sustain, more or less intact, the ideological hegemony of economic liberalism. Finance was, indeed, 'less proud' in the 1930s than it had been after the triumphant re-assertion of normalcy in 1925, but its influence was sufficient to maintain a framework of state policy which precluded systematic industrial modernization. Even where the necessary administrative machinery was created, as it was after the Import Duties Act of 1932, the government proved reluctant to use it for the purpose of forcing necessary rationalization on the productive sector or restructuring the industrial economy. Under the National government, the liberal economy was modified but not transformed. Modernization policies which stressed the primacy of production were powerfully articulated but, in the continuing absence of a coherent producers' alliance, they lacked an appropriate political vehicle. Productionist politics drifted in uncertain cross-party currents or surfaced, with Mosley, beyond the pale of parliamentary democracy.

Notes: Chapter 3

1 Churchill to Sir Otto Niemeyer, 22 February 1925, quoted in Gilbert, 1976, p. 98.
2 Priestley, 1977, p. 295. For general accounts of the crisis of 1929–32 and its impact on the British economy see Aldcroft, 1986, pp. 45–53; Kirby, 1981, pp. 56–65; Peden, 1985, pp. 88–92; Pollard, 1983, pp. 141–5.
3 For the 'Yellow Book' and the 'Orange Book', see especially Booth and Pack, 1985, pp. 35–54; Tomlinson, 1981, pp. 80–7.
4 Mosley, 1968, pp. 252–3; see also Skidelsky, 1967, pp. 167–89; Skidelsky, 1975, pp. 200–20.
5 W. A. Wells, *Imperial Preference: a Short Historical Sketch* (1952), p. 9, a pamphlet published by the Empire Industries Association. For growing protectionist pressure culminating in 1931–2 see Capie, 1983, pp. 61–76.
6 The argument in this paragraph draws heavily on Eichengreen, 1981, pp. 22–37.
7 *A Summary of the Book 'The Next Five Years: An Essay in Political Agreement'* (The Next Five Years Group, 1936), p. 11. For a recent discussion of the group see Booth and Pack, 1985, pp. 64–75.
8 *Summary of 'The Next Five Years'*, p. 31.
9 *A Better Way to Better Times: Reprint of a Statement Issued by His Majesty's Government on Mr Lloyd George's Proposals* (London, HMSO, 1935), p. 37.
10 Chamberlain in the House of Commons, 14 February 1935, quoted in Winch, 1983, p. 59.
11 See the useful discussion of the genesis and nature of regional policy in Parsons, 1986, pp. 1–59.
12 *What's Wrong with South Wales?* (1935), pp. 17, 21. This pamphlet, with a preface by Lloyd George, was first published as a supplement to the *New Statesman*, 27 July 1935.
13 See especially Aldcroft, 1986, pp. 55–9; B. Alford, 'New Industries for Old? British Industry between the Wars', in Floud and McCloskey, 1981, Vol. 2, pp. 330; Pollard, 1983, pp. 54–6.
14 Robertson's *The Control of Industry* quoted in Young, 1973, pp. 26–7.

CHAPTER FOUR

Total War and Industrial Modernization, 1940–1951

The Impact of Defeat in 1940

The performance of the British economy between 1940 and 1951 provides a striking contrast to what was achieved between the wars. Britain began to operate its industry at full capacity for the first time since 1920 and had by 1944 mobilized its economy more completely than any other belligerent nation. The full utilization of all available factors of production stimulated a 64 per cent growth in national income between 1939 and 1946 (Milward, 1977, p. 89; Pollard, 1983, p. 250). In consequence there was an impressive expansion of output, not in coal or steel production, where it actually fell, but in more modern capital-intensive industries such as electricity, aluminium, aircraft and military vehicles.

Such achievements were only possible because of a startling change in the political climate which allowed Britain to move on to a total war footing after 1940. The liberalism which had characterized the conduct of economic policy between the wars was abandoned as the Churchill government made common cause with both sides of industry. The economy was driven to out-produce those of its enemies. To this end public spending was increased from £1,933 million in 1939 to £5,565 million in 1945; the government pumped £900 million into capital investment in the munitions industries; borrowed heavily from abroad to finance its massive import needs; and introduced trade and exchange controls to conserve shipping space and foreign currency reserves. At the same time strategic sectors of the economy were largely run from Whitehall and the government acquired the powers to direct labour and allocate manpower between the services, industry and agriculture.

It would in fact be no exaggeration to say that the Churchill government which came to power in 1940 presided over a revolution in the British political economy. The new administration was able to make such a dramatic break with the past not simply because Britain was at war but because in May and June 1940 its continued existence as an independent country began to appear doubtful. The onset of national emergency justified full mobilization and therefore the repudiation of the basic assumptions underlying the formulation of economic policy after 1920.

These assumptions had not been repudiated between September 1939 and May 1940. Even after the outbreak of war in 1939 Chamberlain had been concerned to protect sterling's international financial probity and as a result the principles of prudent finance governed public spending and overseas purchasing. The government had worked from a 'strategic synthesis', to use Alan S. Milward's term (1977, ch. 2) based on the concept of a limited war fought to preserve the European balance of power. A long conflict was envisaged in which Britain would specialize in investment in warships and bombers rather than in a large army, with Germany's ultimate defeat being assured through military failure in Western Europe along with social disintegration consequent upon the economic blockade. Through this strategic synthesis Chamberlain had hoped to reconcile the demands of national security with the preservation of the British political economy as it had developed after 1920. By attempting to sidestep investment in the army the government believed it could avoid the scale of economic intervention which had been necessary between 1914 and 1918. With a relatively small land force there would be no need to organize and co-ordinate military supply and construct an elaborate regime of economic controls. Hence the war was to be fought according to Treasury rules. Anxiety about an unbalanced budget had been powerful enough to push the War Cabinet into a review of the armaments programme in February 1940. Sir John Simon's 1940 budget was characterized by Gladstonian severity, with sharp increases in direct and indirect taxation. In external economic policy, concern about low foreign exchange reserves had led to the organization of an export drive in the winter of 1939–40; and in April Simon had resisted calls for the intensification of exchange controls on the grounds that they would jeopardize sterling's world role. As late as the Dunkirk evacuation in June spare capacity was large enough to leave 645,000 registered men and women unemployed (Addison, 1975, p. 116).

The limited war strategy was designed to preclude full mobilization. In this if in nothing else it succeeded. Its military inadequacy was, however, exposed in the spring of 1940 as the Anglo-French forces suffered a series of disastrous reverses, first in Norway and then in Belgium and France. Ultimately Chamberlain's government was seen to have failed in the most basic sense of all: it appeared incapable of protecting national security. Commitment to sterling, anxiety about government finances and concern not to extend economic controls counted for little when set against such a fundamental priority.

Chamberlain was no longer prime minister by the time of Dunkirk. But the fiasco in France and Britain's subsequent vulnerability to invasion was taken by both left and right as a comment not merely on his strategy but on the management of British society between the wars. Encouraged by the publication of books such as *The Guilty Men* (Cato, 1940), many now regarded the interwar period as one of failure: failure to appease the dictators, failure to modernize the economy, failure to provide employment. All three failures were subsumed in the disasters of May and June 1940. There was indeed a sense in which many of Chamberlain's opponents, particularly on the left, viewed the events of 1940 as a rough but just verdict not simply on the policies of a government but on a ruling class which had failed the nation.

Given that the national weakness had followed from the pursuit of economic orthodoxy there was something in this view. But it was also rather a simplistic interpretation. Chamberlain, along with his closest colleagues such as Hoare and Simon, was not an incompetent or treacherous individual. Rather, the crisis of 1940 was a judgement on the fallibility of a political economy in which the interests of finance, the middle-class *rentier* and the consumer were equated with the health of the nation. The need in the spring of 1940 was for another definition of the national interest which emphasized the full employment of productive capacity as the foundation of security.

The Churchill government which replaced Chamberlain offered precisely this definition of natonal interest. The new administration was greeted by a groundswell of popular enthusiasm, even among the previously pro-Chamberlain grass roots of the Conservative Party, because from the start it showed itself prepared to accept that the choice facing Britain was now between defeat and the prosecution of total war. The Tory-liberalism of Chamberlain's regime had excluded this choice from the political agenda. But now, with the positive backing of those who had opposed the orthodox policies followed by the National government after 1931, Churchill's Coalition chose total war. The Coalition itself was more genuinely 'national' than its predecessors because far from being dominated by one secton of the Conservative Party it contained Tory imperialists (for example, L. S. Amery and Lord Beaverbrook), Britain's most powerful trade union leader (Ernest Bevin), key members of the Labour Party (Clement Attlee, the leader, along with his deputy Arthur Greenwood, A. V. Alexander, Hugh Dalton and Herbert Morrison) and Lloyd George Liberals such as Sir Archibald Sinclair. Full mobilization held no unwelcome implications for these men. Most of them, particularly those on the left, had been devotees of planning and government intervention during the 1930s, while Beaverbrook and Amery had never accepted the international economic liberalism of the British establishment. Imperialists, industrialists, trade unionists, socialists and radicals were all from their different perspectives committed to maximum production for the war. Just as in 1916 so in 1940: crisis provided a political opportunity for the assumption of power by an alliance of producers.

The War Economy

Full mobilization required a revolution in financial management as well as fundamental changes in trade practice and employment and industrial policy. In 1939 and in 1940 financing the war was regarded as a question of budgetary policy. The government was not averse to borrowing to cover the gap between revenue and expenditure, but it was determined that funds would be raised from the capital market on the voluntary principle. There was accordingly continuing anxiety that serious inflation would result if the government's requirements exceeded the sum the capital market was willing to provide.

Such an approach was not even adequate to cover the government's needs in the first months of the war, and it was recognition of this fact which lay behind the decision to review the arms programme in February 1940. At this point the government had been concerned to adapt the war effort to the demands of budgetary policy. After the crisis of spring 1940, however, it became clear that budgetary policy would have to be adapted to the war effort.

A financial policy more suited to national emergency had been suggested by Keynes in his pamphlet *How to Pay for the War* (1940). Keynes shifted attention away from the narrow issue of government funds to the total amount of national income. His proposals for compulsory working-class savings were rejected by the trade unions, but the basic idea behind his proposals was adopted by the Treasury and became the foundation of financial policy from the 1941 budget until the end of the war. The calculation of national income and expenditure allowed the government to break Gladstonian bonds because it provided a statistical foundation for calculating the difference between the value of goods and services produced and total money demand in the economy. It was this difference which now became the measure of the inflationary gap rather than the discrepancy between government expenditure and revenue from taxation and voluntary savings. Given the determination not to repeat the 1914–19 experience, when this gap had been closed by rising prices which had provoked labour unrest, the only option was to control demand through higher taxation and increased savings. Once the government was able to finance the war by deploying the national income it became possible to sustain a volume of capital investment in manufacturing industry so great as to be unthinkable before 1940.

National income accounting allowed the Churchill Coalition to make full use of the country's financial resources and pursue an anti-inflationary policy. But although 'stabilization budgets' replaced the balanced budget, after 1941 the gap between goods and services produced and the high level of demand generated by the unprecedented level of public spending could not be met by financial measures alone. Consumption goods became relatively scarce, and rather than permit market forces to bid up prices the government introduced price controls to keep down the cost of living and rationing to ensure that no citizen went without the basic requirements of a civilized existence such as food and clothing. Further, in view of the importance of labour in a war where production held the key to victory, controls were an essential component of the government's bargain with the trade unions. An incomes policy was anathema, and it is hard to see how Churchill's administration could have retained the support of the labour movement, so essential to price stability in a fully employed economy, had it not been prepared to exchange physical action against inflationary pressures for wage restraint.

After May 1940 the trade unions were in fact more effectively integrated into decision-making than ever before in British history. The presence of senior Labour Party figures in the War Cabinet had much to do with this, but most important of all was Ernest Bevin's appointment to the Ministry of Labour. Bevin's responsibility for manpower policy made him the most important political figure on the home front. His position as General Secretary of the Transport and General Workers' Union ensured that he had the confidence of trade unionists, and this was a vital asset for a political figure in charge of industrial conscription. The key task was the allocation of workers to the industries most vital to the war effort – munitions, coal, steel, electricity, agriculture. Labour became the country's most vital resource since what was required was a large, semi-skilled workforce operating in capital-intensive factories.

Such a task implied the transformation of Britain's industrial structure. Historically Britain had been the world's workshop rather than its factory (Milward, 1984a, p. 60), and its labour force was still dominated by the figure of the skilled artisan responsible for the production of the metal goods, railway engines and ships which had loomed so large in the Victorian economy. Large-scale, capital-intensive plant producing capital goods with an adaptable workforce had characterized prewar manufacturing industry in Germany and the United States but not in Britain, whose basic industries such as coal, shipbuilding and textiles had been dogged by under-investment and outdated equipment. Only light industry and the service sector, catering for an affluent middle-class society in the south-east, had grown consistently over the previous half-century, and before the war Britain had had to import many of the machine-tools necessary for rearmament from the United States, Such a pattern of production and occupation was by no means adequate to the task after 1940. It became a matter of urgency not simply to direct capital into heavy industrial plant but to reduce the claims on resources of finance and labour made by consumer-oriented concerns. Through manpower budgeting it was possible to divert the labour supply to areas of production critical to the war effort, and between mid 1941 and mid 1943 Britain added two million people to the forces and munitions industries.

It followed from the investment of so much capital and labour in heavy industry that the output of consumer goods would have to fall. Civilian production was accordingly reduced in volume and concentrated in a few factories working full time. The Board of Trade estimated that 290,000 men and women were released from the civilian industries to those essential for the war between March 1941 and March 1944. With over 50 per cent of the national product devoted to the war at peak mobilization it was hardly surprising that spending on consumer goods fell along with their production, which in 1943 was 16 per cent down on its 1938 level (Hancock and Gowing, 1975, p. 324). At the same time output in arms and arms-related industries such as aircraft, vehicles, engineering, metal manufacturing and agriculture expanded. Thus 7,940 aircraft were produced in 1939 and 26,263 in 1945 (Milward, 1977, p. 91). Although it may appear eccentric to locate agriculture in such a category, Britain's ability to feed itself became central to the war effort as the limiting effects on supply of shipping losses and lack of foreign exchange took their toll. And here also the performance was impressive. The combined effect of subsidies, guaranteed profits for farmers, high wages for labourers, the land army and investment in agricultural machinery increased the value of net agricultural output at constant prices by 35 per cent during the war.

None of these achievements would have been possible without the control of manpower. But success would not have come from the exercise of naked compulsion by the state. The co-operation of the trade unions was vital and Bevin won this partly because he was who he was but also because he showed himself profoundly concerned with the welfare of each worker. The Ministry of

Labour proved itself determined to uphold good health and safety standards wherever it could, and the emphasis on welfare eased movement, reduced absenteeism and kept up productivity. Perhaps more than any other department the Ministry of Labour was responsible for the creation of the adaptable, well-paid work-force vital to a modern industrial society at war – and in peace.

The best efforts of the ministry could not of course guarantee completely harmonious industrial relations. Indeed, Correlli Barnett, in *The Audit of War*, has argued that labour troubles were widespread between 1939 and 1945, quoting numerous instances of disruption and unofficial strikes (Barnett, 1986, chs 4–8). The attempt to depict trade unions in the war as militant and sectional, putting their own grievances above the national good, does not convince, although serious disputes and stoppages did occur, notably in the coal industry. Nevertheless, labour relations were much improved on those of 1914–18 (Cronin, 1984, pp. 112–20), and troubles were not peculiar to Britain. The American economy was no less prone to industrial disputes, and the number of man-days lost through strikes in the two countries works out at much the same after allowances for the disparity in size between each labour force (Milward, 1977, p. 243).

Although Bevin became in effect supreme over the home economy the conduct of industrial policy was very much a concern of government and industry working with labour. Tripartite consultation was institutionalized through the National Joint Advisory Council and the National Production Advisory Council, where civil servants met with employers and trade unionists to co-ordinate regional and national planning for the war effort (Middlemas, 1979, pp. 227 ff). At the same time the organization of the productive effort required the development of close government–industry co-operation. Between the wars the Board of Trade had been the only government department to be seriously concerned with industry. Even then its role had been limited and links with organizations such as the FBI and the BEC (British Employers' Confederation) had been vague. Throughout the civil service only 14,700 civil servants had been involved in liaison with industry. During the war the position was transformed. New departments were formed to supervise key sectors and in consequence there was a dramatic increase, to a figure of 113,000, in the number of officials responsible for industry. Many of the new civil servants were drawn from the academic world but many others were from private industry itself because of official need for experience and expertise.

The key new ministries were Supply, covering iron and steel, non-ferrous metals, vehicles, engineering and explosives; Fuel and Power, responsible for coal, gas, electricity and oil; and Food, organizing the procurement, distribution and price controls of vital foods and foodstuffs. Most crucial of all was the Ministry of Productions, formed in 1942 to control the importing of raw materials and their allocation between domestic industries. The administrative revolution formalized links between government and industry: each industry, grouped into a representative trade association, was placed under a sponsoring department whose brief was the influence or control of each phase of production. The trade associations in turn organized the allocation of markets and distribution of raw materials. Yet although private industry retained considerable autonomy within the overall framework of government supervision, there were strong countervailing pressures against any tendency to put the interest of a particular industry before the war effort. There was no point in distributing raw materials to industries deliberately starved of manpower by the government, and sectors whose performance was disappointing were subject to drastic reorganization. The Ministry of Aircraft Production, for example, was responsible for a thorough overhaul of the structure and management of the air industry, and in 1943 forced firms with a poor production record to change all their controlling personnel (Milward, 1977, p. 205). Controls over investment and labour supply in fact allowed the government to run an industrial policy involving expansion rather than rationalization for the first time since 1918. This is not to argue that Britain's industrial performance during the war was a record of unblemished success. Barnett has pointed to major failings, in terms of output, productivity and quality, in coal, steel, shipbuilding, and in aircraft and vehicle production. The British war economy, unlike that of its efficient German enemy, was a vast Heath-Robinson machine, kept together only by American supplies of food, raw materials, machine tools and munitions. The faults stemmed from poor industrial relations, restrictive trade union practices, incompetent management, inadequate prewar investment, and the maintenance of outdated plant and equipment (Barnett, 1986, *passim*).

The general argument is open to serious question, although it is difficult to quarrel with the criticisms made of the coal[1] and steel industries, and of the prewar industrial experience. Yet given the legacy of the years after 1920 a massive improvisatory effort was the only option available to Britain, and within these constraints the overall achievement was very considerable. Naval and landing craft launchings rose from a level of 94,000 deadweight tons in 1939 to one of 600,000 deadweight tons in 1944 (Pollard, 1983, p. 203). Even Barnett admits that the expansion of the aircraft industry was 'an industrial development without parallel in British history in terms of scale, speed and cost' (1986, p. 146). Whatever the imperfections of some British bombers it should not be forgotten that by 1944 the Nazis had themselves abandoned production of medium and heavy bombers and had been forced to concede mastery in the air over large tracts of Western and Eastern Europe to the Allies. German tank production may have exceeded British in quantity and quality, but since from the start of the war Nazi planning had been geared to a 'strategic synthesis' centring on *Blitzkrieg*, it would have been extraordinary if this had not been so (Milward, 1977, ch. 1). The Germans were meanwhile unable to motorize their infantry divisions, most of whom relied upon horse transport even in 1943–4, and were easily outdone by the British in the production of military trucks and half trucks (Barnett, 1986, pp. 164–5). Finally, the comparison of British dependence on supplies from across the Atlantic with a Germany who 'fought her war from first to last out of her own national resources *or the resources of countries her armies could occupy*'[2] is self-evidently dubious. It is grotesque to pretend that the industrial capacity of France, the energy resources of Norway, the foodstuffs and raw materials of Eastern Europe and the USSR, not to mention the armies of slave labour recruited from all over the Nazi Empire, were of no account (see Milward, 1977 and 1965). Only by a selective and partial reading of the evidence can it be denied that after 1940 the British economy was transformed. The process was imperfect and dependent upon external support. Nevertheless, modernization followed from total war as resources flowed to the capital-intensive sectors vital to economic growth in peace as well as to success in war.

Full mobilization generated a demand for raw materials, food, capital equipment and munitions. Britain's requirements were vast and, given the emphasis on production for the war effort, could not be financed through exports. After 1941 lend-lease supplies of munitions, raw materials and food from the United States and Canada were of increasing value to the British war effort. The Mutual Aid Agreement by which the terms of lend-lease were settled stated that Britain would not have to pay for these goods during the war. But lend-lease was too late to prevent strains on the British balance of payments in 1939 and 1940. In consequence, pressure on foreign exchange reserves combined with the physical limitations imposed by lack of shipping space to force the government into the introduction of exchange and import controls. The free convertibility of sterling into other currencies was abandoned for the first time since the Napoleonic wars and throughout the sterling area government approval became necessary for any transaction involving the purchase of foreign currency. After June 1940 state purchasing accounted for most imports into Britain, the remainder being subject to official licensing (Sayers, 1956, p. 246).

Although convertibility had been suspended on the outbreak of war, the exchange control system was not perfected until 1940. From September 1939 sterling area members agreed to pay their earnings of hard currency into a central pool in London in exchange for sterling. The pool itself was administered by the Exchange Equalization Account, and demands upon it were restricted to the financing of essential imports. These arrangements did not, however, add up to the construction of an impenetrable fence around the sterling area, and in the early months of the war foreign holders of sterling had been able to convert their balances into hard currencies, notably dollars. The continuation of this facility had been officially justified by reference to the need to preserve international confidence in the currency. But the maintenance of confidence in this manner could not be squared with the imperative of husbanding all available resources for the war, and it was estimated that $737 million flowed out of the reserves between September 1939 and early 1940 (Sayers, 1956, p. 246). As a result, one of the Churchill government's first acts was to block foreign sterling balances and arrange bilateral trade treaties to curtail the flow of foreign exchange to Britain's suppliers.

Such measures did not stop Britain from ending the war as the world's greatest debtor, with overseas liabilities of over £3,000 million. Most of this was owed to Empire and Commonwealth countries which had provided food, raw materials and military bases to Britain. Given sterling's inconvertibility and the agreement of the creditors not to demand immediate payment for their goods and services, these sterling balances presented no financial threat to Britain as long as the war lasted. Their accumulation, along with lend-lease, in fact allowed Britain to conduct the war with more resources than it alone could command and demonstrated that fighting a total war could not be reconciled with continuing to be an international creditor. Between 1920 and 1939 domestic economic policy had been tailored to the demands of sterling's world-wide financial role. After 1940 the priorities were reversed. Exchange controls, bilateral agreements and the sterling balances all implied a change in Britain's international economic orientation: to insulate itself against the deflationary impact of pressures on the balance of payments and so sustain the productive effort, the country had put itself at the centre of a discriminatory economic bloc.

The Political Economy of Reconstruction

Total war had profound political consequences. The centre-right coalition which had underpinned National governments after 1931 was destroyed. In its place by 1945 there existed a centre-left coalition whose project was the reconstruction of Britain as a socially just, fully employed, efficient modern industrial state. Of all three main political parties it was Labour which identified itself most with this vision and with the shift in popular attitudes which lay behind it. Seen in this light, the Labour Party's landslide general election victory in July 1945 is by no means as surprising as it appeared to many at the time.

Postwar reconstruction plans began to multiply after the fall of the Chamberlain government. An entire issue of *Picture Post* in January 1941 was devoted to the creation of a new Britain, characterized by full employment, comprehensive health care, equal access to educational opportunity and town and country planning. But such schemes were generally proposed by the intellectual progressives and planners of the 1930s, seizing the opportunity provided by the growth of state power to return from the political wilderness. Although Churchill was persuaded to put reconstruction on the agenda he did not accord it a high priority and took the view that winning the war came before social engineering. At the start of 1941 he accordingly made Labour's Arthur Greenwood, a member of the War Cabinet, responsible for studying the issues of postwar reconstruction. The committee over which Greenwood presided was, however, deliberately deprived of the power to act on recommendations it might favour and was soon shunted into a bureaucratic siding.

Yet Churchill's reluctance to discuss reconstruction did not prevent his government from producing its own blueprints. In 1944 the Coalition committed itself to maintaining high levels of employment in peacetime (the *Employment Policy* White Paper), to the establishment of a National Health Service, to comprehensive social insurance, and to providing secondary education for all to the age of 15 (the Butler Education Act). This spurt of reforming activity was provoked not by the intelligentsia but by a perception that there was real popular anxiety that the end of the war might herald the return of the economic depression, unemployment and social insecurity which had characterized the interwar years. Above all a series of left-wing successes in wartime by-elections made it obvious that if the government wanted to retain public support it could not ignore demands for a job, a house and decent living standards after the war. The simple truth was that, whatever Churchill believed, total war implied social engineering, and for many people, particularly those who had lived in the depressed areas before the war, the experience of employment, good wages, a proper diet and decent clothing meant a welcome extension of government influence. Once the state had shown itself capable of benevolence, of tackling deprivation, there was no desire to see its powers contract. In short, the successful state-led productive effort was central to a revolution in popular perceptions of the proper role of government. Non-intervention was now equated with the social inequality and industrial inefficiency of the 1920s and 1930s.

The strength and durability of this popular swing to the left was enhanced by the shift to organized labour in the balance of power in British society. Close co-operation between the Churchill government and the trade unions and redistribution of income in favour of the working class followed from full employment and the emphasis on industrial mobilization. Trade union leaders were drawn into government through the National Joint Advisory Council and the National Production Advisory Council. Collective bargaining arrangements were strengthened by state action in areas of the economy where workers had previously been poorly organized. Whitley Councils were established in the retail and distributive trades and a statutory national minimum wage was fixed for agricultural workers. In the mining industry coal owners were forced to concede authority to a National Reference Tribunal with the power to adjudicate in unresolved disputes between management and labour (Pollard, 1983, p. 224). Between 1939 and 1945 trade union membership expanded from 6.25 million to 8 million, and with the increase in membership and authority the TUC began to assume the air of an official department responsible for the co-ordination of social and industrial policy.

Full employment was responsible for wage rises not just in low paid, poorly organized or unskilled trades but also in the engineering and aircraft industries where demand for labour was high. Weekly earnings rose from an index of 100 in October 1938 to a peak of 181.5 in 1944, falling slightly to 180.5 by the end of the war (ibid., p. 225). Yet wage rises did not by themselves cause the £900 million increase in the share of national income taken by wage earners between 1938 and 1947 (1947 prices). They were in fact strongly reinforced by the progressive taxation and price controls which followed from the new approach to financial policy. After tax, middle-class income fell by over 7 per cent while working-class income rose by 9 per cent, and by 1948 purchasing power in the hands of the best paid one-sixth of the population had fallen by 30 per cent but had increased by 25 per cent for the rest of the community.

Full employment, prosperity and political power all worked together in providing organized labour with the confidence to demand a fair deal after the war. The aspirations of trade unionists were shared by many employers whose expectations of the proper role of the state in economic policy were transformed between 1939 and 1945. The industrial experience between the wars had been generally characterized by limited demand and over-capacity. During the first half of the war the predominant worry throughout organizations such as the BEC and FBI was that once the hostilities were over depressed conditions would return. Although the abandonment of liberal orthodoxy followed from this view it was not replaced by any commitment to state-led industrial expansion. Instead the FBI and the industrialists involved in the Nuffield College Reconstruction Survey argued that after the war the state should help to restrict production so that competitive cost-cutting, leading to lower profits, lower wages and unemployment could be averted. The *National Policy for Industry* (1942) called for 'a positive policy' to meet the problems of overproduction, but all this amounted to in the end was more influence for trade unionists in company direction and government support for the regulation of output and prices by trade associations throughout both the domestic and the international economy.

After 1943 there was, however, a significant change in attitudes. The rejection of old-fashioned free-market capitalism remained, but by this time the wartime performance of industry had stimulated optimism about the future. Investment and the application of scientific techniques to industry led civil servants, politicians and industrialists to feel confident that when the war ended the British economy would be well placed to take advantage of new market opportunities with modern products whose competitiveness would be guaranteed by high productivity. Accordingly the economic problem of the postwar period was now seen to be not the rationalization of a saturated market but the need to maintain the full employment of labour and capital. The state's duty was to provide a framework for modernization and expansion. In consequence the *Employment Policy* White Paper was welcomed and it was accepted that Keynesian economics and state planning would be the inevitable costs of growth in the future (see Blank, 1973, p. 37; Middlemas, 1979, pp. 290–2). Greater intervention was an acceptable price to pay for the avoidance of a return to interwar years, partially because wartime experience had shown that *dirigisme* did not necessarily mean the end of private ownership of the means of production, but mostly because industrialists themselves had played such a central role in the management of the war economy. The state may have become the key source of economic activity, but this had not implied the subordination of industry to government dictation so much as a new undertaking between the two, based on the autonomy of trade associations, the co-operation of businessmen and officials on committees and the prominence of the employers themselves in maintaining controls. Above all, state planning was not particularly objectionable if it could be organized by the well-paid managerial salariat which had developed during the war.

The conversion of employers and managers to planning and expansion ensured that reconstruction proposals from both sides of industry would have much in common. There is little evidence to suggest that the aspirations of trade unions extended to workers' control. Given that the principal concerns were employment, fair wages and good conditions of service, management itself could be left in the hands of an enlightened salariat. The confrontational industrial politics of the 1920s were finally buried by wartime co-operation between employers and unions, by the mutual recognition that the other side had a crucial role to play and by common revulsion to policies which had produced stagnation and unemployment between the wars. It was Ernest Bevin, the political figure most responsible for enhancing the power of British labour after 1940, who ultimately articulated a reconstruction programme which set out the main objectives of the new producers' alliance. Bevin's agenda, set out in 1944, included full employment, fair shares between industrial profits and wages, education for all up to 16, social security legislation and the continuation of the joint consultation schemes developed during the war (Middlemas, 1979, pp. 288ff).

The producers' alliance which had evolved between 1914 and 1918 had ultimately been too weak and divided to overpower an establishment determined to conquer inflation by a return to financial orthodoxy. This pattern of events was not to be repeated after the Second World War. The combinaton of controls to contain rises in the cost of living with the determination of the trade unions to restrain wage demands ensured that employers would not support class confrontation and the use of mass unemployment to bring down prices after the war. This does not mean that nobody feared inflation. The point is that the wartime collaboration between the government and both sides of industry had shown that it was possible to reconcile full employment with low inflation, good wages and fair profits. There was therefore no powerful constituency in British society which favoured returning to a liberal economic policy. Given the identification of national efficiency with the full use of all productive resources, reconstruction proposals were characterized by commitments to preserve the essentials of the wartime system. However much radicals on the right or on the left may have deplored this development, there was by 1944 no prospect that they would be able to mobilize a political constituency strong enough to reverse it. Tory liberals were a discredited minority even in their own party and potential upholders of old-fashioned financial orthodoxy such as the Bank of England were equally isolated. Economically and politically discredited by its interwar support for external financial probity at the expense of domestic expansion, the Bank was forced to make a positive answer to calls that it should channel investment into industry even if this meant public ownership. Within the Coalition, Labour pressure for nationalization was not supported by the Conservatives, but the Bank's unpopularity amongst employers as well as trade unions suggested the postwar inevitability of some degree of public supervision to ensure greater responsiveness to the needs of Britain's producers. To meet these criticisms, many of which went back to the Macmillan Committee, the Governor of the Bank proposed in 1944 the formation of two companies, one to finance reorganization in large-scale industry, the other to provide small businesses with long-term finance (Middlemas, 1979, p. 287).

Bevin's reconstruction agenda came under heavy fire from socialist critics, but although they met with more success than the free-marketeers their achievements were limited. Aneurin Bevan complained that the programme was characterized by corporatism and argued for the nationalization of the economy after the war, with domestic employment to be protected from international fluctuations by state trading and import and exchange controls. The leadership's identification with the ethos of national efficiency and Keynesian-style state intervention, coupled with its willingness to go along with American proposals for the removal of discrimination in world trade after the war, lay at the root of the left's critique. It was argued that a future Labour government would end up under the control of big business rather than vice versa, and that the opening up of the economy would make planning impossible.

Labour Party support for this line was strong enough to ensure that the 1945 election manifesto, *Let Us Face the Future*, contained pledges to nationalize the Bank of England, iron and steel, fuel and power and inland transport. Yet such a project involved nothing specifically socialist and some of the reforms had been supported by many Liberals and even some left-wing Tories for years. At the same time the leadership was not prepared to repudiate international economic agreements made with the United States during the war. Its support for them, however, was conditional on the maintenance of many wartime controls on foreign trade and on the continuation of American aid to Britain after the war, so that the reconstruction programme would not be undermined by a balance of payments crisis, only to be replaced by old-fashioned deflation.

This repudiation both of radical socialist policies based on the eternal verities of the class war and of old-fashioned liberalism was characteristic of the reconstruction consensus which had developed in the years after 1940. The political impact of changes in British society wrought by total war was great enough to marginalize all those who sought a return to the prewar *status quo* along with those who advocated a planned, genuinely socialist future. This represented a dramatic shift to the left since it involved the consignment, for the immediate future at least, of everything the prewar National governments had stood for to the dustbin of history. Backed by a trade union movement which supported the reformation but not the abolition of capitalism, the Labour Party exploited the electoral value of the new consensus for all it was worth. In the 1945 general election the policies it advocated were squarely based on the issue of economic and social reconstruction, involving class collaboration and the maintenance of the wartime system, albeit with an enlarged state sector.

Correlli Barnett has maintained that the fundamental aim of reconstruction was misguided, because, dominated by an anti-industrial ruling elite and a class-conscious labour movement, it placed a higher premium on the creation of the welfare state than on the promotion of industrial modernization. At the same time, national self-deception about the achievements of the war economy encouraged a groundless confidence in the future health of British industry. In consequence the economy performed poorly by comparison with that of Britain's major competitors after 1945 as the Attlee government and its successors persistently deprived industry of resources and devoted a disproportionately large share of the national income to the social services.[3]

This view is at best highly contentious. It skates over the impressive recovery achieved between 1945 and 1950. Given that spending per head of the population on education and health in Sweden, France, West Germany and the United States is higher than in contemporary Britain, the Barnett thesis would not seem to be a convincing explanation of industrial decline. Above all, however, Barnett's argument, stemming from a failure to appreciate either the strength or the nature of the shift in the balance of social forces caused by total war, reveals a serious misunderstanding of the ideology associated with reconstruction. Distinctions between the economic and social objectives of reconstruction are artificial. Commitment to industrial modernization was central to the consensus established after 1940 because it had become obvious that the best guarantee of social reform was the existence of a managerial state geared to the maintenance of full industrial production. The Labour Party's 1945 manifesto stressed the need for a 'tremendous overhaul' of the nation (Rogow and Shore, 1955, pp. 2–12), centring on the modernization and re-equipment of industry, so that Britain would be able to pay its way in the world and generate the wealth necessary to the construction of better homes, schools and social services. The New Jerusalem was to be sustained by economic growth. This determination to build on wartime achievements explains the Labour Party's overwhelming appeal to producers' Britain, vastly grown in size and strength after 1940. So clear-cut a victory would have been impossible without the mobilization of a coalition uniting working-class voters and middle-class progressives with the new official and industrial technocracy.

Protection and Reconstruction

The fundamental problem facing the postwar Labour government when it came to power was how to pay for the reconstruction programme. At the end of the war Britain not only carried sterling liabilities of over £3,000 million but faced a prospective balance of payments deficit between 1945 and 1950 of £1,250 million. The orthodox method of adjustment to so threatening an external financial position of course involved deflation and the sacrifice of all the wartime hopes for industrial expansion, full employment and social security. In view of the political commitment to reform within British society such a drastic adjustment was unacceptable, and the new government determined that Britain should produce its way out of insolvency, aiming for a 75 per cent increase, in real terms, in exports up to 1950. In 1945 as in 1940 Britain faced a national emergency which could only be overcome through the full mobilization of all the nation's productive resources.

The problem in peace as in war was that full mobilization was dependent upon a steady flow of imported raw materials and capital goods for industry. Much of this could only be provided by the United States, but Britain's gold and dollar reserves were desperately low. In consequence the new government immediately went to the Americans in search of an interest-free credit, or even a grant, of $5 billion to cover the likely 1945–50 deficit.

The United States provided the money but on terms which were not congenial to the Labour government. Both London and Washington were committed by wartime agreements to working for a multilateral system of trade and payments. But common policies did not follow from shared principles. Whereas the British favoured the concerted pursuit by nations of domestic expansion the Americans concentrated on the need to remove barriers to the circulation of goods. In 1945 American politicians and officials operated within a framework of liberal-capitalist assumptions about the world which held that the best guarantee of peace and order, not to mention export markets, lay in a regime of free circulation for men, goods and capital. It was therefore hardly surprising that Washington viewed both the imperial preference system and above all the wartime sterling arrangements as major obstacles to multilateralism, insisting that the international convertibility of sterling must be a condition of any loan. With a convertible pound Britian's trading partners would be able to purchase goods from any part of the world; if sterling remained inconvertible money earned from Britain could not be spent automatically outside the sterling area itself.

The financial discussions took place in Washington and were

concluded in December 1945. The upshot was a Financial Agreement, finally approved by Congress in July 1946, by which Britain was to receive only $3.75 billion, repayable over fifty years at 2 per cent interest. The sum was disappointing but it was the convertibility provision of the Agreement which most angered the Labour government. Under the Bretton Woods Agreements of 1944 which led to the establishment of the International Monetary Fund, Britain had been provided with a transitional period of 'several years duration' before it was obliged to make sterling convertible. During this period Britain would have been able to maintain exchange restrictions on current payments, but this entitlement was lost as a result of American pressure at the Washington talks. The British argued that the early introduction of convertibility would force them to accumulate inconvertible foreign exchange while their trading partners gained access to hard currency when they sold goods to the United Kingdom. But American determination to break open the sterling area was so great, and Britain's need for dollars so acute, that in the end the Cabinet was forced to agree that convertibility for current transactions would be introduced by 15 July 1947 (see Newton, 1982, ch. 1).

Sterling convertibility proved a fiasco, as indeed it was bound to given the prevailing international economic conditions. After the war not only Britain but the West European countries and Japan were heavily dependent on the United States for the equipment which would allow their industries to operate and for the consumer goods and food which would provide their populations with a reasonable standard of living. It followed that dollars were in demand throughout the world: the United States estimated in 1947 that it would export $16 billion in goods and services but receive only $8 billion in return. Given the existence of this dollar shortage the central problem facing any nation in deficit with the United States was how to finance imports essential to reconstruction (see Newton, 1984). It was therefore hardly surprising that Britain's trading partners used the opportunity of convertibility to get out of sterling into dollars by stepping up exports to the United Kingdom and by adopting restrictive practices to cut down on imports. Britain found itself taking the strain for the world's demand for dollars, and the dollar drain, running at a rate of $650 million a month after 1 August 1947, was intensified by capital transactions out of sterling by holders of sterling balances. As banker to the sterling area the British also had to finance these operations out of their dwindling reserves. By the start of August, it looked as if the entire American credit would be exhausted within a matter of weeks, leaving Britain with gold and dollar reserves so meagre as to force the abandonment of reconstruction. Treasury studies were forecasting the collapse of industrial output, the onset of mass unemployment and the ruin of the governemnt's reformist social programme.[4]

The government's reaction to the crisis revealed the depth of the commitment to reconstruction. There was no question of adopting pre-Keynesian deflation to cut imports to a level commensurate with the low reserves. Instead Labour determined to insulate domestic economic activity from the precarious external position by resorting to the rapid reimposition of physical controls and a discriminatory trading policy. Convertibility was suspended after just five weeks, on 20 August 1947, and was henceforth regarded as an objective which could be achieved only when the world-wide dollar shortage had been cured. Meanwhile the wartime dollar pooling arrangements were reintroduced, complemented by a series of bilateral trade and payments agreements with countries outside the sterling area. Restrictions on all but the most essential imports from the dollar area were intensified throughout the sterling area. In Britain these controls were particularly effective and reductions made in dollar imports as a result of the crisis produced a fall of over 30 per cent in their value between 1947 and 1948 (Cairncross, 1985, p. 342). This implied a much greater reduction in volume than in value, since 1948 import prices were 13 per cent above those of the preceding year. At the same time the government consciously strove to reduce dependence on American supplies through the encouragement of colonial development. What could be extracted from the colonies, such as cocoa, cotton, tobacco, groundnuts and chromium, need not be purchased with scarce dollars.

Repudiating notions of an early return to international economic liberalism was, however, not popular with the State Department and Treasury in the United States. A second sterling crisis occurred in 1949 when politically motivated speculation against the pound combined with an American recession which caused a sharp temporary decline in dollar revenues to lead to another drain on the reserves. Although the government devalued sterling against the dollar by 30 per cent (from \$4.03 to \$2.80 to the pound), the essentials of its policy were not altered and the devaluation was accompanied by cuts of 25 per cent in dollar imports throughout the sterling area. The discriminatory foreign economic policy could in fact only be abandoned if Labour was prepared to renounce everything it stood for. Controls on the outflow of hard currency, together with American assistance through Marshall Aid, allowed the government to maintain an economic expansion which would not finally self-destruct in the balance of payments crisis to end them all.

The unshakeable commitment to expansion, rather than a comprehensive system of economic planning, was the key to the fulfilment of the reconstruction programme. Protection and unprecedented levels of peacetime public spending (34.9 per cent of the gross national product in 1951 against 19 per cent in 1938; Pollard, 1983, p. 243), together with low interest rates, sustained a consistently high level of demand. Full employment was therefore maintained throughout the postwar years and the buoyant economic climate encouraged rising output throughout industry, to a level of 195 in 1950 (1938 = 100; ibid., p. 252). The expansion in fact fed on itself because widening markets stimulated a wave of innovation which reduced costs and provided a further upward twist to growth.

The wartime trend to economies of large-scale production was maintained and gave encouragement to greater efficiency. Despite a reduction in the length of the average working week productivity rose to an all-time high by 1950 and after the war not even the Americans managed to increase output per man-hour as rapidly as the British. Although the average rate of growth of labour productivity between 1945 and 1951 was only 1.6 per cent per annum, this figure conveys a misleading impression, and would be a good deal higher but for a fall in productivity in 1945–6.[5] Between 1948 and 1951, GDP per head in manufacturing industry rose to a level of 3.5 per cent each year (Cairncross, 1985, p. 19). Reconstruction was particularly notable for the striking increases in output achieved by the industries which had been vital to the war effort and which were to be central to the postwar international boom in investment and exports. Thus 'engineering and allied industries' expanded production by 16 per cent on average each year between 1946 and 1951, metal manufacturing by 8.55 per cent, and chemicals by 13.8 per cent (see Feinstein, 1972, Table 51). Investment responded to boom conditions, keeping pace with high demand and output while fixed investment quickly reached its 1938 level – the prewar peak – and by 1950 exceeded it by 75 per cent, spurred on by the efforts of private companies, public authorities and nationalized industries.

Inflationary pressure followed from high demand as incomes rose to a level which could not be satisfied by domestic output. The government's response to inflation was founded on a determination not to alienate either side of the producers' alliance which had been central to the reconstruction coalition. Policies which either allowed prices to rise freely or reduced economic activity through drastic public spending cuts were clearly unacceptable since they could not be squared with the 1945 commitment to full employment at reasonably stable prices. At the same time Labour did not wish to retain the full panoply of controls which had characterized the war economy. Particularly after Sir Stafford Cripps became Chancellor in November 1947 the government sought to manage the economy through partnership with industry rather than through coercion. By 1950 price controls were mainly limited to non-food goods and consumer rationing had been reduced to basic foodstuffs. High taxation, as in the war, remained an important part of the anti-inflation policy but official efforts were concentrated on securing the voluntary agreement of the FBI and the TUC to hold down prices and restrain dividends and wages. The government in fact linked the problem of inflation with the over-riding need to export; it worried that high wage costs would not only push up domestic prices but simultaneously make British goods uncompetitive in world markets. Trade union leaders made it clear that wage restraint was inconceivable while employers and *rentiers* were enjoying rising profits and dividends. In consequence the employers assented to voluntary price stabilization and dividend restraint in return for the acceptance by the TUC of a wage freeze. This tripartite bargain worked remarkably well until it was undermined by a dramatic rise in the cost of living in 1950, when import prices rose sharply, partially as a result of the 1949 devaluation but mainly because of the explosion in the cost of raw materials which followed the outbreak of the Korean War. At this point the TUC repudiated the wage freeze; but its maintenance between 1948 and 1950 had been central to keeping the annual rate of inflation down to under 3 per cent while physical controls were being reduced in scope.

Adherence to what has been called 'voluntarism' (Blank, 1973, p. 88) characterized the government's approach to industrial reconstruction. Given Labour's commitment to a mixed economy the employers on the whole took the nationalization programme in their stride and controversy about public ownership did not become significant until 1949, when it centred on the strategically vital steel industry. Generally, however, relations were quite close. In part this was because both government and industry were committed to the full employment of resources and rising productivity. But agreement on principles was reinforced by practice. Cripps supported the continuation of self-regulation through the trade associations and encouraged the FBI to become a spokesman for industry as a whole. To this end the FBI was regularly consulted by the government on all industrial matters and between 1945 and 1951 it sent nominees or representatives to thirty-four official boards, councils or committees. Amongst the most important of these bodies were the Anglo-American Productivity Council and the Exports Board. Industrial policy followed naturally from the managerial vision of a reconstructed Britain which had formed during the war. But it also derived from the government's conviction that, in view of balance of payments problems, the new Welfare State could only be sustained by increasing exports and by reducing dependence upon imports.

After 1945 there was certainly no impediment to exporting heavily to the Empire and Commonwealth, because of the sterling balances, which acted as claims on British production. The only effective way Britain could run down its sterling area debts after the war was by payment in goods which the creditors had little choice but to accept in view of their shortage of hard currency. Throughout the first six years after the war nearly one-half of all British exports were sent to the sterling area. This flow of what became known as 'unrequired exports' (since Britain received no payments in cash or in kind by return) helped sustain domestic activity but it caused the government some anxiety. The real need was for dollars and these could not be won if too many resources were devoted to meeting demand in what were to all intents and purposes captive markets. In consequence the real point behind the 'export drive', launched in the aftermath of the 1947 convertibility crisis, was to send goods to western hemisphere countries which would pay for them in hard currency.

'Voluntarism' was vital to the export drive. In September 1947 the government announced agreed targets for 153 classes of exports, to be met by the end of 1948. Over the next few months the targets were reviewed in consultation with the respective industries. But selling products in America was no easy task. The great strides in United States' productivity during the war meant that those who wanted to prise open the American market would have to ensure that exports were competitive. The Labour government was aware of this problem and stressed in its *Economic Survey for 1949* that 'The time has now arrived when we can and must intensify our attack on the North American market . . . Our task is to produce goods which, through design, quality and price, will command buyers in a free market . . .' To encourage this, a campaign for higher productivity was joined to the export drive. The campaign was institutionalized in bodies such as the Anglo-American Productivity Council, established in 1948 to see what lessons could be learned from the experience of the United States. A succession of teams drawn from British industry by the trade associations, employers' federations and trade unions were transported across the Atlantic and came back recommending more research, more mechanization, more standardization, more efficient managerial techniques and improvement in the lay-out of factories. Many of their recommendations were adopted, particularly in the newer industries such as engineering, machine tools, electronics, vehicles and chemicals, which showed the most dramatic increases in productivity after the war. The results of the export drive were extremely encouraging, with exports increasing by 25 per cent between 1947 and 1948. Expansion continued into 1950, by which time exports had exceeded the forecasts of even the most optimistic planners in 1945, having risen in real terms by 77 per cent in five years. The most successful participants in the export drive were the newer industries, where government policy encouraged the continuation of the substantial wartime capital investment. In the motor industry, for example, the level of output attained in the best prewar year, 1937, was reached in 1948, and by 1950 had been surpassed by 90 per cent. At the same time the limitation of domestic demand for cars by a swingeing purchase tax (66.67 per cent in 1951) and the discriminatory allocation of sheet steel to companies producing for the dollar market ensured that 78 per cent of all those made in 1951 were exported. By 1950 the proportion of British exports going to the western hemisphere stood at almost 18 per cent, having increased from 13.5 per cent in 1946. More generally Britain's share of world trade in manufactured goods rose from the prewar level of 17.5 per cent to 20.7 per cent in 1950.[6]

It is of course true that the task was made easier after 1945 because there was no German or Japanese competition. But the available opportunities had to be seized in the first place. This did not mean merely continuing consumer goods' shortages at home. The *Economic Survey for 1949* declared that:

> it is the Government's intention, while maintaining investent in the social services at the 1948 level, to increase to the maximum investment in those industries and basic services where increased output will, directly or indirectly, assist the balance of payments, and, more particularly, serve to increase dollar earnings or reduce dollar expenditures.

Austerity was, however, politically acceptable because the sacrifices were fairly distributed and because the government made it clear that no other policy would guarantee the success of reconstruction. In fact the export drive not only underpinned reconstruction: it was part of it.

The 1945 Coalition was committed to encouraging the continuation of the wartime trend to the modernization of the British economy as well as to constructing the Welfare State. And diminishing dependence on the old staple industries, notably coal and textiles, was testimony to modernization. During the twentieth century the manufacturing sectors best placed to take advantage of international trade growth have been those where high productivity has meant a high ratio of exports to output. It was precisely these capital-intensive industries which had been expanded most rapidly in Britain after 1940, first in response to the demands of total war and subsequently because their success was linked to the creation of an efficient new society which could pay its way in the world. The achievement was considerable and by 1950 the commodity composition of British exports was characterized by a real shift to machinery, vehicles, electrical goods and chemicals, all of which were growth sectors in world trade. Indeed in the early 1950s products for which there was increasing international demand made up almost two-thirds of all Britain's exports (Pollard, 1983, p. 251).

Modernization was not restricted to manufacturing industry. The need to reduce dependence on dollars led the government to maintain the wartime policy of encouraging agricultural production so that Britain could feed itself as far as it was possible to do so. The key to success was the 1947 Agriculture Act by which farmers were assured of markets for about 75 per cent of all their produce and provided with guaranteed prices. In making agricultural policy Labour did not deviate from the principle of co-operating with the relevant association of producers. Markets were guaranteed for about 75 per cent of all farm produce and prices were fixed in negotiations between the Ministry of Agriculture and the National Farmers' Union.[7] In farming as in the rest of the economy there was to be no return to the *laissez-faire* policies which had characterized the immediate aftermath of the First World War. The consequent maintenance of a stable environment led to increased investment in modern machinery, a development assisted by generous tax concessions. Output rose steadily and by 1950 it had reached 146 per cent of the prewar level, with the results that British agriculture became the most efficient in Western Europe.

Postwar reconstruction was in general a success story. The contrasts with the British experience after 1918 were obvious. Neither expansion nor full employment was ever repudiated and a real shift in the pattern of British industry took place. The structural problem of dependence on old, declining industries did not reappear and great steps were taken towards the fulfilment of the technocratic dream in which government, employers and workers all co-operated to build a modern, productive society. Similar aspirations had been evident in the wake of the First World War, but 'the politics of decontrol' had seen to it that they could not then be satisfied. On this occasion the harmony of interests between the Attlee government and Britain's producers underpinned resistance to external calls, mostly from Washington, and internal demands, mainly from the City and the Bank of England, for the comprehensive dismantling of controls. Indeed the commitment to reform throughout society was too powerful to be overcome by the forces of financial orthodoxy. Above all Labour retained mass support because its policies guaranteed the delivery of the Welfare State. Full employment and the extension of social services ensured that the wartime promises to abolish primary poverty were kept:

> B. S. Rowntree, visiting York in 1950 to conduct his third social survey there, found the proportion of the working-class population living in poverty to have dropped from 31.1% in 1936 to 2.8% in 1950; of those living below the poverty line, nearly one-third gave unemployment as the reason in 1936, while not one was found in 1950; in that year 68% attributed their poverty to old age. At the same time Rowntree and Havers calculated that if the welfare provisions (including subsidies) in 1950 had been only those of 1936, the proportion of working class families living in poverty would have been, not 2.8% but 22.2%. (Pollard, 1983, p. 266)

After 1945 the share of the national income occupied by wage-earners continued its wartime growth, having risen by 1949 to 41.4 per cent of the total (37.8 per cent in 1938). The increase was larger than the figures suggest at first sight because between 1938 and 1950 wage-earners actually fell as a proportion of the working population from 71.4 per cent to 66.2 per cent. Despite high taxation profits rose as well, to the highest levels in the history of British industry (Rogow and Shore, 1955, pp. 68–9), and the post-war years as a whole saw gains for the producers of wealth. By contrast the period was characterized by setbacks for the *rentier*, whose share of the national income fell from 22.58 per cent in 1938 to just 10.78 per cent in 1950 as a result of rent controls, low interest rates and dividend restraint. It was this combination of social justice with economic achievement which held together the reconstruction coalition at a time when unprecedented financial difficulties made it inevitable that the going would be tough. Labour failed to lose a single parliamentary seat in any by-election between 1945 and 1951. In Sir Alec Cairncross's words (1985, p. 509), these were 'years when the government knew where it wanted to go and led the country with an understanding of what was at stake'.

Nevertheless, by 1950 strains were beginning to appear in the 1945 alliance. The government's determination to nationalize steel, along with its production of a list of other industries to be taken into public ownership, including sugar, water and cement, was not welcomed by the FBI. But the fatal blow was an economic crisis in 1951, largely resulting from the international impact of the Korean War, whose propaganda value a middle class resentful of high taxation and a financial establishment keen on the removal of controls did not hesitate to exploit.

Notes: Chapter 4

1 Although problems in the coal industry were common to most of the belligerent countries. See Milward, 1977, p. 231.
2 Barnett, 1986, p. 61. Emphasis added.
3 Barnett's book (1986) is challenging and powerfully written. The thesis is, however, flawed by a highly selective treatment of evidence, a strange ignorance of the work of Alan Milward on both the German and British wartime economies, and by a total neglect of the location and influence of finance within the British political economy. The end result is a book whose arguments are contentious but hardly conclusive.
4 See PRO T229/136, Central Economic Planning Staff study, 'Marshall Proposals: Alternative Action in Event of Breakdown', July 1947.
5 Immediately after the war productivity had fallen as a result of the inevitable dislocation caused by industry's transition to production for peaceful purposes. Women workers were replaced by men, and efficient use of labour resources had to await the completion of tooling up for new production. Further difficulties were caused by a tendency on the part of industries subject to raw material shortage to hoard labour in the expectation of better supplies. See N. H. Leyland, 'Productivity', in Worswick and Ady, 1952, p. 393.
6 T. Balogh, 'The International Aspect', in Worswick and Ady, 1952, p. 253; Cairncross, 1985, pp. 35–6.
7 See D. K. Britton, 'Agriculture', in Worswick and Ady, 1985.

CHAPTER FIVE

The Fall and Rise of the Producers' Alliance, 1951–1964

Conservative Freedom, 1951–1958

There was to be no consolidation of the postwar progress towards a modern, productive industrial economy in the 1950s. Despite the existence of full employment and growing prosperity for the consumer the overall performance of the British economy was disappointing. Growth, which had averaged over 3.5 per cent per annum after 1946, became increasingly erratic, did not occur at all in 1958 and averaged only 2.6 per cent per annum for the decade as a whole. Britain's major competitors easily outpaced this: between 1950 and 1960 the German economy grew at an annual average rate of over 7 per cent, the Japanese at about 8 per cent, while even France, supposedly the 'sick man' of Europe, enjoyed a steady advance of 4.5 per cent. At the same time Britain's share of the world market in manufactures diminished significantly. By 1957 it was down to 14.7 per cent, falling to 12.7 per cent in 1961.[1]

There were short-term and long-term factors at work. In the short term, the diversion of large amounts of plant and capacity to rearmament rather than to production for exports after the outbreak of the Korean War meant lost markets. The West German and Japanese economies, neither bearing a heavy defence burden, benefited particularly from the check to the British export drive. In the longer term, Britain's export performance began to suffer from a national failure to invest as much of the GNP as its principal competitors. Gross domestic investment as a proportion of the GNP between 1950 and 1960 reached an average 19.1 per cent each year in France, 24.0 per cent in Germany and 20.8 per cent in Italy. In Britain, however, the average was 15.4 per cent. The international competitiveness of British products suffered from the failure of investment to grow as rapidly and consistently as it did elsewhere. With 60 per cent of the buildings and 38 per cent of the plant and machinery in manufacturing industry and construction dating from before 1948 in 1961, it was not surprising that technical advance was sluggish. The investment failure meant, in short, a failure to embrace wholeheartedly new methods of production, and in consequence British productivity compared badly throughout the 1950s with practically every other advanced industrial country except the United States. Between 1950 and 1960 output per man-hour in manufacturing industry in West Germany rose at an annual average of 5.9 per cent. For Italy and France the increases were, respectively, 4.1 per cent and 3.6 per cent. The British managed to achieve a level of 2.3 per cent. High costs of production followed from low investment and British goods consistently lost ground in world markets.

The collapse of the wartime producers' alliance, and its replacement in the formulation of economic policy by an anti-planning coalition led by the City of London, the Bank of England and the Treasury, provided the background to the unhappy industrial performance. The critical moment was the 1951 general election, fought in the midst of an economic crisis which was attributed to the government's policies even though Labour was by no means wholly responsible for it.

In 1950 Britain had appeared to be on the way to overcoming its persistent dollar problem. The sterling area's net deficit of $1,532 million in 1949 had been transformed into a net surplus of $805 million as a result of heavy American raw material stockpiling in aid of the rearmament programme stimulated by the Korean War. Having achieved a surplus with the dollar area for the first time since the war, in 1951 the sterling area *en masse* relaxed the import restrictions imposed to save hard currency. But the improvement came to a sudden end during the third quarter of the year. By February 1952 the sterling area reserves, which had risen to $3,800 million in June 1951, had fallen to $1,800 million (£643 million). Further deterioration, to $1,500 million (£536 million) by the end of March, was predicted in Treasury and Bank of England forecasts. At the same time the annual rate of inflation leaped to 10 per cent.

The economic crisis arose from a combination of bad luck and poor judgement.[2] The government had embraced an over-ambitious rearmament programme, increasing the share of the national product taken by defence from 6 per cent (1950) to 10 per cent (1951–2), which not only curtailed the export drive but also stimulated a high demand for imports. This would have put pressure on the reserves in any case. But the strain was intensified by the boom in international commodity prices which had followed from the stockpiling of raw materials by the United States. At the same time primary producing members of the sterling area, flush with dollars, expanded imports, purchasing heavily from the United States because Britain was in no position to meet all their demands for capital goods. With gold and dollars flooding out of Britain and the sterling area, senior officials in the Treasury began to worry about the prospects of an 'early bankruptcy'.[3] By the start of 1952 the new Churchill government weighed assets of under $2 billion against liabilities of over $10 billion.

The sterling crisis of 1951 represented a serious setback for British reconstruction. During the general election campaign, Labour's economic competence was challenged by the Conservatives and Liberals, who pointed to the deteriorating external financial position and the high inflation rate. In view of the fact that Attlee could scarcely have chosen a worse time to go to the polls, however, it is remarkable that Labour performed so strongly, recording its highest ever popular vote. But it lost because it registered increased support in its working-class heartland and suffered from a middle-class swing to the Conservatives in marginal seats.[4]

It was no accident that the middle-class vote played such an important part in the general election of 1951. The middle class as a proportion of all adults had risen from 27.1 per cent in 1931 to 30.4 per cent in 1951. Over the same period the share of the adult population occupied by the manual wage class had fallen from 68.1 per cent to 64.6 per cent (Bonham, 1954, p. 113). It was this middle class, composed of office workers, professional groups, managers and businessmen, which came to resent the outgoing government. The charges of incompetence it levelled against Labour implied growing alienation from the policies pursued since 1945 and from the social-democratic philosophy which underpinned them. The system of controls, rationing and high personal taxation, vital to reconstruction, was regarded as a disincentive to work and thrift and as the harbinger of socialist regimentation. The FBI strongly opposed iron and steel nationalization, claiming that it struck at the principle of voluntary co-operation between government and industry. Within the FBI there was growing dissatisfaction with the maintenance of dividend restraint and, outside it, other industrial groups such as the National Union of Manufacturers argued that the free enterprise system itself was now under threat (Blank, 1973, pp. 125–6). Meanwhile many middle-class voters not associated with industry expressed fears that rising prices would erode the value of personal savings. Labour's counter-inflation policy, centring on co-operation with the TUC, was deemed undemocratic and ultimately ineffective. On top of these specific grievances came a more general anxiety that the balance of social and political power in Britain was shifting to organized labour (Bonham, 1952, pp. 183–4).

In these circumstances, and given the demise of the Liberal Party, it was predictable that many middle-class voters would support the Conservatives in 1951. Quite correctly the Conservatives were seen as more tolerant of inequalities in income levels than Labour, biased to economic freedom rather than to intervention, and less concerned to govern with the collaboration of the trade unions. During the election campaign the Conservatives articulated middle-class grievances against the new *status quo*, maintaining that hard work could be rewarded by tax cuts if government spending were reduced. The 1951 Conservative manifesto contained a commitment to 'cut out all unnecessary government expenditure' and claimed that 'British taxation is higher than in any country outside the Communist world'. The project was to create an anti-socialist coalition spreading from the centre to the right of British politics. This coalition's purpose was to unite in defence of free enterprise and freedom of choice at the marketplace all those groups antagonized by Labour's interventionist policies.

The rightward drift of the middle class went with the tide taken by small businessmen (64 per cent of whom voted Conservative in 1951 as against 37 per cent in 1945), large-scale industry and the

City of London (ibid. p. 76). In the postwar era of exchange and import controls the City's voice had been muted, but it possessed a powerful spokesman in the Bank of England, which shared its interest in the preservation of sterling as an international currency. Both the City and the Bank had been forced to accept Britain's rejection of international economic liberalism in 1940 but neither institution had been comfortable with the maintenance of the wartime sterling system after 1945. It was true that the Bank was now nationalized, but the material significance of this act had been minimal. For all its radicalism the Labour government had failed to transform the function and staffing of the Bank so as to make it genuinely responsive to the needs of British industry. The Bank retained its independence, its personnel was unaffected and its politico-economic priorities remained unaltered from prewar days. The advent of a Conservative government dedicated to the restoration of market capitalism therefore allowed the Bank and the City to emerge from what had been little more than a state of suspended animation. In December 1951 London was reopened as a marketplace for international foreign exchange.

Along with the new administraton the Bank viewed the economic crisis as a verdict on the methods and policies pursued since the outbreak of war. The existence of speculation against sterling, a side-effect but hardly a cause of Britain's problems, was seized on by the Bank to reinforce its ideological distaste for a regime of continuing controls. It was argued that the speculation could only be suppressed if sterling was kept out of foreign hands and thus lost its status as an international currency.[5] In reality there was no need to take such drastic action and speculation declined in intensity as the balance of payments gradually improved during the spring of 1952. The real problem was not the unacceptable cost of measures to prevent speculation but Britain's adjustment to balance of payments difficulties via continuing inconvertibility and the planning of foreign trade. It was the maintenance of this system which could not be tolerated: restricting the use of sterling would diminish its international attractiveness, resulting in the City's inability to draw foreign funds.

The enthusiasm of the City and the Bank for a return to liberalism was matched in the Treasury, which was ultimately responsible for managing the balance of payments and maintaining the value, and hence world-wide attractiveness, of sterling. It followed that senior Treasury officials were seriously concerned about the worsening external balance, and throughout the autumn of 1951 they argued for spending cuts, accompanied by a rise in the bank rate to damp down demand. Financial restraints would mean reduced imports, lower inflation and resurgent international confidence in the currency. Deflation was, however, not enough to satisfy independent sterling area members which had done well out of the commodity boom and now wanted to spend freely in the western hemisphere. At the January 1952 Commonwealth Finance Ministers' Conference, delegates from Australia, Ceylon and South Africa attacked continuing controls on dollar purchasing and called for an early return to convertibility. The pressure worried the Treasury. It came to fear that the sterling area might disintegrate and Britain's historic international financial role finally disappear if it seemed that inconvertibility was to be the rule for the indefinite future. One Treasury official specifically argued that 'it *must* be in our interest to have sterling convertible for we cannot possibly trade and ship and insure and all the other things we do unless sterling is convertible'.[6] These sentiments represented a rebirth of the prewar orthodoxy which had identified the vitality of finance and of commercial capitalism with the health of the national economy.

Such views had in fact never been absent from the Treasury during the 1940s, but at moments of crisis as in 1947 and 1949 they had not prevailed because the government's priority had been a sustained industrial expansion incompatible with the liberal objectives of Britain's financial community. The 1951 election result had, however, meant the abandonment of this priority and its replacement by a determination to integrate Britain into the international economy. This was not because the Conservatives explicitly rejected putting reconstruction and modernization first, but because their victory was also a triumph for all sections of British society hostile to the controls which had insulated the domestic economy from external pressures. The change in the political climate let the Treasury liberals off the leash. They now argued to a receptive government that Britain's postwar recovery had not been a genuine one. The dollar shortage was not exogenous but a reflection of Britain's inability to adjust to the level of costs and prices prevailing in the United States, a failure exacerbated by anti-dollar discrimination and sheltered markets in the sterling area. What was damaging to finance was therefore also counterproductive for industry. The adjustment necessary to real and lasting recovery could only be secured through competition in the international marketplace, and the best way to achieve this would be by making the pound a convertible currency once again (Newton, 1986, p. 14).

Despite its enthusiasm for liberalism the new government took time to return to full convertibility. A plan to make the pound convertible for non-residents of the sterling area at a floating rate, code-named Operation Robot, was discussed and rejected by the Cabinet in 1952. The Chancellor of the day, Rab Butler, was enthusiastic but his colleagues feared that the domestic consequences of its implementation would involve mass unemployment (ibid. p. 29–31). Although the Tories strongly believed in *laissez-faire* they were committed to protecting the Welfare State and maintaining full employment, and even if they had been willing to return to the policies which had made them so unpopular in 1945 the 1951 election result provided them with no mandate to do so. The shift to the right in the balance of social forces in Britain had not gone so far as to permit a return to pre-Keynesian orthodoxy. The Conservative version of Keynesianism was therefore a liberal one, characterized by growing de-regulation within the domestic and external sectors of the economy. Subsidies were vastly reduced in scope, dividend restraint was ended, middle-class voters were rewarded with tax relief and consumers granted more freedom in the marketplace by the gradual lifting of rationing, which vanished altogether in 1954. As the dollar shortage abated because of the world-wide expansion of the American military machine and growing investment in Europe by multinational corporations centred in the United States, the old trade and exchange controls were gradually removed. Bulk purchasing arrangements were scrapped and the commodity markets re-opened. More freedom was provided to those wishing to transfer capital abroad, and by early 1955 sterling was effectively convertible into dollars and other foreign currencies for all non-residents. Full convertibility was finally reintroduced in 1958. At the same time the government manipulated the overall level of economic activity by control of credit, increasing the bank rate to reduce demand and attract foreign capital when the balance of payments was weak, lowering it and reducing taxes when the external position was healthy (Brittan, 1964, Chapter 6).

The government's two priorities were the opening of the British economy and the preservation of expansion. When Butler expressed a hope that the nation's standard of living might double in the next twenty-five years, he appeared to be making consistent long-term growth a goal of policy no less definite than the encouragement of the widest possible international use of sterling as a trading and reserve currency. Yet in fact these two policies were ultimately contradictory. What would the government do if the balance of payments problems reappeared? Impose physical controls to maintain domestic activity, as after the war, or deflate so that any adjustment did not infringe the canons of liberal orthodoxy? Given the fundamental commitment to *laissez-faire* it was not likely that the answer to this question would satisfy employers and unions seeking steady expansion. For a time, however, there was no need to make a choice between the two aims. The period from 1952 to the start of 1955 was characterized by growing prosperity and a healthy external balance, with Britain benefiting from a shift in the terms of trade away from commodity producers after the end of the Korean War boom. Demand increased steadily at home and the existence of a sellers' market internationally disguised declining competitiveness *vis à vis* German and Japanese exports.

Industrialists took the coincidence of rising profits and growing markets with the re-established primacy of the marketplace as clear evidence that the economic problems of the beginning of the decade could be blamed on excessive state interference. Boom conditions were testimony to the fact there was no longer any need to worry about the maintenance of full production and the modernization of industry to make new products for the international market. It followed that de-regulation was welcomed throughout industry. There were few complaints as the consultative machinery established to ensure close co-operation with government after 1940 fell into neglect. The FBI lost its pre-eminence in the formulation of economic policy as the Conservatives sought to regulate economic activity by financial rather than by physical controls and therefore left the allocation of resources to the market. Yet this development was not regretted, since after

1949 the leadership of the FBI had come under increasing criticism from members who felt that their organization had become a department of state rather than an independent representative body. Greater autonomy for industry seemed to be reconcilable not only with the full use of productive capacity but also with the guarantee of a safe future for private enterprise in Britain.

The reaction against tripartite consultation continued through the mid-1950s as industrialists and managers came to believe that the economy was a productive machine whose efficiency could be assured if it was left to tick over by itself. Obstacles in the path of expansion were now seen to be mainly political, stemming from government behaviour. Inflation, which remained a concern of the FBI and its sister organization, the British Employers' Confederation, was attributed to excess demand resulting from high public spending. It was accordingly argued that the pressure of rising prices would be weakened if spending cuts were implemented even if this meant slightly higher unemployment than had been usual since the war. Nobody was proposing a return to the 1920s and 1930s but it was felt that if labour was rather less scarce employers would be able to force through wage settlements which did not push up costs and prices. The alternative way of holding down inflation, involving an incomes policy along Crippsian lines, was anathema. High taxes, price controls and dividend restraint only reduced incentives, lowered profits and weakened the willingness to invest.

In fact the rejection of Crippsian methods was common to both sides of industry. The TUC was committed to the maintenance of free collective bargaining, with voluntary income restraint held in opprobrium after its collapse in 1950. Union leaders did not, however, share the analysis accepted by industrialists of what caused inflation. Pointing to the high level of profits, they claimed that the government should press industry to charge lower prices, and in addition called for the extension rather than the reduction of subsidies. The government, meanwhile, called for a greater sense of partnership between employers and unions but itself followed policies which inevitably destroyed the prospects of co-operation. The last food subsidies were ended in the 1956 budget, and the Cabinet decided to take a tough line with wage demands in the public sector. In consequence the nationalized industries became a focus of serious industrial disputes. Private employers followed the government's lead and the result by early 1957 was the worst wave of industrial stoppages to afflict the economy since 1926.

The consensus forged in the war between government, industry and the unions had broken apart by the mid 1950s. The old reconstruction coalition had been able to unite around a common commitment to full employment, modernization and growth. Each member of that coalition now came to feel that these *desiderata* had been achieved and did not require constant re-affirmation. In any case the prosperous, expanding Britain of the 1950s was faced by new economic problems which each party to the wartime alliance tended to view in different terms. Common ground on the proper objectives of national economic policy no longer existed. Industry and the employers were preoccupied with the issues of profits and inflation. Trade union leaders concentrated on the need to ensure that wages kept pace with increases in the cost of living. The government's aim was to manage an increasingly open economy at full employment without provoking a balance of payments crisis.

Industry's reaction against Labour in 1950 and 1951 had resulted from animus against intervention but not against expansion. The Tories had been welcomed because they were believed to be liberal expansionists. But after 1955 it became increasingly obvious that liberalism came before expansion. The government identified national economic health with a sound balance of payments and its corollary, international confidence in the currency, and to achieve these ends it was prepared to put all kinds of obstacles in the way of sustained growth. In the autumn of 1955 a weak balance of payments encouraged international speculation against the pound. The government did not react by imposing physical restrictions on imports but instead reduced internal demand by pushing up the bank rate and by drastically reducing investment programmes for the nationalized industries (Pollard, 1984, p. 44). The deflationary policy worked in that it brought about a reduction in imports, but the price was stagnant output and investment in 1956 and 1957. These measures were not, however, enough to satisfy the increasing number of international holders of sterling, who started a new wave of panic selling in September 1957. Slow growth notwithstanding, the City and the Bank of England blamed the new crisis on lax credit conditions at home and maintained that only the complete absence of domestic inflation would satisfy external holders of sterling that they possessed a reliable asset. A particular anxiety seems to have been the willingness of the international financial community to desert the pound for the German mark, a worrying development in view of the plans in the City and the Bank to restore London fully to its prewar international financial pre-eminence. In response the Chancellor, now Peter Thorneycroft, pushed through further reductions in public spending, tightened the credit squeeze, cut investment and raised the bank rate to what was then the sensationally high level of 7 per cent.

There is no need to invoke either incompetence or conspiracy theories to explain why the government was prepared to follow policies damaging to the real economy. Its true loyalties had from the start lain with the traditional centres of politico-economic power in Britain – the City, the Bank and the Treasury. The liberalization of sterling and the re-establishment of London as a commercial entrepôt had indeed encouraged the inflow of foreign funds to the City and the wider international use of sterling in the 1950s. By 30 June 1957 the sterling balances were worth £4,154 million. Much of this money was quite speculative, and investors could move it in and out of the country according to their expectations both of the returns from interest rates and of the currency's stability. A weak balance of payments therefore meant trouble because it created fears of devaluation, and rather than see the value of their balances reduced by millions of pounds at a stroke foreign holders of sterling would ship them right out of Britain. As the de-control of the external sector proceeded Britain became more and more vulnerable to unstable capital flows of this kind, particularly because its own gold and dollar reserves, totalling only £850 million in June 1957 (Jenkins, 1959, p. 69), were never large enough to justify its vast liabilities. With the wartime and postwar control system dismantled the only way the government could prevent a large movement out of sterling was by making Britain a thoroughly attractive place for the owners of capital. The alternatives – devaluation or an about-turn on the march to full convertibility – were obviously counterproductive, given the Conservatives' overall project. In consequence the government was forced into the deflationary policy whose logical conclusion was Thorneycroft's 1957 measures. As a result economic growth came to a standstill and the level of industrial production actually fell, from 67.8 in 1957 to 67.2 in 1958 (1975 = 100; Nevin, 1983, p. 182). It was this willingness to contract the economy and cut investment to hold the line on sterling which was at the root of Britain's poor economic record during the 1950s.

The Conservatives suffered no electoral damage as a result of this policy and easily won the 1959 general election. Full employment was maintained, largely as a result of boom conditions in the international economy. And while the pursuit of de-regulation, a sound currency and zero inflation naturally squared with the City of London's desire to expand its cosmopolitan activities, it also suited the needs of the many middle-class consumers and *rentiers* who were so prominent in the anti-planning coalition which had brought the Tories to power in 1951. For those with money to spend there were more and more goods available, and the overriding concern was to ensure that they stayed cheap. The collapse of expansion under the Conservatives was 'celebrated amidst a

Table 5.1 Rent, Dividends and Net Interest as a Percentage of the GNP (at Current Market Prices), 1946–1960 (£m)

	GNP	Rent, dividends and net interest	Percentage of GNP*
1946	8,855	1,274	14.39
1947	9,458	1,357	14.35
1948	10,469	1,217	11.62
1949	11,204	1,204	10.75
1950	11,762	1,268	10.78
1951	12,942	1,268	9.80
1952	13,994	1,285	9.18
1953	14,485	1,393	9.62
1954	15,812	1,447	9.15
1955	16,987	1,534	9.03
1956	18,244	1,547	8.48
1957	19,231	1,633	8.49
1958	20,082	1,844	9.18
1959	21,180	2,056	9.70
1960	22,965	2,372	10.33

* The 1946 figure of 14.39% in itself represented a sharp fall from the 1938 level of 22.58%. The continuing substantial decline in *rentier* incomes as a proportion of the GNP up to 1952 reflected the policies of cheap money and dividend restraint followed by Labour to support its reconstruction programme.

Source: Feinstein, 1972, Tables 1 and 10.

growing chorus of frenzied middle class voices shouting that no sacrifice of real wealth was too great so long as the price tags on goods in the shops could be kept the same' (Schonfield, 1958, p. 248). For the owners of capital the end of dividend restraint and the reliance on the bank rate to manipulate economic activity meant a halt to, and then a reversal of, the decline in incomes experienced during and after the war (see Table 5.1).

Ultimately, in January 1958, Thorneycroft was forced to resign along with his two main subordinates at the Treasury, Nigel Birch and Enoch Powell. Their calls for real cuts in public spending were not supported in a Cabinet where there was no enthusiasm for using mass unemployment as a tool of economic policy. The liberal Keynesian synthesis achieved after 1951 survived. But the priority which Thorneycroft had given to sterling was not questioned, even though the events of 1957 revealed what was to become increasingly clear: defending the international status and acceptability of sterling involved creeping deindustrialization at home.

The Stagnant Society and its Enemies

By 1962 the complacancy which a few years earlier had led Harold Macmillan to announce that 'most of our people have never had it so good' had disappeared. It was in 1962 that the National Economic Development Council (NEDC) was established in response to mounting calls for economic planning not just by the Labour Party and the unions but by prominent journalists, academics and the FBI. *Laissez-faire* was out of fashion again and in the 1964 general election both major political parties advocated economic planning as the key to faster growth and the modernization of Britain.

Concern about slow growth had first been most cogently expressed by Andrew Schonfield in his classic study, *British Economic Policy since the War* (1958). Schonfield argued that only sustained high investment could guarantee uninterrupted domestic expansion and international competitiveness. As it was, however, the government's increasing resort to deflationary policies to protect sterling whenever the balance of payments went into the red had acted as a disincentive to investment. High interest rates made borrowing prohibitive, tight credit control took demand out of the home market, and the sudden changes in economic policy meant that the climate of long-term stable growth which made investment worthwhile to industrialists was absent. In addition to all this, the government had deliberately encouraged cuts in spending on new plant and equipment at the first sign of trouble out of the conviction that such measures would reduce the demand for imports and bring the trade figures back into balance. Schonfield therefore proposed the removal of external constraints on expansion. Britain should introduce exchange controls on the outflow of capital to the sterling area, impose discriminatory taxes on companies which invested abroad and negotiate with all governments holding sterling balances to limit the amount which could be withdrawn in any year to an agreed figure. These actions would lead to the availability of more capital for productive investment at home and reduced speculative pressures on the pound. Having created an international environment which would protect domestic growth, an expansionist British government would be able to increase spending on investment directly, by treating the nationalized industries generously, and indirectly, by granting tax concessions to private industry. All this time inflation would be held down through a wages and prices policy negotiated with the TUC (Schonfield, 1958, pp. 267–96).

Schonfield's commitment to faster growth derived from increasing anxiety about the politico-economic implications of stagnation. In his concluding chapter he pointed to prices which rose more rapidly in Britain than elsewhere, to worsening industrial relations, to the number of people who 'have come to be positively afraid of full employment' and to the meanness of public provision for culture by comparison with West Germany. The Labour Party was receptive to many of Schonfield's ideas and some of them reappeared in *The Labour Case*, written by Roy Jenkins in 1959. Jenkins was particularly impressed by Schonfield's argument about the deleterious consequences for home investment of acting as banker to the sterling area – an irony in view of his own conduct at the Treasury between 1967 and 1970. In general, however, warnings about the poor state of the British economy made little impact in 1959. Quite apart from the fact that Schonfield's recommendations contradicted the basic tenets of financial orthodoxy so dear to the Bank and the Treasury they evoked no popular response. In 1959 the government easily secured its re-election by taking all the brakes off the economy, and talk about slow growth and fragile prosperity appeared to have small contact with the everyday experience of many voters.

In 1960 and 1961 the position was transformed. Treasury fears about the inflationary consequences of the election boom led to a credit squeeze and to an increase in the bank rate, from 4 per cent at the start of the year to 6 per cent in June. Predictably production stopped rising. The government then performed a *volte-face* and over the next few months eased credit and lowered the bank rate to 5 per cent. But expansion was short-lived. As in 1957 the pound was buffeted by speculation in favour of the mark, and to protect sterling the Conservatives changed course yet again. The familiar contractionist measures were all reintroduced – another credit squeeze, another rise in the bank rate (back up to 7 per cent this time), pledges of cuts in public spending – along with a 'pay pause' introduced over the heads of the trade unions to stop wage and salary increases.

These continual oscillations in policy, known as 'Stop–Go', provided the background to the emergence of a consensus in government, industry and the unions in favour of economic planning. The FBI had in fact abandoned its support for *laissez-faire* after 1960, first of all because it had become increasingly obvious that the industrial autonomy which had resulted from the arm's-length approach to the state following Labour's demise was purely nominal. In particular after 1955 industry had been subject to all the government's policy changes without in any way being able to influence them. Secondly, by 1960 it was clear that economic growth on the continent had for some time been higher and smoother than in Britain, and that industrial organizations were in close touch with government even in supposedly liberal countries such as West Germany. What was most striking, however, was the revelation that the French economy had outperformed the British for most of the 1950s despite colonial wars and political instability. It was noted that throughout all these vicissitudes the major parties in France, together with industry and the unions, had retained the commitment to economic growth made after the liberation. Above all no one had challenged the central position of the *Commissariat Général du Plan* in the formulation of French economic policy. The Commissariat, which had brought together government ministers, civil servants and representatives from both sides of industry, had been responsible for the reconstruction and modernization of basic sectors in the French economy such as coal, steel, transport, agriculture, cement and electricity. With the state dedicated to the maintenance of long-term expansion it had been possible for public and private industry to plan levels of investment and output several years ahead. In consequence the interwar stagnation which had rendered France so technologically backward and socially divided in 1940 was now just a traumatic memory and a warning of what could happen to a country which neglected to make economic growth a priority of policy. Moreover advocates of planning in Britain used the example of the continental economies to point out the correlation between expansion, low costs and increasing exports. At the Brighton Conference held by the FBI in 1960 to discuss the development of the British economy over the 'Next Five Years', Chancellor Heathcote Amory argued that growth was dependent on a strong, internationally respected currency, stable prices, rising investment and higher production – in that order. His views were frostily received and they were openly contradicted by the FBI president Sir Hugh Beaver, who maintained that higher growth was the key to lower inflation and a sound balance of payments rather than the other way round (see Brittan, 1971, pp. 217–18; Blank, 1973, p. 151).

Changes in the structure of British industry also help to explain the FBI's reassessment of planning in and after 1960. During Labour's period in office the most vociferous opposition to government–industry co-operation had come from small and medium-sized businesses. These had become increasingly worried that the semi-corporatist system of liaison between trade associations and economic ministries was favouring large-scale concerns and would result in the establishment of monopoly control throughout industry. The prominence of allegations that genuine free enterprise was being stifled had contributed to the breakdown of accord between Labour and industry. It had been particularly hard for the FBI leadership to ignore the charges, with the voice of small and medium-sized industry being amplified as a result of an increase in number after 1930. In 1935 the hundred largest firms had taken 23 per cent of net manufacturing output and this share had declined to 21 per cent by 1948. During the 1950s, however, there was a trend to concentration and an increase in the size of many businesses, so that by 1963 the hundred largest firms occupied 38 per cent of net manufacturing output. The composition of the FBI altered accordingly: by the early 1960s its membership had doubled and embraced almost three-quarters of the 'Top 200' companies listed by *The Times* (Ingham, 1984, p. 210). It followed that industrial opinion turned against the risks of the free market in favour of a managed economy characterized by steady growth. Predictability was essential to large corporations contemplating heavy investment in research and development, the mass production of sophisticated products, and substantial advertising to manipulate consumer demand. The government's role now became essential, for it alone could guarantee the climate of long-term expansion which not only encouraged investment but made it worthwhile.

Calls by industrial organizations for more rapid growth and planning were echoed and encouraged in contemporary critiques of British society stimulated by alarm at Britain's poor economic performance in comparison with what its major competitors had achieved. Examples of this literature include *The Establishment*, edited by Hugh Thomas (1959); *The Conservative Enemy*, by Anthony Crosland (1961); *The Stagnant Society*, by Michael Shanks (1961); *Suicide of a Nation?*, edited by Arthur Koestler (1964); and *The Split Society*, by Nicholas Davenport (1964). Common to all these texts was a commitment to modernization, which by making Britain more efficient and competitive would allow future governments to increase spending on health, social services, education and culture. Prosperity and growth were identified with the creation of a more dynamic and less unequal society. Shanks warned that the continuing neglect of the search for material progress would lead to the development of 'an impoverished society' breeding 'intolerance, repression, meanness and insensitivity to cultural and aesthetic values'. At the end of his book he asked, rhetorically, 'What sort of an island do we want to be? . . . A lotus island of easy, tolerant ways, bathed in the golden glow of genteel poverty? Or the tough, dynamic race we have always been in the past . . . ?' (1961, p. 232).

None of the radical critics would have dissented from these words, but their recipes for change were by no means identical. Shanks's manifesto, indeed, was one of the more conservative. Unlike Schonfield he supported Britain's commitment to the sterling area. He placed much of the responsibility for slow growth in the 1950s on the shoulders of the trade unions. Working-class conservatism had encouraged resistance to technical innovation throughout industry, obsession with obsolete distinctions between different crafts had led to wasteful demarcation disputes, and apathy on the factory floor had allowed political extremists to become shop stewards. These militants had then proceeded to disrupt production by fomenting unofficial strikes. Accordingly Shanks suggested trade union reform, isolating in particular the importance of strengthening the authority of the TUC over the movement as a whole. He argued that the TUC General Council should be able to investigate reports of abuses, encourage amalgamations between unions, provide binding arbitration in inter-union disputes, and commit all its members to a wages' policy. He emphasized that some redundancy and labour mobility was central to the creation 'of an expanding dynamic economy', but stressed that redundancies should be negotiated with union representatives and not introduced by management fiat.

Exasperation with trade union attitudes was not peculiar to Shanks, but he was the only significant commentator to devote so much space (69 pages out of 236) to articulating it. His remaining proposals, for better technical training, for more public investment including support for research and development and the purchasing of shares in profitable private companies by the state, and for the establishment of a central planning agency which included representatives of government, the employers and the unions, all appeared elsewhere. Other writers, however, maintained that no modernization plan would succeed unless a radical government was prepared to challenge the authority of key sections in the British establishment. Hence Davenport, whose analysis bore many resemblances to Schonfield's, attacked Britain's moneyed ruling elite which placed the fortunes of 'finance capital' above those of the working class. The objectives of full employment, modernization and fair shares had been placed second to policies designed to enhance sterling's international status. British society was split between financiers and producers to the detriment of the latter: the pursuit of 'hard money' policies to protect the pound had increased the wealth of *rentiers* at the cost of slow growth. In these circumstances it was not surprising that trade unions had developed a bloody-minded trait (Davenport, 1964, pp. 177–8).

Measures to heal the 'split society' therefore meant faster growth by definition since they involved the priorities of the productive economy first. Davenport called for a more *dirigiste* approach to industrial policy, with trade union support for wage restraint being bought by increases in the social wage and tax reforms to ensure a more equitable distribution of wealth. At the same time it would be necessary to intervene in the City to prevent unpredictable flows of money in and out of Britain. Either the government should physically restrain the issues of foreign securities on the domestic capital market or, on the Swiss model, the practice of making interest payments on unwanted foreign deposits in London should be terminated. Such measures would insulate the bank rate at home from external influences and allow it to fall to a level which would encourage private and public investment but discourage the accumulation of savings more rapidly than they could be put to work (Davenport, 1964, pp. 150–3).

The conviction that the British establishment neither knew nor cared very much about the needs of industry was shared by Thomas Balogh. In a famous essay entitled 'The Apotheosis of the Dilettante', first published in 1959, Balogh lamented the 'amateurism' of Treasury officials. They were recruited immediately after an academic career, usually in the public schools and ancient universities, from which most of them graduated with liberal arts degrees. In consequence few had any expert knowledge of economics, industry or the applied sciences when they began to work in the civil service, yet no steps were taken to educate them in subjects of central importance to the administration of an advanced industrial economy after their recruitment. The justification for this was that civil servants were bright people with well-trained minds and they could therefore turn their hands to anything. Balogh deplored this cult of the generalist: 'no one would be mad enough to advocate the periodic interchange of dentists and surgeons, solicitors and barristers, engineers and musicians.'[7] He argued that the use of non-specialists to administer Britain was a legacy of the Victorian era, when it was believed neither necessary nor desirable for the state to intervene in the management of the economy. As a result Treasury officials were characterized by addiction to outmoded *laissez-faire* ideas, hostile to public spending of any kind and socially tied to the most privileged and conservative circles in British society. A government committed to growth could not therefore count on the support of the department with overall responsibility for economic and financial policy because its loyalty was to the health of sterling, the traditional concern of Britain's ruling, financial elite. It followed from Balogh's critique, which was developed in a Fabian pamphlet called *The Administrators* (1964), that civil servants should be professionally trained and recruited much more from state schools and provincial universities. Promotion to senior rank should be made dependent on personal merit and the old hierarchical division between the mainly public school, Oxbridge-educated administrative class and the executive grades, most of whose staff had not been to any university, should be abolished. The modernization of the civil service, above all of the Treasury, was a prerequisite for the modernization of Britain.

The government was sympathetic to demands for faster growth and economic planning to provide a framework for it. The Cabinet, and particularly the prime minister, Harold Macmillan, was worried about the disparities between growth rates in Europe and Britain, an anxiety intensified by rising unemployment in the north-east. Macmillan's first response to relative decline had been to commit the government to membership of the European Economic Community (EEC), a move supported by the FBI and the BEC. It was believed that the expansion of the French, German, Italian and Benelux economies had been assisted by the existence of the Community because of the large market created by the progressive reduction of barriers to trade in Western Europe. Along with the government, large-scale industry in Britain wanted to join the EEC out of a conviction that the British market was now too small to provide worthwhile returns on investment in new products requiring major initial outlays. But going into Europe was not regarded as a cure-all, and both Macmillan and his new Chancellor, Selwyn Lloyd, appreciated that the economy would have to be in a healthy condition to take advantage of new opportunities.

To begin with the Treasury responded to criticisms of its past management of the economy by accepting the reforms outlined in the Plowden Report on the Control of Public Expenditure. After Plowden the Treasury retained overall financial control over government departments, but allocated resources between them according to long-term spending programmes designed to last four or even five years. At the same time the Treasury itself was split into two sides, Pay and Management, dealing broadly with civil service salaries and administration; and Finance and Economic. The Finance and Economic side was subdivided into three groups: Finance, responsible for balance of payments policy and the defence of sterling; the Public Sector Group, in control of state spending; and the National Economy Group, concerned with macro-economic questions such as inflation, unemployment, growth and incomes. There was no accident about the timing of these changes. They were introduced when they were because they reflected the government's determination to secure more rapid economic expansion. This was now to be facilitated by making growth an explicit concern of the Treasury and by guaranteeing a measure of continuity in public investment schemes which had hitherto been exposed to all the uncertainties of 'Stop–Go'.

The final government concession to the new mood of anxiety about Britain's economic prospects was the creation of the National Economic Development Council (NEDC). The first steps in the creation of the NEDC came in the aftermath of the 'Stop' and pay pause of 1961, when the Chancellor had spoken of the need for tripartite agreement on the formulation of national economic policy. At the same time his views had been influenced by traditional Treasury fears about inflationary pressures in the economy. These might be controlled if improvizations like the pay pause could be institutionalized through the formulation of a permanent incomes policy. Not surprisingly the TUC was unimpressed by this and had little to do with early talks on planning, feeling that the word was just a euphemism for yet more wage restraint. The FBI, on the other hand, quickly took up Lloyd's suggestion and in discussions with him emphasized the importance of *concertation* on French lines if growth was to be achieved. Initially cautious, the Chancellor was persuaded, not least because the French experience showed that the existence of an independent planning council did not mean the adoption of socialist policies. With the support of the prime minister, Lloyd convinced the cabinet of the need for a planning body in which government, industry and the unions could discuss investment and incomes policy in the light of an agreed target for growth (Brittan, 1971, p. 220).

TUC distrust delayed the first meeting of the NEDC, which in accordance with the wishes of the FBI was to be independent of the Treasury, until March 1962. It should not be inferred from this that the labour movement was hostile to planning. Its support for free collective bargaining during the 1950s had been justified by reference to the Tories' *laissez-faire* policies: 'if there is a free for all we are part of the all' as Frank Cousins, General Secretary of the TGWU, had said. This was perhaps not entirely convincing, given that the unions had actually rejected wage restraint before Labour had fallen from power in 1951. Nevertheless, once Lloyd had made it clear that the NEDC was not going to concentrate on the subject of pay to the exclusion of everything else the TUC joined it. Membership of the NEDC was seen as a way of regaining influence over government policy, of extracting firm pledges on future levels of public investment and of linking action to restrain profits with any move to control the rise in incomes. Above all, however, the value of the NEDC rose in the estimation of trade union leaders when they discovered that their national economic policy prescriptions had much in common with those of industrialists. Both sides of industry argued for increased economic expansion and during 1962 were frequently in accord that the government was not doing enough (Blank, 1973, p. 179). Government words had not been matched by deeds: industrial activity remained low and unemployment continued to rise throughout the year. Deflation persisted and it became clear that the Treasury reforms had not tipped the balance of power away from the officials who regarded domestic health as a function of external financial probity. In these circumstances the NEDC was distinctly useful as an instrument of pressure on the government to take action which would put people back to work and alleviate the growing problems of regional deprivation in northern England and Scotland. By 1964 union leaders were enthusiastic supporters of the NEDC: never before had the representatives of productive industry possessed within the framework of the state itself an institutional forum to make the case for growth and employment.

The new consensus between both sides of industry was expressed in the work of the NEDC. It called for commitment to a growth rate of 4 per cent per annum and issued a report,

Conditions Favourable to Growth (1963), which emphasized the importance of increasing investment in scientific research and education to British modernization. The government's response was positive. Continuing stagnation was damaging its ratings in the opinion polls and its performances in by-elections. The external solution to low growth, membership of the EEC, had been ruled out in January 1963 when General de Gaulle had vetoed Britain's application. A general election was approaching and Tory prospects did not look good. What was particularly disturbing was the lack of support for the Conservatives in the growing ranks of white-collar workers. Industry's desire to keep abreast of technical change had led to the employment of more scientists, engineers, draughtsmen and technicians throughout the 1950s. In 1951, 30.9 per cent of the work force had been white-collar employees; by 1961, the proportion had risen to 35.9 per cent (Pollard, 1983, p. 342). This expanding salariat was on the whole composed of people who had worked their way through the state schools and provincial universities from relatively modest backgrounds. As a rule they were believers in meritocracy and professionalism. They were receptive to critiques of Britain such as *The Stagnant Society* (Shanks, 1961) and blamed the Conservatives, identified with the maintenance of a social order where wealth and status depended on inherited privilege rather than on innate personal ability, for the unsatisfactory economic performance. It was clear that the only way to win the loyalty of this new middle class of technicians and engineers was to pursue policies designed to foster efficiency and rapid growth. With electoral politics reinforcing industrial pressure the new Chancellor, Reginald Maudling, opted for economic expansion after 1963 and declared the government's determination to deliver the NEDC's objective of 4 per cent growth.

Between 1963 and 1964 the government therefore made a real effort to prove its credentials as a modernizing administration to the emerging coalition of industrial producers and frustrated technocrats. *Laissez-faire* was abandoned as regional development plans were approved for Scotland and north-east and south-east England. The Robbins Report, calling for the expansion of higher education, was endorsed in a drive to extend equality of opportunity and enlarge Britain's pool of skilled and scientifically qualified workers. The role of the NEDC was enhanced, with the creation of the Economic Development Councils, or 'Little Neddies', for particular industries. Each little Neddy, composed of representatives from management, the unions and the relevant government department, was to provide the NEDC with information and forecasts and to make suggestions for improving productivity in its particular sector. At the same time Maudling reflated the economy by easing credit restrictions, by introducing generous tax relief for middle and low income families, equivalent to a wage increase of 2 per cent for many workers, and by increasing investment allowances for industry. These measures to stimulate the economy were most effective: industrial production rose by 8 per cent between the end of 1962 and the autumn of 1963, and unemployment fell from over 3 per cent of the workforce to 1.4 per cent by February 1964. Growth was rapid indeed and exceeded 5 per cent per annum at the start of 1964, although it slipped back to about 4 per cent in the summer.

During the election campaign the government claimed that the boom was a triumph for its version of planning. This was hardly justifiable because the expansion, as in 1955 and 1959, was led by increasing consumer demand. Indeed, the much-vaunted conversion of the Conservatives to planning on the French model amounted to very little. The little Neddies notwithstanding, there was no real, direct intervention in industry, and the NEDC's role was largely confined to exhortation and the announcement of the growth target. The *dirigiste* side to French planning was entirely ignored, possibly because the government believed that it was not compatible with the survival of free enterprise. Equally the Conservatives may not have noticed the existence of *dirigisme* at all because of a conviction that there was by definition no room for it in a capitalist country. This suggests that the liberal prejudices with which the Conservatives had come to power had not disappeared by the early 1960s, that they neither knew nor wanted to know what economic planning really meant. France was undeniably a capitalist society but the state there was not seen by any significant party, right or left, as an institution which was set apart from the economy. It was rather believed to be the agent of economic development: this meant that it did not just create a 'favourable climate' and then leave industrialists to get on with the job of producing goods and making money. On the contrary: the government in France was the principal source of finance for investment, owning the major financial institutions, insurance companies and savings banks. Funds were allocated between different sectors of the economy by the Ministry of Finance as part of a deliberate attempt to encourage industries with a growing international market. To this end also the state continually supervised industrial policy, encouraging mergers and concentration in an effort to secure the competitive advantage which comes with economies of scale (Brown, 1980, pp. 59–75). All this was a far cry from the indiscriminate system of investment allowances favoured by the Conservatives. Whereas the French concentrated on ensuring that there were goods available for the people to buy, in Britain 'the idea was still that prosperity could be created by giving people money to spend' (Pollard, 1984, p. 342).

The policy of modernization through reflation was beginning to run into the sands by mid 1964. The expansion of consumer spending was sucking in imports and the export performance had been disappointing. The weaknesses stemming from the failure to secure continuous high levels of investment in the past were in fact intensified by present policies. The increasing demand for products such as electrical household goods, chemicals and man-made fibres could not be matched by domestic output because of shortage of capacity. Above all it became increasingly clear that the boom was reaching its limit because there were not enough machine-tools to go round. Inadequacy here as in so much else was a result of 'Stop–Go': the frequency of contractionist measures to defend the pound had resulted in erratic demand and had ultimately acted as a disincentive to investment.

Bottlenecks and rising imports were taken as a sign of excess demand by the government. Instead of tackling this problem by genuinely following the French example, ministers called more and more urgently for wage restraint. The only alternative they could see was another period of deflation – a sure sign that the 'Stop–Go' priorities and mentality had not been swept away – and this was clearly out of the question just before an election. The unions refused to consider an incomes policy in any case, and along with the Labour Party blamed the problems on the inadequacy and tardiness of Conservative planning. Nicholas Davenport noted that there was a whole range of modern products which Britain had either failed to develop or had been forced to copy from other countries. He mentioned transistors, acrylic fibres and new metals, blaming inadequate investment in plant, equipment and technological research (Davenport, 1964, p. 44).

During the election campaign the Labour Party claimed that it alone was capable of modernizing Britain. After its third successive defeat at the polls in 1959 it had deliberately tried to attract white-collar votes and broaden its popular appeal so that it was not seen purely as the party of organized labour. In many respects it was attempting to put together a coalition in favour of planning and growth not unlike the one which had brought it to victory in 1945. The leaders, Hugh Gaitskell, until his premature death in 1963, and then Harold Wilson, worked for closer links between Labour and the growing body of scientists, administrators, managers and professional people. They claimed that under the Tories Britain was missing all the opportunities afforded by the new scientific revolution and argued that Conservative planning was a charade (Davenport, 1964, pp. 145 ff). Labour had thoroughly absorbed the radical critiques and commentaries of the enemies of the stagnant society, and sought to convince voters that it now offered a programme for a more efficient and socially just nation.

The appeal was successful. Labour's commitment to 'planning with teeth' impressed not just the unions but the salariat and even industrialists, whose fear of nationalization was assuaged by the party's managerial and non-doctrinaire approach to the problems facing Britain. It was an approach which contrasted sharply with the one offered by the Tory leader Sir Alec Douglas-Home, a hereditary peer who became prime minister after Macmillan's retirement from ill-health in 1963. Douglas-Home developed public-school *insouciance* to a fine art during his tenure of office, unblushingly stating that he needed to use matchsticks to understand economics. Against this, Labour announced that it would reform the civil service and rely on professional economists and on the service of enlightened industrialists for the implementation of its policies, in order to break the power of Treasury officials in Whitehall. Indeed, the Treasury monopoly over economic policy was to be brought to an end completely, with the creation of two new departments to manage Labour's scientific revolution. Economic planning was to be the concern of the Department of Economic Affairs while the expansion of high technology sectors and of scientific research and development would be left to the

Ministry of Technology. Treasury responsibilities were reduced to financial and balance of payments policy. Production and modernization, it seemed, were to be liberated from their old subordination to Britain's international financial role. This was a complete reversal of the priorities to which the Tories had been committed throughout their years in office and the transformation reflected the disintegration of the old anti-planning coalition of 1951 and its replacement by a reborn producers' alliance. Yet the overall majority enjoyed by the parliamentary representatives of the producers was small – only five seats – and the new Labour government inherited a balance of payments deficit of £700 million (thought at the time to be £800 million). This combination of political vulnerability with economic crisis meant that Labour's determination to build what Wilson called a 'New Britain' would quickly be put to the test.

Notes: Chapter 5

1 Cairncross, 1985, p. 36; Cambridge Economic Policy Group, *Economic Policy Review*, no. 1, 1979, Table 4, p. 35.
2 For an account see Mitchell, 1963.
3 PRO T236/3240, minutes of a meeting held on 27 November 1951.
4 Labour won 48.8 per cent of the poll but only 295 seats whereas the Conservatives captured 321 seats with 48.0 per cent of the poll.
5 Bank of England, Adm. 14/30, 805/1, paper by Thompson-McCausland, 31 October 1951; see also Newton, 1986.
6 PRO T236/3240, memorandum by R. W. B. Clarke, 'Convertibility', 25 January 1952. Emphasis in the original.
7 Balogh, 'The Apotheosis of the Dilettante', in Thomas, 1959, p. 99.

CHAPTER SIX

Modernization Frustrated, 1964–1979

The 'New Britain' Aborted, 1964–1967

The general elections of 1964, 1966, 1970 and 1974 (when there were two) brought into power a succession of administrations committed to industrial modernization. In each case, however, the discrepancy between aspiration and performance was considerable. The years between 1964 and 1979 were characterized by low growth, balance of payments crises, rising inflation, and, after 1975, by mass unemployment.

The technocratic consensus which had developed on both sides of industry in the early 1960s notwithstanding, attempts at planning were either quickly aborted or gestural. Sustained economic expansion was pursued only once in the entire period, from 1971 to 1973. The power of the Treasury and the Bank of England remained strong enough to squash suggestions that Britain's traditional international economic liberalism be sacrified in order to protect domestic activity. Each external financial crisis was met by deflationary measures. Not surprisingly the level of investment in industry was consistently disappointing. The international competitiveness of British exports continued to deteriorate, and in the mid 1970s a rapid and alarming rise in import penetration began to compound the problems created by a falling share of world trade in manufactured goods.

As 'Stop–Go' gave way to prolonged periods of 'Stop', manifested in tight credit, high interest rates and wage controls, class conflict rather than class co-operation became the norm. Trade union militancy increased in response to tough pay policies. At the same time industry's desire for full employment of resources was steadily overshadowed by disillusionment with the idea of state intervention and by determinaton to prevent what was seen as attempts by organized labour to undermine managerial authority. By 1979 the modernization consensus was dead, with the producers' alliance which had sustained it in ruins.

Labour's 1964 manifesto had claimed that the party was 'poised to swing its plans into instant operation'. This turned out to be something of an overstatement, but the first year of the Labour government was characterized by institutional innovations. The Department of Economic Affairs (DEA) and the Ministry of Technology were both quickly established, so that work on planning and industrial modernization could begin at once.

In political terms the conditions for a determined attempt at planned growth had not been so favourable for twenty years. First of all, the man directly responsible for carrying out the modernization strategy was George Brown, Deputy Leader of the Labour Party. Brown was a committed expansionist and his views could only be given weight by the powerful position he occupied as Wilson's second in command. Secondly, the government's apparent determination to break out of the old 'Stop–Go' cycle brought it the goodwill of many industrialists, who quickly showed themselves willing to collaborate with Labour. Never before in peacetime had there been such a large influx of high level businessmen into government (Blank, 1973, p. 224). Most were absorbed by the DEA's Industrial Policy Division or by the Ministry of Technology. Thirdly, the trade union leaders had already signalled that, to use Frank Cousins's phrase, they would accept a 'planned growth of wages' in return for economic growth, price and dividend restraint and improvements in social security benefits. Given that employers' associations had declared themselves prepared to accept voluntary price restraint and that the government's entire *raison d'être* was expansion, with the proceeds distributed to the less well off, the attitude of the trade unions clearly implied an end to free collective bargaining.

So great a consensus between government and both sides of industry was rare, and Labour did not hesitate to exploit such a favourable moment. The government moved quickly to fulfil its pre-election promises on social reform. In its first weeks it increased old age pensions, abolished prescription charges, put up income tax and announced proposals to introduce a corporation tax. The measures were testimony to Labour's determinaton to build a fairer society as well as a more efficient one. They had the effect of strengthening the producers' alliance by helping to secure the commitment of the TUC to the *Joint Statement of Intent on Productivity, Prices and Incomes* signed in concert with the government and the employers' associations in December 1964. In approving the *Joint Statement* the TUC committed itself to restraining increases in salaries and wages so that they would not exceed the growth of real national output. This was the first time that employers and unions had ever taken a common public stand on the issue, and the way was prepared for the establishment of the Prices and Incomes Board (PIB) in 1965. Both sides of industry accepted the existence of the board, which was given the task of advising whether pay or price rises referred to it by the government were 'in the national interest'. In practice this meant deciding whether there were any grounds – for example, in terms of productivity – for wage and salary rises of over between 3 and 3.5 per cent, the figure taken by the government to represent the 'norm' for increases in incomes justified by the growth of the economy. The Board had no statutory powers, but if it found against a pay rise the union in question was expected to settle in accord with the 'norm'. The same principle applied to price increases, which the Board would only approve if they resulted from unavoidable increases in costs. The *Joint Statement*, and the subsequent acceptance of the PIB, offered a real prospect of non-inflationary growth underpinned by tripartite agreement.

At the same time the DEA's administrative machinery was rapidly put into place. The principal functions were allocated to two Divisions, one dealing with industrial policy and the other concerned with economic planning. The task of the Industrial Policy Division was to encourage efficiency and greater productivity throughout the economy with the co-operation of unions and management. To this end a chief industrial adviser was appointed, with access to the Prime Minister and to the Cabinet. Under the chief industrial adviser worked a team of industrial advisers, most of whom were drawn from the private sector, each of them representing the DEA or the little Neddies. The little Neddies were in turn increased in number and by the end of 1966 twenty were operating, covering about two-thirds of all the firms in private industry. The Economic Planning division was meanwhile given the task of preparing Labour's National Plan for the development of the economy up to 1970. Its establishment meant a downgrading for the NEDC, whose function was effectively reduced to that of commentator on policies for development in specific industries worked out in the little Neddies. Labour had never been entirely happy about the NEDC, justifiably regarding its independence as a fatal flaw because it allowed the government to disregard any recommendations not to its liking. The new system involved the subordination of the NEDC to the DEA, signalled by Brown's presence in the chair, but it also meant that industrial policy and economic planning would receive the political imprimatur of a major department of state.

The rapid construction of a planning apparatus geared to industrial modernization was revolutionary in the context of British history. This was not lost on George Brown, who later wrote that the establishment of the DEA 'was also the opening campaign of a major social revolution' (1971, p. 95). The next stage in the revolution was the publication of the National Plan in September 1965. The Plan was the centrepiece of Labour's economic strategy, and on its success or failure hung Britain's chance of transformation into a dynamic economy whose growth was founded on high technology and manufacturing industry. It envisaged a 25 per cent growth in the economy up to 1970, or an annual growth rate of 3.8 per cent.

One problem, however, was that the term 'Plan' was a misnomer. The document merely provided information about what would happen to the economy if it grew by 25 per cent up to 1970. The information was based on an inquiry in which industries were asked to provide assessments of investment, manpower and import requirements, and of export levels, based on the assumed rate of growth and on forecasts of public spending and consumption. In consequence the Plan appeared internally consistent: a 3.8 per cent per annum growth rate implied an increase in export volume of 5.25 per cent each year to pay for all the imports that would be needed, and responses to the inquiry indicated that the figure could be as high as 5.5 per cent. If the Plan worked there would be startling improvements in Britain's economic performance. Exports would grow at twice the rate of recent years, with investment in manufacturing and construction industries rising by 7.5 per cent each year while other forms of investment would be held down to an annual increase of 4.0 per cent. It was assumed that the incomes policy would succeed in restraining private consumption to a yearly growth of 3.2 per cent, so releasing resources for investment and exports. All this was very encouraging on paper but the trouble was that the optimistic scenario was based on an assumption in itself question-begging. How was such a sustained high level of growth to be achieved? The Plan provided no answers, had no powers, and could only flourish, anti-climactically, a 'check-list of action required' if it was to succeed (Lernez, 1975, pp. 170–3).

Nevertheless the document was greeted with goodwill. The Confederation of British Industries (CBI, created out of a merger between the FBI and the other employers' associations in February 1965) welcomed it. So did the TUC. But goodwill alone would not be enough. The key to the success of the National plan was high economic growth and it was up to the government to create the conditions which would allow this to happen. At no stage in its career did Labour commit itself to the necessary degree of economic expansion. The economy in fact grew by just 14 per cent up to 1970, an annual average of little more than 2 per cent. Far from breaking out of the 'Stop–Go' cycle Labour presided over the most prolonged period of deflation since the war. By 1970 hardly any of the projections set out in the National Plan had been achieved because the harsh economic regime had discouraged rather than stimulated investment (see Table 6.1).

The trouble was that Labour had willed the end of modernization but not the means. On coming to power Wilson was confronted by the £800 million deficit, almost twice as large as he had anticipated. During the 'Stop–Go' era Labour spokesmen had always claimed that they would make growth a priority over the balance of payments because only through sustained, high growth would Britain be able to export its way into the black. After eighteen months of expansion under Maudling it was beginning to appear that this assumption was not going to be justified; but, unprepared for the scale of the inherited external deficit, Labour had made no assessment of its implications for the modernization strategy. Indeed, there were no plans to deal with it at all. The new government was thus in an extremely weak position when it came

Table 6.1 Some Indicators of Economic Performance, 1964–1970

	National Plan projections (1974 = 100)	Actual in 1970
Gross domestic product	125	114
Personal consumption	121	113
Gross fixed capital formation	138	120
Investment		
Manufacturing and construction	155	127
Public corporations	130	105
Housing	132	94
Exports	136	142
Imports	126	132

Source: Derived from Opie, 1972, p. 174.

under pressure from the City and the Bank of England, in the person of the governor, Lord Cromer, as well as from the Treasury, to take orthodox measures which would satisfy the international financial community and so leave confidence in the currency intact.

Orthodox measures naturally implied cuts in spending programmes, dearer money and tax increases. Their implementation would jeopardize the fulfilment of Labour's hopes for the economy. However, alternative ways of reducing the balance of payments deficit, without inflicting a deflationary shock on Labour's programme, did exist and were canvassed by some Cabinet ministers and most of the academic economists who had settled into Whitehall with the new government. One option was to devalue the currency; another was to impose physical controls on imports, in the form of quantitative restrictions. The Treasury, the City and the Bank would have found it difficult to stomach either course of action. Devaluation would have been taken as evidence not just that Labour was incapable of preserving the international reserve currency status of the pound but that it had no intention of doing so anyway. Quantitative restrictions would have implied a retreat from the liberalism which had been characteristic of British economic foreign policy since 1951. The alternatives, in short, meant choosing growth rather than maintaining the external orientation of the economy. They were rejected out of hand. Quite apart from the fact that they were unpopular with the financial establishment the Prime Minister himself was opposed to them. Wilson was never slow to accuse domestic and international speculators of selling Britain short, but his protests were empty because in the end he believed in the same set of priorities, centring on the maintenance of the world-wide role of sterling, which had made the productive economy so vulnerable in the first place. He ruled that the subject of devaluation was not to be discussed in Cabinet meetings and committed the government to defence of the existing sterling parity of $2.80 to the pound. No radical steps were taken and Labour moved to cut the deficit and protect the exchange rate by imposing a 15 per cent tariff on all imports of manufactured goods, and by borrowing $3 billion from the central banks of the United States and of European Community members. Wilson's hope was that this action would allow Britain to adhere to its global economic obligations without sacrificing domestic modernization. The move was clever but the hope was forlorn. It began a long process of humiliation by which Labour gradually lost control over the British economy and was forced into increasingly deflationary measures to satisfy foreign creditors. The prime minister had allowed damage to be done to the National Plan's chances of success even before it had been formulated, a dubious achievement made possible by Labour's pre-election balance of payments policy vacuum.

Devaluation in 1964 would not have been an easy option. Quite apart from the government's narrow parliamentary majority there were about £4,000 million of sterling balances in London and there was a risk that a fall in the exchange rate might precipitate a massive capital outflow which would only be contained by the imposition of stringent wartime style controls.

Nevertheless, Labour's position was a strong one because of the backing it had received from both sides of industry for its modernization plans. In the last resort a snap general election on the theme of a 'bankers' ramp' would have been a worthwhile gamble. But although Labour was making the most of support from employers and trade unions in building the institutional framework for its programme it did not exploit the political power of the producers' alliance. Indeed, the decision to borrow abroad strengthened the opponents of the New Britain because it meant that the financial establishment's commitment to low inflation, a sound currency and a healthy balance of payments was now reinforced by foreign bankers who had no more confidence in Labour's radical plans than the City, the Bank of England and the Treasury. Neither the domestic nor the international financial community believed that their priorities could be squared with state-led expansion, based on new, interventionist ministries, on increases in public spending and on higher taxes for the wealthy, and there was particular concern lest Treasury hegemony over Whitehall be brought to an end by the DEA.

The financial establishment had no need to worry. The struggle between the DEA and the Treasury was no contest. Once the decision had been taken to defend the existing exchange rate and the international role of sterling the state of the balance of payments and confidence in the currency became the criteria by which the government judged the success or failure of its policy. In these circumstances it was inevitable that the Treasury would retain its dominance over Whitehall because its responsibility for finance and the balance of payments had survived the coming of the DEA. In consequence every budget until the government's fall in 1970 revealed that domestic economic policy was dependent on the external financial position. In July 1965 the government announced cuts in public investment and intensified hire purchase controls. At the same time, to satisfy external creditors, it embarked on a series of talks with the CBI and the TUC with the intention of winning their support for providing the PIB with legal powers. The projections of the National Plan looked decidedly optimistic on its publication in September, and the following year, after another dose of 'July measures' in response to yet more speculation against the pound, the Plan was aborted. Despite the security of an overall parliamentary majority of ninety-seven after the March 1966 election, the government continued to put the needs of finance first: the bank rate was increased from 6 to 7 per cent, taxes were raised and there were further reductions in expenditure programmes. George Brown was forced to tell the House of Commons that the growth targets of the National Plan for 1970 were now unattainable and shortly afterwards left the DEA for the Foreign Office. Brown, along with a group of Cabinet ministers, notably Anthony Crosland, Richard Crossman and Roy Jenkins, had tried to push for devaluation rather than deflaton, but they were overborne by Wilson and the Chancellor, James Callaghan. The 'July measures', along with Brown's departure from the DEA, effectively marked the final collapse of Labour's attempt at a social revolution.

It is of course true that sterling was devalued to $2.40 to the pound in November 1967. But it was three years and £1,500 million of borrowed money too late. And even then there is some evidence to suggest that Wilson only countenanced the move because he was aware that London's international financial business could flourish even if sterling was in decline as a world-wide reserve currency. The proportion of the world's official reserves held in sterling declined from 25 per cent in 1948 to 8 per cent in 1969. Yet in the middle and late 1960s transactions in London grew rapidly and overseas earnings rose by 150 per cent. City commentators drew attention to this trend at the time, and it became clear that devaluation need not involve a panic flight of capital (Ingham, 1984, p. 286). Devaluation, in short, did not mean any reorientation of policy by the government and was undertaken only when the financial sector was ready for it. Deflationary measures continued as the government endeavoured to keep the confidence of foreign bankers by paying off the large external debt. The bank rate went up to 8 per cent and with Roy Jenkins as Chancellor financial policy became austere: 1968 and 1969 were years of public spending cuts and tight credit restriction. The prime minister himself spoke of these years of massive disappointment[1] as if they were part of some crusade for national moral regeneration. He described the 1969 budget, proudly, as 'the most punishing' in British peacetime experience. By 1970 the external position was sound and the balance of payments was in the black, much to the gratification of Wilson and Jenkins. Yet the achievement was largely symbolic because the real economy had been worn down: industrial production rose by just 2.5 per cent on average each year between 1964 and 1970, or by 15.7 per cent for the period as a whole, while the comparable figures for France and for West Germany were, respectively, 38.9 per cent and 41.6 per cent. The contractionary economic climate offered no incentive to investment, which completely failed to occur on a scale which would stimulate rapid technological advance. In 1970 gross physical investment per head reached a postwar high, at £172; in France it was £356, in West Germany £371, and in the Netherlands

£279 (Ham, 1981, pp. 91–2). Under Labour, therefore, finance prospered while industry continued its relative decline.

However, Labour's investment in the ideology of modernization had been profound, and the demise of the National Plan did not mean the abandonment of the attempt to build a New Britain. Having rejected the option of stimulating growth by increasing demand for British goods, the government sought to promote technological change through structural intervention in the economy. Its chosen agents were the Industrial Reorganisation Corporation (IRC) and the Ministry of Technology. The IRC was an independent body, established in 1966, financed from public funds but run by private businessmen. It was created out of concern that sectors of the economy manufacturing products for which there was a growing international market, such as the motor industry, electrics or computing, were not competing effectively because of their relatively small size. Economies of scale were needed to enhance efficiency and generate the resources for substantial investment in research and innovation. Accordingly the IRC was given the task of promoting mergers where it considered them to be in the national interest, usually defined in terms of the need to develop import substitution and increase exports, and it was provided with a budget of £150 million so that it could encourage rationalization and undertake selective investment.

The IRC was abolished by the Tories in 1971. Given its limited funds and short life its impact was bound to be modest. Nevertheless there were some achievements. By the end of its career the IRC had been involved in more than fifty mergers. This was a very small proportion – about 2 per cent – of the overall total from 1967 to 1970 but it included some of the most significant. In the electricity industry GEC was transformed into a major international corporation after taking over AEI and then English Electric. The car industry, hitherto an area of wasteful competition, with too many products for a limited market, was rationalized with the creation of British Leyland out of a merger between BMC and Leyland. The IRC also took the initiative in electronics and was directly implicated in the establishment of International Computers Limited, the largest manufacturer of computers outside the United States (Lernez, 1975, p. 213).

The encouragement of innovation was not confined to the IRC.

In 1968 the government passed the Industrial Expansion Act, which gave the Ministry of Technology the power to lend money to or even assume a direct stake in concerns manufacturing products whose immediate commercial prospects were doubtful. The act was an interesting departure, but its outcome was disappointing, mainly because its active life was only two years and partly because once again finance was limited. Only £150 million was made available and most of this was channelled to companies which were already well established such as Rolls Royce. Like the IRC, the Ministry of Technology could probably have done much more to promote modernization in an expansionary context. As it was, both had to swim against the tide, a task made no easier by the modest financial provision which was a function of the government's determination to contain public expenditure.

Limited as they were, the experiments in direct intervention did not go down well with private industry. The CBI began to complain about state interference and some of its leaders accused the government of using the IRC and the Industrial Expansion Act as back doors to extending public ownership throughout the economy. These fears were preposterous, but they were deeply held and their articulation by the CBI showed that the producers' alliance which had underpinned Labour's triumphs in 1964 and 1966 was falling apart. One factor in this was unquestionably disappointment with the overall thrust of Labour's economic policy. Another was the nature of the CBI itself. Labour had assisted in its creation, hoping that it would become a powerful spokesman for productive industry, an equal partner with the TUC in the formulation of national economic plans. But the problem was that the CBI did not represent only manufacturing industry: its membership had been expanded by banks, finance houses, firms from the distributive sector and small businesses (Blank, 1973, pp. 228–9). The ideology of *laissez-faire* was particularly strong throughout these organizations and, just as in the period between 1949 and 1951, planning was seen as a euphemism for the suffocation of private enterprise. This ideological distaste for intervention was reinforced by the impact of high taxation and legislation on prices, and in 1967 a group of doctrinaire liberals led by Arthur Shenfield (previously executive director) tried to push the CBI into a strongly anti-government stance. The revolt was defeated by John Davies, the director-general, who remained committed to the concept of planning throughout. Davies himself, however, distrusted the statism of the IRC and the Ministry of Technology, and sought to appease the malcontents by emphasizing the importance of the NEDC. At the same time he became drawn into a series of increasingly acrimonious rows with the government, and by 1970 the CBI had come out in support of the Conservative proposals to reintroduce indicative planning and trim the powers of the unions.

By 1968–70 the arena of industrial politics was characterized by conflict between the government, the CBI and the TUC, and all that remained of the 1964 consensus was the rhetorical commitment to modernization. Labour's determination to hold down the level of consumption had left pay and price controls the focal point of its economic strategy. By 1968 the statutory powers of the PIB were policing a limit of 3.5 per cent on increases in prices, wages, salaries and dividends, with flexibility being allowed only where justified by improvements in productivity. This rigid policy was deeply resented by trade unionists, and TUC attempts to ensure compliance with it on the factory floor were steadily undermined by a growing number of unofficial strikes. The government itself became so concerned at this turn of events that in 1969 it introduced proposals, entitled *In Place of Strife*, which included legal sanctions against unofficial strikes, but fierce resistance from the TUC, the Parliamentary Labour Party and from senior Cabinet members forced a retreat. Having fallen out with industry the government now lost the support of the trade union movement. Both the Trades Union Congress and the Labour Party Conference passed motions calling for the abandonment of statutory wage controls in 1968, and it became clear that the continuation of any incomes policy into 1969–70 would be politically impossible. Sustained deflation had made the concept of a 'planned growth of wages' a sour joke and no effort was made to extend the life of the incomes policy. Not surprisingly three years of restrictions were followed in 1969 and 1970 by an outburst of militancy from the unions: between the fourth quarter of 1969 and the fourth quarter of 1970 average earnings rose by 13 per cent. Instead of harmony between the two sides of industry there was class warfare on a scale not witnessed since the 1920s. There were nearly 4,000 strikes in 1969, twice as many as in 1966 or in 1967, and 7 million working days were lost. In 1970 the number of working days lost grew to 11 million as pay disputes spread throughout the economy, taking in sectors where strikes had hitherto been uncommon, such as the engineering and motor industries (Stewart, 1978, p. 107).

Harold Wilson should not have been surprised by the result of the 1970 election. In practice Labour's economic policy had been a repudiation of almost everything the party had stood for in 1964 and in 1966. By 1970 all challenges to the power of the Treasury had failed. In consequence Treasury rules had prevailed throughout and the government's determination to make the economy observe them undermined the coalition which had brought it to office. The failure to modernize had alienated the technocrats, the pay policy had disillusioned working-class voters, and the disenchantment of the CBI was completed by the collapse of the attempt to curb shop steward militancy. In these circumstances the abstention of many of Labour's traditional supporters on polling day was predictable (the party received 900,000 fewer votes in 1970 than in 1966, a decline of 7 per cent). At the same time there was nothing unexpected about the enthusiasm of industrialists for a Conservative programme which offered growth without intervention and legislation designed to restore the authority of management over labour.

The Failure of Heath's Revolution, 1970–1974

The defeat of Labour in 1970 did not imply the removal of industrial modernization from its leading place on the political agenda. The new prime minister, Edward Heath, was acutely conscious of Britain's decline as an industrial power and saw the reversal of that process as a personal mission. Heath's commitment to growth was profound and it was reinforced by the support he received from CBI leaders and from managerial salariat. The 1970 Conservative government saw itself at root as the political embodiment of large-scale capital and based its programme for expansion firmly on the aspirations of large-scale capital, as expressed by organizations like the CBI during the late 1960s.

These aspirations centred on the reduction of state intervention in the economy, on membership of the EEC and on curbing the power of the trade unions. The hostility to intervention, of course, derived from resentment at the activities of the IRC and the Ministry of Technology. It certainly did not extend all the way to enthusiasm for complete *laissez-faire*, and the importance of indicative planning was never denied. Indeed, both the government and industry put faith in the NEDC, viewing it as the body which could help employers plan for the future by providing them with access to information about national economic trends and with forecasts of future growth. The policy was in many ways similar to the one followed between 1961 and 1964: investment allowances were brought back and most of the interventionist agencies introduced in the Wilson years were either wound up or emasculated. Thus the IRC and the PIB were abolished and much of the Industrial Expansion Act was repealed. Both the government and the corporate sector were convinced that one precondition for growth was greater competitiveness and efficiency throughout industry. Labour's *dirigisme* involved a misuse of finance: instead of allowing incomes to grow in the pockets of the people and of encouraging personal enterprise it had wasted taxpayers' money on supporting firms that were by definition uncompetitive if they could not stand alone.

At the same time the enthusiasm for giving the market a larger share in the allocation of resources was intensified by the dictates of class interest. Big capital in Britain has tended to be more international than in other advanced capitalist societies. In 1970, eleven of the world's hundred largest businesses were British, while the members of the EEC could between them muster only eighteen. Of the two hundred largest non-American companies fifty-three were British, forty-three Japanese, twenty-five German and twenty-three were French. All the top hundred British manufacturing companies were multinational by 1970, a legacy of empire and of the successful cultivation of imperial and financial connections going back at least to the 1920s (Rowthorne, 1975, pp. 31–51). This pattern of development had two implications for modernization policy in the 1970s. First of all it created a large constituency opposed to interventionist policies because of the risk that these might involve attempts by the nation-state to plan investment and restrict the ability of the corporation to shift resources freely throughout the world. Secondly, given that the corporations needed expanding and assured markets, it meant that the government would try to resolve the problem of modernization through strengthening Britain's integration into the international economy rather than through state-led national planning. The obvious way to do this was by joining the EEC. Although British multinationals had been operating in the EEC since the early 1960s they shared a common anxiety that if Britain remained outside the Community they might become subject to measures discriminating against companies from non-member states. Within the Community they could compete on equal terms with corporations based in the Six. A move into Europe, moreover, had been long wanted by medium-sized industry in Britain and could easily be justified in terms both of the healthy impact on domestic firms of competition with continental businesses and of the opportunities presented to British manufacturers by the large market. Heath immediately began talks to secure entry to the EEC and Britain formally became part of it on 1 January 1973.

The legislation to curb trade union power, embodied in the Industrial Relations Act of 1971, gave the government authority to order compulsory ballots before strikes if it considered the 'national interest' to be at risk; undermined the principle of the closed shop; and established a National Industrial Relations Court to arbitrate on unfair industrial practices. To a large degree the legislation stemmed from a determination to restore the 'right to manage' after the labour unrest of the later 1960s. It had a deeper purpose, however, in tune with the desire to open up the economy to more competition. Some of the technocratic literature of the early 1960s, notably Michael Shanks's *The Stagnant Society* (1961), had argued that the restrictive practices of many trade unions had prevented innovation in the economy. By the late 1960s this conviction, no doubt reinforced by the experience of conflict, had spread throughout industry. With Heath as leader, the Conservative Party committed itself to reducing the power of organized labour in the hope that more discipline on the factory floor would not only mean fewer strikes but more investment by capitalists. It was all part of the attempt to prepare British industry and workers for the shock they would receive when the full impact of integration with Europe was felt. In his early days Heath appeared to believe that the trade union movement had to be publicly humiliated if it was properly going to learn the gospel of efficiency according to corporate capitalism. In consequence a number of disputes were needlessly prolonged, such as the 1971 postmen's strike, and Heath forfeited what little trust there was for him within the ranks of organized labour for the rest of his premiership.

If Heath had been deflationist this policy would have been logical if distasteful. The next Conservative prime minister had no compunction about seeking to destroy the power of organized labour, both by allowing unemployment to rise and by introducing legal sanctions against unions. The context was, however, one in which Britain was reduced to industrial wreckage, and such an outcome was the last thing Heath wanted. The harsh rhetoric of 'Selsdon man' notwithstanding (Stewart, 1978, pp. 111–12), Heath was at heart an expansionist and believed that the key to higher growth was reflation. This commitment was strengthened by anxiety about the rising level of unemployment, which peaked at over 900,000 in January 1972, resulting in large part from the orthodox economic policy followed by Labour. Having inherited a large balance of payments surplus the new government therefore took a series of measures to increase demand. Income tax was reduced, particularly at the top end of the scale, and purchase tax was cut by 20 per cent. These fiscal measures were accompanied by the provision of easier credit: the bank rate was lowered from 7 per cent to 5 per cent between January and September 1971 and all hire purchase controls were abolished in July. At the same time the government reformed the financial sector with the introduction of the 'Competition and Credit Control' measures designed to encourage a larger volume of bank lending to industry than had generally been the case in the past. The new regulations effectively reduced the minimum ratio of assets to liabilities which each bank was required to retain from 28 per cent to between 15 and 20 per cent, and stimulated competition to provide financial assistance and services to the public. In consequence bank advances doubled in the period from mid-July 1971 to mid-July 1973 and a heavy dose of demand was injected into the economy. True to their managerial constituency and to their market-centred philosophy, the Tories aimed to expand national output by creating a boom in private consumption and investment. The hope was that industry would respond positively to the more buoyant domestic climate, fighting off foreign competition with the aid of the new policies designed to improve efficiency.

Heath's objectives were 5 per cent growth and full employment.

By late 1971 both the Prime Minister and his Chancellor, Anthony Barber, had become convinced that the latter objective was not going to be achieved merely by stimulating private consumption. The government therefore decided on a substantial increase in public expenditure in order to increase demand throughout the economy. In these circumstances Heath's early display of political contempt for the unions proved to be a major political blunder for it became increasingly clear that his policies needed their support. Rapid economic expansion was now being pressed on top of an inflation rate of 9 per cent. The Industrial Relations Act had not quelled the understandable determination of trade unions to protect members' living standards from rising prices. On the contrary: it had worked along with the regressive taxation policy to stimulate both bitterness towards the government and a determination to see that the working class received its share of any bonanza on offer. During 1971 wage rates rose at about 12 per cent per annum and in 1972 this figure rose to 16 per cent. There was serious danger that in the absence of an incomes policy a sharp rise in private consumption would be inevitable, leading to a massive import boom and higher inflation. It would in consequence be necessary to try to reassemble the pieces of the producers' alliance and return to tripartite consultation about national economic policy. Given organized labour's distrust for Heath's administration this was never going to be easy. But the Conservatives were not to be deterred and offered the unions a whole series of concessions, including a commitment to 5 per cent growth, legislation to help the low paid, price controls and subsidies for nationalized industries, in an effort to win support for wage restraint based on a £2 a week pay increase across the board. Although the policy was more radical than anything suggested by Labour it remained unacceptable to the unions, both because of the Industrial Relations Act and because the experience of 1966–9 had resulted in disillusion with any form of pay restraint. But by the autumn of 1972 Heath was determined to control pay and prices, and, thwarted in his attempt to achieve a bargain with labour, he introduced a statutory policy in November. This statutory policy, policed not by the PIB but by a Pay Board and Price Commission, remained in place until the government's fall from power. Until the winter of 1973–4, when it was challenged by the miners in particular and undermined by imported inflation, it worked quite smoothly and helped to prevent the annual rate of inflation from reaching 10 per cent.

Trade union acquiesence in the policy was facilitated by the government's substitution of an interventionist industrial strategy for the old liberal approach in 1972. Given the hostility towards statism felt by the government's supporters in large-scale industry this was a courageous move, but not a surprising one in view of the priority which both the CBI and the Tories had throughout accorded to industrial modernization. By 1972 it was clear that this objective was not going to be achieved on the basis of non-intervention. Between 1971 and 1972 industrial production in Britain increased by just over 2 per cent but rose by 4 per cent throughout the EEC, by almost 10 per cent in the United States and by 7 per cent in Japan. There was no sign here that stiff competition was going to stimulate an industrial revival. Indeed, the evidence suggested that it might lead to an acceleration of decline. In 1971 Rolls Royce, a major employer in the forefront of technological innovation, producing sophisticated engines for civil and military aircraft all over the Western world, went bankrupt. Its collapse would mean unemployment, lost export markets and the demise of many smaller industrial concerns which depended on Rolls Royce for business. Beyond this the international prestige of Rolls Royce was such that its closure would be taken as symbolic of the fate of manufacturing industry in Britain. Nevertheless, all these consequences would have to be faced had the Conservatives remained committed to the view that subsidies to ailing firms involved a waste of resources. That they did not, that they even took the company into public ownership, revealed that non-intervention had never been taken as an end in itself but as a means to modernization. But what kind of industrial modernization involved the loss of a large firm whose products were based on advanced technology? The answer was self-evident, and in 1972 the Conservatives adopted a much more positive, interventionist industrial strategy.

The change in course was marked by the 1972 Industry Act. The Act provided tax incentives for investment and regional development grants for depressed areas, and gave the secretary of state freedom to invest public money in any industry or firm if he considered such action to be in the national economic interest. If necessary grants could be made conditional on state shareholdings. Shortly afterwards, in June 1972, after a wave of speculation against the currency, the government allowed sterling to float rather than follow in Labour's footsteps and sabotage its expansionary policies by defending an uncompetitive exchange rate. Both the Industry Act and the decision to float the pound revealed the depth of the commitment to expansion and modernization but they did not involve any challenge to the government's supporters in corporate industry or to the priorities of the City. In part this was because of industry's desire for high growth. More importantly, however, neither move implied any challenge to the traditional external economic orientation of the British state. Formal membership of the EEC was only months away, and Britain's accession was eagerly awaited not only by multinational companies but by the City, which anticipated a vast expansion of its already major role as an offshore banking centre for funds held by foreign governments, corporations and speculators (Nairn, 1973, ch. 2). Sterling was no longer a significant international reserve currency, and Britain's large foreign debt did not exist any more, so there was no need for the City, the Bank of England and the Treasury to frighten the government into orthodoxy in order to retain the confidence of the international financial community. Above all the expansion was to take place within the framework of the open economy. Joining the European Community meant more freedom for capital movements, and there was no thought of resorting to physical controls if reflation sucked in imports. A downward float of sterling, making imports dearer and exports cheaper, would protect the balance of payments.

The results of expansion under Heath and Barber were on the face of it extremely encouraging. The economy grew at a rate of almost 6 per cent in 1973. Industrial production was up by 9 per cent compared with 1972, and unemployment fell back to 500,000. But below the surface there were mounting problems and in late 1973 and early 1974 these combined with an unforeseen external shock to destroy the experiment and bring an abrupt end to the last sustained attempt at industrial modernization in recent British history. First, the level of investment of industry in fact fell from 6.2 per cent to 3.6 per cent of industrial production between 1970 and 1973 while net investment outside industry rose from

19.4 per cent to 24.8 per cent. In part this disappointing performance followed from the government's determination to stimulate private spending, so that too much of the national income was devoted to consumption rather than investment: 'the encouragement of a spending spree led to a spending spree' (Pollard, 1984, p. 46). The low level of industrial investment was also, however, a function of the property boom which had followed from the 1971 Competition and Credit Control reforms. Between mid 1971 and mid 1973 finance companies had taken advantage of the availability of easy money to increase their borrowing from banks from £1.3 billion to £4.8 billion (Stewart, 1978, p. 141). Much of this was ploughed not into industry, where output was never going to rise rapidly enough to yield quick profits, but into property and houses, which had the benefit of being hedges against inflation. The consequent speculation on the property market pushed up house prices by 70 per cent in the two years following the implementation of the reforms. From 1970 to 1973 investment in new plant and equipment rose by just 25 per cent while private investment in property increased by 83 per cent.

The property boom was evidence that the simultaneous expansion of private consumption with public spending and investment had injected into the economy a level of demand which could not be matched by production. The growing domestic market was a disincentive to exports and acted as a magnet for imports, which increased in volume by 27 per cent between 1971 and 1973. As a result there was increasing pressure on the balance of payments, which swung from a surplus of £1,000 million in 1971 to a deficit running at an annual rate of £750 million by the summer of 1973. This deteriorating external position was made worse by an international boom in food and raw material prices stimulated by the simultaneous expansion of the major industrial economies in 1973. As with Maudling, so with Heath and Barber: modernization within the context of Britain's traditionally open economy was generating a mounting balance of payments deficit. This time the problem of the foreign balance was magnified by the sudden quadrupling of the price of oil, as a result of the Arab–Israeli war, between October 1973 and January 1974. Within the Treasury it was estimated that the oil price rise would add as much as £2.5 billion a year to the balance of payments deficit.

Nothing short of an export drive unprecedented since the early postwar years was going to wipe out this deficit and at the same time ensure the maintenance of full employment. Such an achievement would require severe restraints on domestic living standards, something that could only be done through co-operation between the government and the trade unions. Unfortunately for Heath the winter of 1973–4 saw the chickens of his industrial relations legislation come home to roost. The government's failure to control rising food prices (up by 20 per cent in 1973 while average earnings increased by 13 per cent), on top of the Industrial Relations Act, stimulated a series of protests against the pay policy by powerful unions. First the electricity power workers took action, then the railwaymen, then the miners. Early in February 1974, against the background of the miners' strike, Heath called an election on the theme of 'Who governs?' in an attempt to isolate the militant trade unions. He could not, however, dictate the agenda of the campaign and Labour turned the tactic against him by pointing to rising inflation, speculation and the failure of the modernization strategy, the balance of payments deficit, and class conflict.

Harold Wilson returned to power as a result of the general election, held on 28 February 1974. But the outcome represented not a victory for Labour but a defeat for Heath. His appeal to the country had been rejected. The trouble was that by early 1974 his modernization strategy lay in almost total wreckage: the Industrial Relations Act had not restored managerial authority, membership of the EEC had increased the economy's vulnerability to import penetration, and the early non-interventionist approach to industry had been abandoned anyway. Never able to gain the positive support of the unions the government lost its final claim to legitimacy in the winter of 1973–4 when it was effectively deserted by the CBI. Campbell Adamson, the director-general, appeared on television shortly before polling day, criticizing the Industrial Relations Act, and maintaining that it had been quite counterproductive. Given the prevailing politico-economic crisis there is some evidence to support the view that big capital might prefer a Labour government committed to co-operation with the trade unions rather than the continuation of a Conservative regime whose inability to avoid confrontation had only succeeded in turning the field of industrial relations into a battleground. In the short term, at any rate, crisis management was a more welcome prospect than crisis intensification.

The Struggle over Labour's Industrial Strategy, 1974–1975

Labour returned to power with a radical economic programme designed to achieve the regeneration of British industry. During its years in opposition it had identified the low level of investment in manufacturing industry as the key to Britain's poor economic performance. The February 1974 general election manifesto stated that to reverse the trend Labour would introduce limited measures of public ownership, including mainly the ports, shipbuilding and the aircraft industry; introduce a system of planning agreements with industry; and establish a National Enterprise Board. Trade union co-operation in restraining pay demands would be ensured not through a formal incomes policy but through a 'social contract' involving generous welfare provision for the poor and high taxation for the wealthy, and through the introduction of industrial democracy. The government would abandon all attempts to coerce organized labour, and the statutory prices and incomes policy would be abolished along with the Industrial Relations Act.

The novel elements in this package were planning agreements and the National Enterprise Board (NEB). Both involved a greater degree of *dirigisme* than had ever before been contemplated outside wartime. The innovations were designed partly to supersede the private capital market, which had manifestly failed to allocate an adequate supply of funds to industry since 1970, and partly to ensure that the government retained control over a national economy increasingly dominated by multinational firms capable of switching investment from one country to another. Planning agreements were designed to provide the government with the power to influence the development of major firms throughout industry. It was originally envisaged that they would be compulsory. In return for grants and advice from the state, companies would produce detailed projections of future investment and import and export levels in conjunction with government representatives. The NEB was meanwhile to act as a large version of the old IRC, performing many of the same tasks but with more money at its disposal. The hope was that it would be able to take either a partial or even a total shareholding in firms whose future was believed by the government to be central to the development of the national economy in terms of output, overseas sales and employment. It was part of the NEB's brief that it should act as a venture capitalist, sponsoring products even to the extent of establishing its own companies if the immediate commercial prospects were not encouraging enough to stimulate private investment. Remembering what had happened to the expansionary plans of 1964 and aware that the new programme would almost certainly incur the hostility of the City and of the multinationals, its proponents were committed to a strengthening of exchange controls in order to prevent damaging speculative movements. Although no mention was made of import controls the determination to restore the control of the national government over an economy increasingly vulnerable to international shocks implied a significant shift from the liberal economic policy followed by successive administrations since 1951.

The strategy was never implemented in any recognizable form. Although Labour enacted a wide range of social reforms and repealed the Industrial Relations Act, the modernization programme enshrined in the 1975 Industry Act was, to put it mildly, an emasculated verson of the original proposals. Given the political context of Labour's return to power this was not surprising. The government had taken over with a radical programme but it had received no electoral or parliamentary mandate for the transformation of British society. The administration elected on 28 February was a minority one. A second general election was won in October 1974 but this only resulted in an overall majority of three for Labour in the House of Commons. Whatever Labour Party ministers and backbenchers may have wanted, they were elected with the negative task of crisis avoidance. Productionist though the manifesto may have been it never received the positive support of private industry. The circumstances of 1964 and 1966 were not to be repeated. The interventionism of the industrial policy was not particularly drastic by French or even Japanese standards, but British employers were so frightened that they mounted a relentless campaign for its abandonment. They favoured indicative planning and the consensus politics of tripartite consultation within the NEDC. The CBI was so determined to fight off what it regarded as an assault on the private enterprise system that it even made plans for an investment strike.

The CBI's growing concern about 'socialism' was rather hysterical since the government was dominated by social-democrats such as Wilson, Denis Healey (Chancellor), Jim Callaghan (Foreign Secretary), Roy Jenkins (Home Secretary), and Tony Crosland (Environment Secretary). It had no intention of endangering the mixed economy, whatever some of its more radical spokesmen, including occasionally the Industry Secretary, Tony Benn, may have said. The fears of the CBI were, however, symptomatic of mounting political and economic insecurity throughout private industry. Although industrialists had consented to the repeal of the Industrial Relations Act they soon began to feel that the government's reforms, notably the Employment Protection Act, along with its commitment to industrial democracy, would shift the balance of power in British society decisively towards organized labour. Self-interest alone would have been enough to make the CBI resent such a prospect. But ultimately anxiety stemmed from a belief that bound up with the maintenance of managerial authority was the survival of British capitalism. This moral panic was reinforced by anxiety about profits, which, it was believed, were collapsing under the pressures of taxation, high wage costs and the price of fuel. Writing in the *Financial Times* of 24 October 1974, Sam Brittan argued that profits before taxation between the first half of 1973 and the first half of 1974 had fallen by 88 per cent, and that profits after tax for the first half of 1974 were negative. The basis of the calculations which had yielded such apocalyptic results was later challenged,[2] but nothing short of the government's abandonment of the policy set out in the February 1974 manifesto would satisfy the CBI.

The leading members of the government were sympathetic to this pressure. Wilson had apparently shifted leftwards between 1970 and 1974 in order to preserve party unity, but at root he had no intention of departing from the corporatist approach to economic planning which had marked the period from 1964 to 1970. In 1974–5, with Treasury and Foreign Office support, Wilson exploited the opportunity provided by crisis, not to introduce the modernization scheme but to abandon it in favour of a strategy which involved no radical changes in domestic or foreign economic policy.

Britain's current balance of payments deficit approached £4 billion in 1974. Nonetheless, to begin with Wilson and Healey set their faces against deflation as well as against the control of imports. Instead they allowed the government to run up a large borrowing requirement (the difference between public spending and revenue) financed to a large extent by money placed in London by the rich oil-producing states. In addition to favourable capital flows Britain received a loan of $1,200 million from the Shah of Iran. The hope was that Britain's commitment to expansion would be matched throughout the industrialized world and that a buoyant international climate would sustain high demand for exports. The external deficit would begin to close and would in time be transformed into a surplus once Britain itself became an oil-rich country as a result of developing the North Sea fields.

This strategy increased Britain's vulnerability to international speculative movements. The acid test for any policy as far as the Treasury was concerned was whether or not it would disturb the confidence of Britain's creditors and precipitate a massive capital outflow. In consequence the framework for policy became orthodox. The interventionist industrial strategy could not be allowed, partly because foreign bankers would be unlikely to finance measures held by the British private sector to be the nearest thing to state socialism outside Eastern Europe, but mostly because of its external implications. London was an extremely attractive banking centre for oil-rich countries because of the financial expertise of the City and because of its freedom from government regulations. The strengthening of exchange controls would destroy this liberal climate and restrict the ability of overseas investors to move their money into whatever assets they felt would provide a secure rate of return. It might, suggested Treasury officials, even cause the capital outflow which everyone wanted to avoid.

Wilson and the Treasury won the first stage of the battle over Labour's industrial strategy in the summer of 1974. A White Paper entitled *The Regeneration of British Industry* was published in August. The White Paper rejected compulsory planning agreements and made it clear that these would be made with private firms on a purely voluntary basis. The NEB's powers were to be very limited: any acquisition of shares would have to have the approval of the companies in question, and the provision of grants would be made according to strict financial criteria, projects lacking good commercial prospects would not receive support.

The White Paper represented a political defeat for Tony Benn and was a source of great disappointment to the radical left of the Labour Party. But its publication was not the end of the struggle over the government's strategy, which now came to centre on the issue of British membership of the EEC. The 1964–70 Labour governments had looked with growing favour on the idea of joining the Community and had led an application in 1967, only to be refused entry by de Gaulle. During the early 1970s, however, hostility towards the EEC began to spread throughout the Labour movement. The Common Agricultural Policy was blamed for high food prices which gave an upward twist to inflation. The EEC itself was viewed as no more than an instrument by which large corporations and inefficient farmers could come together to exploit the public. But above all there was a mounting conviction in the unions as well as in the party that membership of the EEC would multiply the difficulties of national economic planning and accelerate industrial decline. Given the relatively weak position of British manufacturing the commitment to free trade in the EEC would be more likely to result in factory closures and unemployment at home along with a movement of capital abroad than to stimulate an industrial revival through increased competition. By 1973 opposition to British participation in the Common Market was so intense that Wilson had committed a future Labour government to holding a referendum on the subject after renegotiating Britain's terms of entry.

There was a good deal of evidence to support the case against membership. The ending of the old cheap food policy on British entry to the Common market had not helped the Heath government's attempt to negotiate a deal on incomes with the unions. But more disturbing than this was the deterioration of the balance of Britain's trade in manufactured goods in the early 1970s. In 1971 Britain's imports of finished manufactures totalled £2,382 million. By 1974 this figure had grown to £3,871 million, and of the overall increase of £1,489 million, £888 million had occurred in 1973 alone (1970 prices).[3] These statistics reinforced the view, implicit in the original industrial strategy, that modernization would require a fundamental change in Britain's relationship to the international economy. By early 1975 the Tribune Group in the Labour Party was calling for public investment in a British economy protected by tougher exchange restrictions and import controls to 'encourage the growth of firms concerned with import substitution, to ensure that key industries have the raw materials and components they need, to see that the whole plan is not frustrated by excessive import bills and to maintain full employment'.[4] The implementation of these controls would cut across Britain's commitment to the Treaty of Rome. Withdrawal from the EEC was therefore seen as the first stage of a process by which British governments would be able to reassert control of the national economy and implement the programme for reversing industrial decline with which Labour had come to power.

The Foreign Office was appalled by this programme. Britain's leading role in NATO notwithstanding, the Foreign Office identified membership of the EEC with commitment to the Western alliance. Its hostility to withdrawal reinforced that shown by private industry, the Treasury and the financial establishment.[5] In these circumstances there was a distinct probability that departure from the EEC would be greeted by a capital outflow, a run on the pound and a vast reduction in the availability of finance from abroad. In the short term, therefore, the radical industrial strategy would imply the establishment of the most rigid exchange controls since the early 1950s and, given the likely shortage of hard currency, a reduction in living standards so that money could be spent on vital imports. The plan would require very considerable public support, well beyond the size of the vote recorded by Labour in October 1974, and this the left hoped to mobilize during the referendum campaign.

The attempt to use the referendum as a way of changing the course of British economic history was a total failure. The public voted by a majority of two to one for the *status quo*. This was precisely what Wilson, Callaghan and Healey had wanted because they were themselves opposed to any move which threatened the liberal orientation of the economy. During the campaign the government commended the new 'terms' of membership to the people and claimed that remaining in the Community was now on balance in Britain's advantage. In fact the renegotiation exercise had been almost entirely spurious, resulting in some minor concessions on EEC regional policy, on the level of the contribution to the Community budget, and on imports of dairy produce from New Zealand. Of these only the third had any meaning. The first proved to be of very modest benefit and the second, in the light of later events, to be practically worthless. Nothing substantial had changed and none of Britain's negotiators had seriously intended otherwise. The real purpose of the renegotiation was cosmetic. In reality the government was deeply committed to participation in the EEC with everything this implied for domestic and foreign economic policy. But the arguments had to be sold to the public. This task could only be achieved effectively if the case for remaining in the Community looked as if it were founded on a dispassionate analysis of the renegotiated 'terms'.

The 'Yes' vote in the referendum was taken by the government as an endorsement of its orthodox approach to managing Britain's economic crisis. Benn was demoted from the Department of Industry to the Department of Energy and replaced by Eric Varley, a Wilson protégé. The Industry Act quickly appeared and gave legislative authority to the proposals of the 1974 White Paper.

Benn's fall was greeted with dismay by the radicals but in truth he had contributed to his own downfall. Although he never had the chance to preside over the introduction of planning agreements and the establishment of the NEB he did have Heath's 1972 Industry Act. Yet in providing grants to a whole range of firms he never appeared to have any set criteria for public investment. On the one hand he authorized the financing of modernization in industries central to Britain's future as a manufacturing nation, such as machine-tools and ferrous foundries. On the other hand he gave money to some firms merely because they were worker co-operatives and therefore met with his ideological approval. Supporting the *Scottish Daily News*, for example, made no contribution to the regeneration of British industry. The decision to help the co-operative of Norton–Villiers–Triumph in Meriden, conversely, could have been vital to saving the motorcyle industry. But as it was the funds were largely wasted because they were not tied to the development of new models to replace the old ones which fewer and fewer people wanted to buy.

This erratic conduct gave the establishment ammunition to use against a policy it wanted to kill. Yet the radical modernization strategy had more potential than the one which replaced it. In making planning agreements voluntary the government ensured that they would be used not to further a modernization plan but, if at all, to prop up private corporations in financial difficulty. So it proved. The one agreement concluded with a private sector firm was with the ailing American-based car manufacturer Chrysler in 1975. Having taken the money Chrysler subsequently sold their British operations to Peugeot, the French company, with the government having no control or even influence over what became of the firm. The only other planning agreement signed up to 1979 was with the National Coal Board (NCB), a baffling move since the NCB was nationalized anyway.

The NEB did have a more distinguished career, but its operations were small by comparison with what had been envisaged. Its finance was restricted by the Treasury to £1,000 million for its first four years, and such a sum was never going to be enough to transform the state into one of the economy's leading entrepreneurs. Within its rather limited brief it did perform useful work, helping to reconstruct British Leyland and so ensure the survival of the car industry, and taking the lead in financing development in high technology. Its most notable achievement was the establishment of the successful computer manufacturer Inmos, but for the most part the initiatives were small scale. The NEB made no impression on the basic structure of the investment market. It lacked the power and resources to give the government influence over the development of manufacturing industry, and its interventions were generally piecemeal.

After the EEC referendum, therefore, the *dirigiste* aspirations of 1974 were finally abandoned in favour of an industrial policy which involved a return to indicative planning. From 1975 to 1979 action to encourage investment and to improve productivity throughout industry was taken on the basis of tripartite discussions in the NEDC. Selective intervention was accompanied by measures to improve the competitive position of British exports. There were tax concessions designed to increase company profitability and an incomes policy was introduced to reduce the pressure of wage costs on British manufacturers. The introduction of formal wage restraint, albeit without a statutory framework, was not unwelcome to Labour, but it was forced on the government from outside. By mid 1975 prices and incomes were both rising at an annual rate of over 25 per cent. The social contract had failed to check pay rises, and union leaders as well as government ministers were becoming worried about the possibility of a hyperinflation, fuelled by an unending spiral of increases in prices and wages. Foreign holders of sterling were also anxious about such a prospect, and at the end of June began to sell the pound in favour of other currencies whose value appeared to be more reliable. On 30 June the value of sterling fell in just one trading session by 1.3 per cent, and it was only the government's announcement of an incomes policy, albeit not with a statutory framework, to reduce inflation to below 10 per cent by the end of 1976 which brought the speculation to an end.

The Collapse of the Modernization Consensus, 1975–1979

Britain's vulnerability to foreign creditors had been increased by international economic developments. The government's early commitment to expansion within an open world economy had not been matched in practice by other major industrial states, notably the USA, Germany and Japan, which had introduced deflationary measures to reduce their import bills. In consequence the world had plunged into a recession. Britain had been one of the few countries to try to buck the trend. Given the government's aversion to protectionism the only way to sustain domestic activity in these circumstances was by allowing the public sector borrowing requirement (PSBR) to increase, and by mid 1975 it was approaching £10 billion, or nearly 10 per cent of the national income. Labour had drawn on overseas monies to meet a considerable fraction of its borrowing requirement but it was not clear how long it could rely on this in view of the attractions of a stable dollar, yen or Deutschmark to international financiers. By 1975–6, therefore, it was clear that the creditworthiness of the British government in the eyes of the world's financial community was dependent on both an incomes policy and a reduction in domestic demand.

All this made for the imposition of a heavy set of constraints on the government, but with unemployment, largely as a result of the world recession, now over one million, it did not wish to pursue drastic deflation. Healey's March 1976 budget was accordingly fairly neutral. At much the same time the government persuaded the Bank of England, against the wishes of the Governor, Sir

Gordon Richardson, to sell sterling and organize a controlled fall in its value of just under 10 per cent (from $2.05 to $1.85–1.90 to the pound). With protection and expansion out of the question a managed devaluation was the only strategy left to a government seeking to modernize industry. The hope was that a reduction in the value of the exchange rate would lead to increased demand for British exports, and that growing markets overseas would stimulate higher investment and output. Productivity was to be improved by measures agreed in the NEDC, and the incomes policy was to continue in combination with curbs on government spending in order to prevent private and public consumption from claiming resources needed for the export drive.

The strategy, liberal and vaguely Keynesian, was a disaster. Instead of leading to a managed decline in the exchange rate the government's decision to sell sterling precipitated an uncontrolled collapse in the value of the currency to $1.50 to the pound in early October. Confidence in the policies of the Labour government had been fragile to begin with. The devaluation was taken as a sign that Britain's financial authorities did not believe the pound could be maintained anywhere near the $2 level rather than as part of an attempt to set in motion export-led growth. Throughout the spring and summer, therefore, there was a steady movement out of sterling on the part of the speculators, banks, multinationals and institutional investors whose deposits in London had grown so substantially over the past few years. So vast was the volume of these funds that subsequent attempts by the Bank to buy sterling and halt the decline were unavailing. The Cambridge Economic Policy Group estimated in its *Economic Policy Review* for 1977 that as much as £1,488 million of short-term capital flowed out of Britain in 1976 (Table 5, page 107). Under pressure from the Bank and the Treasury the government, which had hoped to achieve an annual growth rate of 4.5 per cent in the GDP and an annual expansion of 8.5 per cent in manufacturing production, was driven into deflationary measures which made a nonsense of its objectives. Foreign credits of $5.3 billion were negotiated in July at the price of cuts worth £1 billion in spending programmes for 1977–8, and the interest rate (previously the bank rate) was increased to 13 per cent. These steps were, however, inadequate to stop the haemorrhage. In the autumn the interest rate was put up again, to 15 per cent this time, and an appeal for a loan of $3.2 billion was made to the International Monetary Fund (IMF).

Much has been written about the discussions between the British government and the Fund, and there is no need to repeat the details here.[6] However, it should be stressed, first, that the encouragement of economic expansion has never been the Fund's concern. Its basic purpose has always been ideological: to help sustain the liberal economic order established in the Western world after 1945. This role has been performed through the provision of foreign exchange to countries with large balance of payments deficits, in return for rigidly orthodox policies designed to reduce demand for imports. Secondly, though nominally independent, the Fund has generally behaved as an arm of American economic foreign policy, since throughout the postwar era the United States, like Britain before 1914, has seen itself as the ultimate guarantor of liberal capitalism. Thirdly, the politico-economic priorities of the Fund and of successive American administrations have squared with those of Britain's financial establishment and its guardians in the City, the Bank and the Treasury. The two major evils are inflation and protectionism. Inflation is subversive of the market order because it undermines confidence in money, the medium of exchange through which all transactions are made. Protectionism is anathema because it involves barriers to the free flow of goods and capital. Economic growth is not an objective of policy because the belief is that it flows automatically from the rational allocation of resources which only the unfettered market can provide.

The United States Treasury welcomed Britain's approach to the IMF. The collapse of sterling had led to anxiety that Labour would take radical measures, involving the imposition of trade and foreign exchange controls and the suspension of convertibility. Assistance for Britain was therefore essential; through maintaining Britain's liberal economic orientation the United States would be averting what it believed to be the greatest challenge to the international trading system since the era of Marshall Aid (Ham, 1981, p. 124).

The IMF made it clear that it would provide the money, but only on condition that Labour make the reduction of inflation its priority rather than pursue growth and modernization. Although the rate of inflation had in fact fallen from 24.2 per cent in 1975 and stood at 16 per cent by the end of 1976 the Fund was not satisfied. Whatever the government's achievement, the verdict of the financial markets was what mattered and the capital outflow had shown their disapproval. By putting inflation first Labour could restore confidence in sterling and resolve its external financial difficulties without turning to heretical measures. A drastic reduction in demand was therefore essential, and to this end the IMF required a package of public spending cuts worth £4 billion (ibid.).

The Bennite left of the Labour party and radical social-democrats such as Anthony Crosland, now Foreign Secretary (Callaghan had become prime minister after Wilson's retirement in March 1976), fought against the programme. Both maintained that aid on the terms set down by the IMF was unacceptable, and argued that Labour's commitment to jobs and to increasing output could only be fulfilled if imports were restricted by protectionist measures. Crosland's programme was more modest than Benn's since it involved the avoidance of cuts and the introduction of import deposits rather than outright controls and the direction of investment. Both strategies, however, provoked horror in the Bank and the Treasury, where the Fund was seen as a powerful ally and source of external pressure on the government in the struggle to salvage Britain's international creditworthiness and reduce inflation. The Governor of the Bank of England strongly supported the IMF package. Sir Douglas Wass, the Permanent Secretary of the Treasury at that time, later said that taking either the Benn or the Crosland option would have led the country into an 'abyss', which was to him synonymous with 'very drastic changes in our external economic policy, with implications for our membership of the European Community and our continued participation in the open free trading system'.[7] The alternatives suggested by Benn and Crosland therefore conflicted with the Bank and Treasury view of the national interest and were fiercely opposed by a Whitehall and Threadneedle Street establishment which now had the backing of the international financial community, articulated by the IMF.

The upshot of the debate was of course acceptance of the IMF loan. Crosland abandoned his resistance because he feared the resignations of the Prime Minister and the Chancellor and the collapse of the government if the IMF were rebuffed. Benn was left isolated. The pill was sweetened to some extent by the withdrawal of cuts worth £1,000 million. It was, nevertheless, a formidable deflationary package and implied the burial of the government's early commitment to modernization, a process which had started with the abandonment of the *dirigiste* industrial strategy in 1975. Forced at last to make a conclusive choice between economic liberalism and economic expansion the government had decided in favour of the former.

It followed that from the start of 1977 until its fall from power in May 1979 the government's priority continued to be the conquest of inflation. Credit remained tight and public spending programmes were cut. Revenue from North Sea oil was not invested in industry but was instead used to improve the balance of payments. By 1978 Britain was £1,000 million in the black. This turnaround in the external balance together with sterling's status as a petrocurrency encouraged an inflow of capital from abroad. Keen to see the pound appreciate on the foreign exchanges because the consequent lower import costs would help the counter-inflationary policy, the government did nothing to stop the increase in the exchange rate, which stood at more than $1.90 to the pound in 1978–9.

The complete abandonment of Keynesian ideas that expenditure should be increased in a recession was justified by resort to the newly fashionable doctrine of monetarism, which held that inflation followed from the overexpansion of a country's money supply by its government. By restricting domestic credit and by reducing its own borrowing requirement a government could therefore bring about a fall in the domestic price level. No incomes policy would be necessary because a tight monetary policy would lead trade unionists to moderate wage demands on the assumption of a falling rate of inflation. At the same time any group of workers which stood out for high pay increases would have to face the prospect of unemployment because there would not be enough money in the economy to support a large labour force at wage levels beyond what could be justified by sales of goods and services.

Although this theory was frequently wrapped up in mystifying and technical jargon there was nothing very new about it. It was in essence a rehash of the pre-Keynesian orthodoxy which had prevailed before the war and above all in the 1920s. Shorn of pretentiousness all it involved was the acceptance of mass unemployment, at whatever cost to national output, in an effort to reduce wage costs so that British goods would become internationally competitive. Healey never went along with this view in its entirety and sought to complement the government's restrictive economic stance with the maintenance of the incomes policy.

The strategy reduced inflation to 8 per cent by 1978. The City thrived, and in 1977 £3.8 billion flowed into London. But the deflationary climate made sure that there would be no reversal of Britain's relative decline as a manufacturing nation. Between 1975 and 1979 industrial production rose to an index of 115 (1975 = 100) against indices of 129, 133 and 119 for the United States, Japan and West Germany respectively. Whatever competitive advantage may have accrued to British exports as a result of the 1976 devaluation was quickly wiped out by the subsequent rise of the exchange rate, which encouraged continuing import penetration. By 1978 Britain's share of world exports of manufactures had slipped to 7 per cent. While the volume of manufactured exports increased by 6 per cent between 1977 and 1978 that of imports rose by 16 per cent. Particularly hard hit were some of the industries which had led postwar expansion in Britain and in the world economy, such as motor vehicles, electrical engineering and instrument engineering. In these three sectors the percentage of home demand met by imports rose dramatically between 1971 and 1980, from 15 per cent to 39 per cent for vehicles, from 18 per cent to 37 per cent for electrical engineering, and from 37 per cent to 61 per cent for instrument engineering.[8]

As had been the case for so long, the competitive position of British industry was worsened by low investment. In 1978 it was estimated that fixed assets per worker in Britain 'were only £7,500, compared with £23,000 in West Germany and £30,000 in Japan' (Gamble, 1985, p. 16). The cautious industrial strategy did little to improve matters and indeed the government itself was forced to discourage investment in order to maintain trade union commitment to the incomes policy. Given the need to cut public spending it was politically expedient to reduce capital expenditure rather than current programmes, many of which went to finance unemployment benefits and the social wage. Between 1975–6 and 1978–9 government outlays on fixed investment dropped by £4,900 million.

Despite the attempt to shield welfare benefits the incomes policy could not be sustained. In 1978 Callaghan and Healey tried to gain TUC approval for another year of pay restraint, centring on a pay norm of 5 per cent. Pointing to the inflation rate of 8 per cent trade union leaders made it clear that they could no longer acquiesce in a policy which continually kept living standards from rising in line with price increases. They were in addition profoundly disappointed by the orthodox nature of Labour's economic policy, and particular grievances were the rejection of Jack Jones's[9] proposal for a state investment fund and the shelving of the Bullock report on industrial democracy. The pay policy was in short accompanied by no real political or economic inducements, and during the winter of 1978–9 it collapsed in a welter of bitter strikes, many of them in the public sector and causing more hurt to the public than to the employers.

The withdrawal of trade union support for Labour was evidence that the last vestiges of tripartite collaboration were rapidly disappearing. First, the commitment of organized labour to government policy had become increasingly difficult to secure throughout the 1970s, in part because the institutional mechanisms which had allowed powerful national union leaders such as Bevin or Cousins to control developments on the factory floor had disappeared. With the rise of the shop steward the strength of rank-and-file unionists had increased and their willingness to countermand the wishes of head office had grown with the years of pay restraint. Secondly, the later 1970s were characterized by a reaction against corporatist policies throughout the CBI. At first the expression of hostility even to indicative planning was restricted to the traditionally Poujadist small business sector, but it later began to spread to the leadership of the CBI. This was partly because of continuing slow growth in the economy: indicative planning could make no serious contribution to dramatic increases in the level of output against a macro-economic backround of deflation and a high exchange rate. Yet the disenchantment with *concertation* and the concomitant rise in real opposition to the Labour government stemmed mostly from the persistence of anxieties that the expansion of trade union power threatened the survival of private industry. The events of 1978–9 strengthened the conviction that managerial authority had to be restored, even if this could only be achieved at the expense of other objectives, notably that of economic growth. In consequence the CBI had by 1979 swung round to a broad identification with the monetarist philosophy of Mrs Thatcher's Conservative Party. Mass unemployment would be acceptable if it weakened organized labour to such an extent that a government committed to free enterprise could introduce anti-union legislation powerful enough to shift the balance of class power in favour of capital.

Industrial modernization as a policy objective had been abandoned by the government in 1976. By 1979 it had been rejected by private industry. During the 1979 general election union leaders continued to stress their commitment to modernization but it was not easy to see what this would mean in practice, given their determination to substitute the return of free collective bargaining for an incomes policy of any description. No consensus existed to sustain tripartite consultation. Broad agreement between industry and labour on the desirability of growth and full employment had lasted since 1940. The persistence of politico-economic crisis after 1973–4 had eroded practically all this common ground. While the common ground remained it had always been possible for the producers' alliance to re-form after it had been undermined by conflicts of interest between its members. Its disappearance in 1950–1 had been temporary; its demise in 1968–70 had merely been partial. Disappointing as the 1974–9 Labour government had been it is hard to criticize it too fiercely for failing to resolve a crisis which it had only been elected to manage. Nevertheless its defeat in 1979, rejected by industry and deserted by many trade unionists (only 47 per cent of all skilled workers supported Labour at the general election), formally marked the end of an era which had unofficially closed in 1976.

Notes: Chapter 6

1 This is not to deny that the government passed important measures of social legislation which left Britain a more civilized and compassionate society in 1970 than it was in 1964.
2 Cambridge Economic Policy Group, *Economic Policy Review*, no. 1, 1975, ch. 3.
3 ibid., p. 78.

4 For details of the Labour Party and the referendum see Newman, 1983, pp. 224–40.
5 ibid., interview with Sir Bryan Hopkin (Chief Economic Adviser to the government, 1974–7).
6 See for example Fay and Young, 1978.
7 Quoted in the *Daily Telegraph*, 2 November 1983.
8 Article written on the British economy for Vickers da Costa, November 1978, by Wynne Godley; see also Pollard, 1983, p. 284.
9 General Secretary of the Transport and General Workers' Union, 1972–8.

CHAPTER SEVEN

The Political Economy of Deindustrialization, 1979–?

The New Liberal Consensus

Economic decline had been unchecked through the 1950s, 1960s and 1970s. By 1979 GDP per head in Britain was lower than in any other country in industrial Western Europe except Italy. Italy had been held back by its underdeveloped south but nevertheless its annual average growth rate of 5.1 per cent from 1951 to 1973 and then of 2.1 per cent from 1973 to 1978 was rapid enough for it to overtake Britain in the 1980s. Indeed the annual average rate of growth in Britain from 1973 to 1978 was so low, at 0.9 per cent, that given a continuation of the trend there was not one nation on the entire continent apart from Albania which was likely to be poorer by 2010 (Pollard, 1984, p. 6).

The continued existence of growth did at least mean that decline was relative: living standards were rising, albeit much more slowly than just about anywhere else in the developed world. Some writers saw no harm in this and believed that it augured well for the quality of life in Britain. Once the first industrial nation, Britain would soon become the first post-industrial state (see, for example, Nossiter, 1978). The tyranny of the assembly line and the dirt of pollution would give way to reveal a thriving society whose people earned a living through the production of services – banking, tourism, leisure for the masses and arts for the world. Other countries would soon follow where Britain led because in all developed nations the trend was for increasingly affluent populations to spend a rising proportion of their incomes on leisure, their basic needs for housing, food, warmth and transport having been satisfied. There was no reason why this process of deindustrialization should involve balance of payments deficits. The proceeds of North Sea oil, services and invisibles would make up for falling income from manufactured exports, and Britain would remain in the black, able to afford all the imports of food and raw materials necessary to sustain living standards.

This superficially beguiling argument was in fact fatally flawed, and by the end of the 1970s there were plenty of economists prepared to say so. Ajit Singh pointed out that given the persistence of manufacturing decline, manifested in import penetration and a falling share of world markets, income from services would not be enough to sustain external balance at anything approaching full employment. These views received considerable, although not unanimous, support at a conference called by the National Institute for Economic and Social Research in 1979 to discuss deindustrialization. Here it was observed that with North Sea oil at about two-thirds of its likely total output, Britain was suffering from a level of unemployment unparalleled in postwar history and was running only a small balance of payments surplus. The continuation of present trends once the windfall gains of oil had disappeared would mean that Britain would only be able to stay in the black at the cost of low output and even higher unemployment (Singh, 1978).

Britain's competitive position was already weak. Booming production of steel and of motor vehicles had been characteristic of the postwar reconstruction period. Both industries are critical to the health of a modern industrial economy, and Britain's success in each sector was testimony to the transformation achieved in the 1940s: in 1950 only the United States produced more cars per head; of European nations only Belgium made more steel per head. But by 1978 the picture was bleak, with Britain having fallen behind Italy and Spain in production of steel and cars respectively. Higher investment, and thus higher growth of productivity, was essential in these industries as in so many others if the decline was to be reversed. This was, however, precisely what would not be forthcoming if increasing balance of payments difficulties forced governments to reduce the level of demand. There was real danger that the fate of industrial Scotland, already reduced to near dereliction, would overtake the whole country in subsequent decades.

The Conservatives turned the theme of economic decline to their advantage in the 1979 general election. Labour's record on growth, unemployment and prices was an easy target, and with the winter of industrial disputes and bitterness still fresh in the public memory the outgoing government was accused of giving excessive power to the unions. Above all the Tories concentrated on the issues of inflation and strikes, arguing that these were not merely the results of Labour's incompetence but the end products of economic mismanagement stretching back to 1945. Inflation was seen as the root cause of decline. Strikes were symptomatic of the social breakdown which occurred as money lost its value and groups of workers tried to protect themselves against rising prices. The 1979 Conservative manifesto claimed that

> The pound today is worth less than half its 1974 value. On present form it would be halved in value yet again within eight years. Inflation on this scale has come near to destroying our political and social stability.

Inflation not only threatened the social order but created unemployment because in seeking to defend themselves against it trade unions priced their members out of jobs.

For a generation after the war economists had maintained that unemployment could be cured by increasing demand, even if this meant allowing prices to rise. Now the Conservatives, under the influence of monetarist teaching, argued that expansion was no answer to joblessness because it merely gave another twist to inflation, sucked in imports and ultimately necessitated a drastic contraction which put many more out of work. It was the misguided pursuit of such policies which had led Britain into the mire of 'stagflation', whereby unemployment of 1.3 million, low growth and industrial contraction coexisted with endemic inflation. No government could or should try to preserve full employment. The only way to provide jobs was to obey the laws of the marketplace and produce goods of quality at a price the consumer could afford. The fundamental aim of economic policy was to root out inflation, a task well within the power of the state because of its control over the money supply. In the short term, this might involve more contraction and unemployment, following from tight credit and the planned reduction of public spending over several years. But this painful period would not last long because once employers and workers realized that the government was not going to bail them out again they would have to adjust to the low level of demand by cutting costs and reducing wage demands, or face bankruptcy and even higher levels of joblessness. With inflation conquered, industry driven by market forces to be more competitive, and with workers having to price themselves back into employment, the economy would recover. Customers at home and abroad would start to purchase an increasing volume of British products and a new era of non-inflationary growth would commence (Pollard, 1984, pp. 166–7).

The obverse side of the monetarist coin was distrust for bureaucracy and the state. The growth of government's power over the economy since the war had not only fuelled inflation but had stifled private enterprise. Small businesses had become entangled in a maze of red tape. Given the absence of fast growth, the expansion of public spending to finance the health service, social benefits and subsidies to industry had meant an increasing burden of taxation on middle- and working-class voters. The Conservatives claimed that in consequence the incentive to work had been reduced, with damaging consequences for productivity throughout industry. At the same time the growth of government borrowing from the financial markets in the 1970s had 'crowded out' private investors because competition for funds had driven interest rates up to a level which only the state could afford.

The Conservatives therefore went into the 1979 general election offering a free-market cure for British deindustrialization. By rolling back the frontiers of the state a new administration would conquer inflation and simultaneously encourage the growth of private enterprise. Industry would be able to borrow money at favourable interest rates. Company profitability would rise. Tax cuts, facilitated by reductions in public spending, would encourage saving and investment and would simultaneously lead to a more efficient allocation of resources throughout society. Consumers would be able to spend money on what they wanted rather than have their needs identified for them by a clumsy bureaucracy.

It was, however, acknowledged that monetarism alone might be a necessary but not a sufficient condition for the reversal of economic decline. An old-fashioned demand reflation was obviously out of the question but what were called 'supply-side' measures to help businesses adjust to market conditions by improving productivity and output were perfectly acceptable. Such measures included tax concessions for enterprise, improved industrial training, and above all legislation which weakened the trade unions. Although unions might not be responsible for inflation they could still use their monopoly power both to extort crippling wage settlements from employers and to enforce restrictive practices on the factory floor. Accordingly the Tory manifesto promised that a new government would undermine the influence of organized labour by outlawing secondary picketing, by drawing up an informal code of conduct to reform the closed shop, and by introducing postal ballots so that union elections could not be manipulated by an unrepresentative group of militant workers.

There were serious misapprehensions and false assumptions which lay behind the Conservatives' reading of Britain's postwar economic history and the cure they were proposing for the long decline. First, there was no evidence for the central contention that the state had grown so large that it was pre-empting resources which could have been used by private industry. In the mid 1970s two writers, Roger Bacon and Walter Eltis (1976), had alleged that Britain's fundamental problem was 'too few producers': the expansion of the public sector had attracted so many workers that the 'market sector', which alone created wealth, was shrinking because of a shortage of labour. This charge, which was seized on by the monetarists as evidence that big government and deindustrialization went hand in hand, did not stand up to serious examination. Most of the new jobs created in the public sector during the 1960s and 1970s were taken by poorly paid women workers. Employment in manufacturing industry certainly had contracted in recent years, falling at a rate of 1.1 per cent each year between 1966 and 1974, and then at an annual rate of 3 per cent. The jobs lost, however, had belonged to skilled males who were not in a position to compete for jobs in the public sector (Keegan, 1984, p. 36). And while the public sector had expanded since the war its share of the national income was by no means out of line with those of other Western countries with far more impressive economic records than Britain.

A second criticism of the monetarist thesis is that no one has been able to produce a convincing definition of what money really is. Given this confusion, control of the money supply is by no means a simple operation. Is the government to limit the growth of currency and current accounts (known as M1)? Or a range of liquid assets (M3)? Or notes and coins (M0)? At various times after 1979 the Conservatives tried to use each of these definitions for controlling the money supply. As it became clear that there was in fact no obvious correlation between monetary expansion and inflation, M1 and M3 were replaced by M0, a measurement possibly appropriate in a primitive economy but one which was astonishingly crude for a society in which there were many different forms of credit available. The government itself tacitly admitted the inadequacy of all these 'Ms' by concentrating on using high interest rates to limit the demand for credit, a traditional deflationary policy which had predictable consequences for industry.

Thirdly, the reduction of inflation had been the priority of economic policy ever since 1976. There was nothing new about monetarism. Nor was there anything encouraging about the results of monetarist policies. Prices were rising much more slowly in 1979 than in 1975 but this had been achieved in part at least because of Labour's incomes policy. Furthermore, in view of Labour's overall record, it was difficult to argue that the revival of the real economy followed naturally from a fall in the rate of inflation.

Neither the government nor its supporters in the financial establishment were deterred by the fact that monetarism was a threadbare intellectual construct. Given that monetarism automatically implied *laissez-faire* and deflationary policies it was congenial to the City. In particular, however, City dealers

> wholeheartedly embraced the basic theoretical propositions underlying monetarism – the idea that government borrowing leads to an increase in the money supply, which, in turn, causes inflation – because, whether accurate or not, their simplicity meant that quick decisions could be made to buy or sell according to the state of some simple indicators such as the

> latest statistics on the money supply or public sector borrowing. (Coakley and Harris, 1983, p. 205)

Meanwhile, under Mrs Thatcher, a committed convert to monetarism, the Tories manipulated history in order to legitimize an ideological project. This project involved nothing less than the transformation of Britain into an 'enterprise society', characterized by a small state, a sound, stable currency and a thriving free market. The ultimate objective was the establishment of a political economy akin to that of mid-Victorian Britain. Through following policies designed to turn back the clock by over a century the Conservatives hoped to recreate the conditions which they believed had once allowed Britain to become the world's most successful industrial nation; what had worked in the past should be no less effective in the present.

Many voters were prepared to support a party which was determined to turn this liberal dream into a reality. As in the early 1920s and to a lesser extent in the 1950s the effect of inflation had been counterrevolutionary. The balance of social forces had swung to the right, and the Conservatives were able to recruit behind them a coalition of different groups all prepared to make the reduction of unemployment a poor second to the conquest of inflation. Throughout the campaign, opinion polls revealed greater public concern about rising prices than about joblessness. In part this was obviously because everyone was affected by inflation, whereas only 5.5 per cent of the working population was unemployed. Yet while all suffer from rising prices some groups are more disadvantaged by inflation than others. Particularly threatened are those with savings, and during the 1970s the percentage of real disposable personal income taken by savings steadily increased, from 9.3 per cent (1970–2) to 14.7 per cent (1979). At the same time personal savings as a proportion of all savings increased from an average level of 27.7 per cent (1970–2) to one of 53.4 per cent (1978–80; Pollard, 1983, p. 383).

Consumers and those with savings were not alone in having a vested interest in the crusade against inflation. Their priorities were shared by employers and managers seeking to cut costs and reduce the strength of organized labour. A government which was prepared to tolerate mass unemployment and legislate against the unions was a potent ally in the struggle to assert managerial authority in the work-place. Thatcher's prospectus seemed to many who worked in private industry the last hope of destroying the threat to free enterprise presented by the combination of an overblown state and militant workers. Monetarism provided a solution to all the problems of the last fifteen years: taxation on profits would fall and the terms of borrowing in the financial markets would improve as the government's requirement was reduced. The likelihood of sluggish, or even low demand in the economy was a reasonable price to pay for victory over labour in the latest bout of overt class conflict. By supporting the Conservatives it would be possible to elect a government dedicated not merely to managing but to resolving Britain's politico-economic crisis in the interests of the owners of capital.

Despite the emollience of James Prior as Conservative spokesman on employment there can be little doubt that the broad thrust of the manifesto was hostile to organized labour. Nevertheless, many working-class voters were attracted by the promise of tax cuts and by pledges to restore free collective bargaining. On polling day the national swing to the Conservatives was 5.2 per cent. The pro-Conservative swing among trade unionists and unskilled workers, at 7 per cent and 6.5 per cent respectively, exceeded this figure. On the whole, working-class support for Mrs Thatcher was strongest in the affluent south of the country, while the Labour vote held up well in Scotland, northern England and Wales, areas which were feeling the full impact of manufacturing decline and in consequence experiencing levels of unemployment in excess of the national average.

The popular basis of Conservative support therefore rested on the 'haves', composed of affluent workers, middle-class consumers, managers, businessmen and people with savings, rather than the 'have-nots'. This was hardly surprising, because it was precisely these more prosperous members of society who stood to lose most from inflation and gain from policies designed to roll back the state, cut taxes and reduce the power of the trade unions. In 1975 and 1976 the Treasury, the City and the Bank of England had succeeded, with the help of the IMF, in forcing Labour to pursue sound money and liberal external policies rather than embrace *dirigiste* strategies to reverse Britain's industrial decline. With the election of the Conservatives in 1979 the priorities of the financial establishment were endorsed by a popular coalition whose anxieties about the frustrations with the *status quo* were skilfully articulated in the Poujadist rhetoric of Mrs Thatcher.

Thatcherism: *Cui Bono*?

The incoming Conservative government lost no time in the pursuit of its liberal economic experiment. It immediately introduced tax cuts for the well off, counterbalanced by an increase in VAT to 15 per cent to prevent an increase in the government's borrowing requirement. Perversely, this move had the effect of increasing inflationary pressures but it was justified by reference to the need to encourage people to save money rather than spend it. At the same time the shift towards a fiscal policy which would inevitably enhance inequalities in wealth was in line with Conservative commitments to reward those who were already successful.

The rise in VAT notwithstanding, the aim of the government was of course to eliminate inflation from the economy. To the Conservatives this implied pruning back the activities of the state and they introduced a programme of cuts in public spending, falling mostly on investment, in their first budget. More reductions, worth £3.5 billion, were announced in November 1979, with monies to be raised for the Treasury by the sale of state assets worth £1.5 billion. The new Chancellor, Sir Geoffrey Howe, made it clear that the intention was to bring down the level of public expenditure by 5.5 per cent between 1980 and 1984, and early in 1980 unveiled the Medium Term Financial Strategy (MTFS), designed to lower the proportion of the GDP taken by the PSBR from 4.8 per cent in 1979–80 to 1.5 per cent in 1984–5. The depth of the commitment to the counter-inflation policy was meanwhile signalled by successive increases in interest rates, which stood at 17 per cent by the end of 1979. The tight monetary policy was maintained throughout 1980, and it attracted a steady flow of foreign funds to London, pushing up the value of sterling until it stood at $2.42 to the pound by February 1981. The government welcomed the favourable shift in terms of trade, believing that falling import costs would work along with the MTFS to reduce inflationary pressures in the economy.

Inflation did indeed fall, to 5 per cent by early 1983, but at the cost of the most spectacular slump in the British economy since the Great Depression. The world economy was in recession, and low levels of demand internationally were bound to make the going tough for British manufacturers in search of export markets. To this deflationary pressure was now added a devastating combination of restrictions in government spending, high interest rates and a high exchange rate. The problems created for industry by domestic contraction were magnified by the rise in sterling, as British products were forced to compete on disadvantageous terms at home and abroad with foreign goods. The 'real' exchange rate, reflecting the explosion in wage costs following the demise of Labour's incomes policy, exceeded its 1976 value by 50 per cent and even surpassed its 1972 value by 30 per cent in February 1981.[1] Between 1980 and 1981 the government piled on the agony in the effort to meet its PSBR targets. As spending on unemployment benefit and social security payments rose and tax revenues fell because of mounting joblessness (the level increased from 1.3 million in 1979 to 3.2 million by the end of 1982),[2] public investment programmes were ruthlessly pruned. In 1979 the government's contribution to gross fixed capital formation accounted for 2.1 per cent of GNP, with investment by public corporations taking up 2.3 per cent. By 1981 these shares had dropped to 1.3 per cent and 2.2 per cent respectively, falling in constant money terms from £6,850 million to £4,350 million (Pollard, 1984, p. 167).

Far from creating room for the expansion of private enterprise the cutbacks in government activity merely helped to guarantee a collapse in demand and hence in investment and output. In the words of one critic, 'From the point of view of the British economy as a whole the package was about as subtle in conception, and salutary in effect, as if one had driven a bulldozer into a symphony orchestra' (Jay, 1985, p. 166). Gross fixed capital formation on the part of the private sector, measured in 1980 prices, slumped from £30,579 million in 1979 to £27,567 million in 1981. True, the share of the GNP taken by private gross fixed capital formation only fell slightly, from 12.9 per cent to 12.1 per cent, between 1979 and 1981. This was, however, deceptive because the GNP itself fell by 4 per cent over these two years. Meanwhile industrial production, which had stood at a level of 113.1 in 1979 (1975 = 100), fell to 100 in 1982 and over the same period of time manufacturing output plummeted by 15 per cent. Abysmal as this record undoubtedly is it would have been even worse but for oil and gas production, since, if those industries are excluded, Britain had not even returned to the level of industrial production achieved in 1973 by 1982. Unemployment apart, the only measure of economic activity which rose dramatically in the early 1980s was the level of company liquidations, rocketing from 6,890 in 1980 to an annual rate of 13,000 in 1983 (ibid., p. 167).

After 1982 some of the details of government policy were modified. Hire purchase controls were abandoned and a consumer boom, to be enjoyed by the 87 per cent of the working population in employment, was encouraged. Howe and his successor after the 1983 general election, Nigel Lawson, attempted to find room for tax cuts without expanding the PSBR by selling more state assets to the public. The exchange rate was allowed to float down, although determination to keep inflation low prevented it from falling as far as it should have if it was to be an accurate register of Britain's international competitiveness. In consequence interest rates remained high and in 1985–6 the real exchange rate was still no lower than it had been in 1976. The fundamental thrust of economic management was therefore unaltered: there was no state-led reflation, and the government pointed to improvements in productivity and the resumption of growth as evidence that its *laissez-faire* policy had been successful in encouraging greater efficiency throughout industry and in leading to the expansion of the tertiary sector. The balance of payments enjoyed a healthy surplus (£6.2 billion in 1981, £4.3 billion in 1982 and £2.1 billion in 1983, at 1980 prices).[3] With the rate of inflation falling at the same time the Conservatives claimed that recovery was now at hand.

Growth did occur, partly on the basis of revenues from North Sea oil, partly because the world recession came to an end for a time, and partly because of the consumer boom whose effects were felt most strongly in the south-east. Borrowing was encouraged by banks seeking to take advantage of the lenders' market created by high interest rates, and the consequent availability of credit stimulated personal consumption. This in turn led to expansion in the retail and distributive sectors, marketing goods demanded by the affluent such as houses, cars, electronic equipment, food and furniture. The volume of sales in the retail trade by 1984 stood at 110.7 (1980 = 100), with its largest annual jump taking place in 1982–3 when it rose from 102.2 to 107.1. In the catering sector alone the number of businesses rose from 109,471 in 1980 to 114,563 in 1983, an increase of 5,092.

Given low inflation and a broken trade union movement this was a record appealing to the electoral coalition which had voted Mrs Thatcher into power in 1979. The ability of the Conservatives to depict themselves as the party which had reversed economic decline and put Britain back on the road to greatness was enhanced by the victory in the Falklands conflict of 1982. The 1983 general election was therefore a mere formality for the government, with triumph made particularly easy by the condition of the Labour Party, enfeebled after four years of infighting and a series of defections to the new Social Democratic Party. Opposition commitments to expansion and to the reduction of unemployment proved less persuasive than Tory pledges to control inflation, particularly in the densely populated south of England, where Labour was for the time being at any rate eliminated as a political force. Although the Conservative vote fell back slightly from its 1979 level the split in the opposition combined with the eccentricities of the electoral system to provide the Tories with a massive parliamentary return of 397 seats, compared with 209 for Labour and 23 for the Liberal–Social Democratic Alliance. Labour was driven back into the inner cities and to the declining industrial regions of Scotland and northern England while the Conservatives' success in the shires and the suburbs was not just a testimony to their popularity among the middle class but revealed their increasing identification with the service sector of the economy.

The 1983 general election result therefore turned to a large extent on the skill of the Tories in cultivating support among sections of the community unaffected by industrial decline. It also followed from their ability to mask its effects. For those at work the early and mid 1980s were years of great prosperity: tax concessions after 1979 had left company directors, senior managers, middle managers and even skilled manual workers better off, by 43.0 per cent, 19.0 per cent, 7.5 per cent and 3.1 per cent respectively, than they would have been had their taxes and duties risen in line with inflation (Leys, 1985, p. 10). The fact that so many people experienced rising living standards appeared to make nonsense of warnings about impending disaster offered by economic forecasters such as the Cambridge Economic Policy Group.

Yet industrial decline was no illusion. Productivity improvements were a function of mass unemployment rather than of higher investment. Indeed, in June 1986 the level of investment in manufacturing industry was still over 17 per cent below what it had been when the Conservatives came to power in May 1979. Between 1978 and 1984 manufacturing output fell by 8 per cent, though the output of services rose by 10 per cent. The share of the GDP taken by manufacturing output, standing at 28 per cent in 1972, had fallen by 1984 to 21 per cent, with the trend still pointing downwards. While it is true that manufacturing has declined as a proportion of GDP throughout the advanced industrial world, in no country except Britain has it fallen in absolute terms. The government has argued that this development is merely characteristic of the transition, bound to occur in every advanced society, from an economy founded on manufacturing to one based more on services. Yet the British people have generally devoted about 37 per cent of all domestic spending to manufactured goods since the early 1960s. It cannot therefore be maintained that what has befallen British manufacturing in the recent past is 'natural'. The absolute contraction has happened not in fulfilment of some economic law but because for a long time now imports of manufactures have risen relative to exports. By the mid 1980s Britain's share of world trade in manufactured goods was not much more than 7 per cent. The proportion of domestic spending on manufactures taken by imports has meanwhile doubled, rising from 25 per cent in 1975 to about 50 per cent ten years later. Hardly surprising, then, that Britain actually ran a manufacturing trade deficit in 1983 for the first time since the industrial revolution and has continued to do so ever since. The 1985 deficit was £3 billion. Only an oil surplus of £8 billion kept the external balance in surplus and allowed the country to finance the imports of food and raw materials which sustained living standards.

The fundamental problem facing British manufacturers has been lack of competitiveness. Conservative policies after 1979 in fact made this much worse, with investment collapsing in the wake of deflation and the crippling exchange rate. The lack of investment meant an ageing stock of capital, which in turn weakened competitiveness even more, leading to further erosions of market shares at home and abroad. Far from modernizing British industry the Conservatives drove it down into a vicious circle of low investment and low growth. At no stage has the government seriously attempted to break out of this circle. The macro-economic climate remains uncongenial for manufacturing. A review published by the National Institute for Economic and Social Research in August 1986 reported rising spare capacity in the economy in the first half of 1986 and forecast an increase of just 1.7 per cent in the gross domestic product of the non-oil economy for 1986 as a whole.[4] The consistent failure of industry to achieve a sustained revival reflected low levels of spending not just on plant, buildings and machinery but on research and development, which fell as a proportion of GDP from 2.34 per cent to 2.19 per cent between 1981 and 1983 (Smith, 1986, p. 247). Here again the government set the pace by expenditure cuts, stretching all the way to industrial training and education. In consequence the British economy failed to show the rate of innovation which characterized its rivals, and, incredibly at a time of mass unemployment, a shortage of skilled labour began to develop.

The industries worst hit by the poor level of technological innovation were those Britain could least afford to lose. They tended to be the advanced, capital-intensive sectors such as electrical and electronic engineering, vehicle production and metal manufacturing, rather than the more mature industries such as timber, clay, glass, rubber and leather (see Table 7.1). This was a profoundly disturbing trend since, throughout the century, international demand has grown more rapidly for advanced than for mature products, which have tended to become areas of specialization for the less developed countries. Deindustrialization therefore implied relegation to the status of a developing society dependent on imports of sophisticated manufactured goods from advanced industrial nations. By the middle of the 1980s Britain was moving rapidly towards this state of affairs, sustaining growing deficits in particular with West Germany, Japan and Italy (House of Lords, 1985, pp. 16–21).

Some manufacturers did complain bitterly about the Thatcher government's attitude to industry. In 1980 Sir Terence Beckett, director general of the CBI, threatened a 'bare-knuckle fight' with

Table 7.1 Crude Balance of Trade in Selected Industries (Overseas Trade Statistics basis, summary by class)

		Exports minus imports (£ million)			Change in balance
		1978	1983	1984	1978–84
Class 32	Mechanical engineering	2,345	1,934	1,965	–380
Class 33	Office machinery and data processing equipment	–213	–947	–1,050	–837
Class 34	Electrical and electronic engineering	697	–1,036	–1,398	–2,095
Class 35	Motor vehicles and their parts	334	–2,535	–2,502	–2,836

Source: House of Lords, 1985, Table 2.1, p. 17.

the government over the interest and exchange rates. In 1985 John Harvey-Jones and Lord Weinstock, the chairmen respectively of ICI and GEC, attacked the government for its seeming lack of concern about deindustrialization.[5]

Yet these protests have either been muffled or ignored. Beckett's 'bare-knuckle fight' never materialized because he failed to swing the CBI behind him. Only after 1983 did the CBI seriously begin to criticize government policy. Superficially this is curious, given that the organization is dominated numerically and financially by industrial firms, supplying 70.1 per cent of the subscription income in 1981, and that anxieties about the extent of trade union power had been removed. It should, however, be remembered that 30 per cent of the CBI's funds are provided by non-industrial firms, including companies involved in the distribution of imports and banks eager to expand their overseas operations, all of whom gained as a result of the high exchange rate. Manufacturers catering for the export market were not able to dominate the CBI and transform it into the industrial pressure group it had once seemed likely to become. Instead the CBI was a microcosm of the economy itself, characterized by an increasingly powerful community of firms in the commercial, retailing and distributive sectors. Not until these businesses became alarmed about the state of the infrastructure on which they, like manufacturers, depended did attitudes begin to change.

Unsurprisingly the government was not shaken by Beckett's anger. Throughout its first term it adhered to the market strategy, refusing to return to tripartite consultation, reducing support for industry (though assistance continued for British Leyland, British Steel, the railways and the National Coal Board at the cost of fairly drastic truncation), and replacing the NEB with the shadowy and ineffective British Technology Group. Inmos, which could have pioneered the expansion of the high technology sector, was sold to the electronics corporation Thorn-EMI. Closures, bankruptcies and unemployment were all justified as the price Britain had to pay for the purge, without which the economy would never become internationally competitive, of inefficient and overmanned plant.

The exposure of the economy to the free play of market forces was intensified by its growing external orientation. The key moment came in October 1979 when all remaining exchange controls were abolished. The move gave financial institutions and multinational corporations the freedom to export capital to any part of the world and was clearly consistent with the liberal ideology which informed the government's whole approach to economic policy. Defending the decision against criticisms that it would encourage an outflow of investment at a time when British industry needed more funds, government spokesmen argued that it would help exporters by restraining the rise in the exchange rate caused by oil's contribution to the growing balance of payments surplus. This was entirely bogus: high interest rates, not oil revenues, pushed up the pound after 1979 and the exodus of capital which followed the removal of controls did nothing to restrain sterling's rise. Other justifications included the claims that the decision would allow Britain to acquire a cushion of invisible earnings to protect the external balance when the oil ran out, and that as in the late nineteenth century trade would follow in the wake of overseas investment. Above all, however, the abandonment of controls was a symbol of the government's conviction that given the rejection of *dirigisme* only the full integration of the British into the international economy would lead to the degree of restructuring which would make the country competitive.

The decision was therefore the logical outcome of the trend towards the internationalization of the economy over the previous thirty years. In consequence it squared with the long-term interests of the financial establishment which had welcomed the arrival of Mrs Thatcher's monetarist regime. Reactions in the City and the Bank of England were entirely favourable. With investors now able to accumulate assets overseas without hindrance the City's position as the world's most open financial market was guaranteed, and this was bound to attract international business to London. At the same time City institutions now had the opportunity to make billions of extra pounds each year by expanding the range of their overseas activities. This prospect was particularly welcome to pension funds and insurance companies, prominent in the lobby for the abolition of exchange controls. The assets at the disposal of these institutions had mushroomed since the late 1950s, those held by insurance companies rising from £4.9 billion in 1957 to £52.2 billion in 1979. Over the same period pension fund assets grew from £2.1 billion to £41.8 billion (Coakley and Harris, 1983, Table 5.1, p. 96). So great an accumulation of wealth inevitably amplified voices calling for freedom to export capital since the returns from investment in flourishing overseas companies could only increase the wealth of the institutions. Banks interested in overseas expansion and multinational corporations, by their very nature committed to direct investment abroad, also took part in the favourable reception accorded to liberalization.

The effect of abolition was dramatic. While the British economy slumped and investment in domestic manufacturing industry collapsed, capital flooded out of the country. Net overseas investment rose from £2,726 million in 1978 to £7,281 million in 1981. In 1985, the figure exceeded £14,000 million and Britain briefly became the world's largest creditor nation. The outflow coincided with London's increasing monopoly of the Eurodollar market, swollen as a result of the surpluses earned by the oil-producing states during the period from 1974 to 1982. Over these years 45 per cent of the new-found wealth was deposited in banks in London; in 1981 all of it was. Taken together the expansion of overseas investment and the growing volume of foreign currency business transacted in London were testimony to the City's increasing detachment from the fate of the productive economy in Britain. It did indeed take on the form of an offshore island, handling vast amounts of money (£1 trillion in 1985) as industry declined (Anderson, 1987, p. 69).

Prosperity in the City of London reinforced the growth of the service sector in south-east England. Demand for solicitors, accountants, estate agents, private education and private medical treatment followed from the fortunes which could be made out of a career in finance. For the old London proletariat employment opportunities were increasingly narrowed to meeting the needs of bankers and the affluent new professional class. This meant jobs in trading, domestic service and in the manufacture of luxury items such as clothes, cutlery or furniture.[6] There were distinct parallels with the economy and society of late Victorian and Edwardian Britain. The turn of the century, like the 1980s, had seen great prosperity for the City, for overseas investors and for the service sector while industry stagnated. The major difference was that in the 1980s manufacturing industry underwent absolute contraction while in the early years of the century the export trades at least had flourished. Regional disparities between the green and affluent south and a poorer industrial north were exaggerated by the disappearance of manufacturing not just from large parts of Scotland and northern England but from the areas of postwar growth such as the West Midlands.[7]

The pursuit of the *laissez-faire* policies catering for a coalition of non-producers, including financiers, *rentiers*, employers in the service sector and middle-class consumers, was catastrophic for manufacturing industry even as it modernized British commercial capitalism, historically characterized by a vigorous entrepreneurial ethos. Speaking to the Institute of Bankers in 1900 the (then) staunch apostle of free-trade imperialism, Halford Mackinder, had looked ahead to a period when 'the financial importance of the City of London may continue to increase, while the industry, at any rate of Britain, becomes relatively less' (quoted in Semmel, 1960, p. 169). Thatcherite policies have brought this time ever closer. The government has largely accepted the onset of dereliction over large parts of the country as the verdict of the market. True to its liberal views it has offered no serious industrial policy apart from the encouragement of inward investment by multinational corporations centred in Japan, West Germany and the United States. Its main initiative has been to encourage the service sector, notably tourism, a departure made possible not just by Britain's comparative advantage in historic buildings and pleasant countryside but also by industrial decrepitude. Rather than invest in new plant and machinery it has sought to transform areas once distinguished by manufacturing such as the Black Country into museums, as if Britain now has no products left to sell except its past. And, given the vagaries of the British climate and a road and rail network deteriorating after years of neglect, problems exist even with the attempt to market failure.

Alternative Strategies

Mrs Thatcher's claim that 'there is no alternative' to her government's policy has been challenged. Throughout her years in office economists, politicians, trade unionists and, latterly, some industrialists have argued for a different approach. Overall they have held in common a commitment to the Keynesian view that the aim of economic policy should be the fullest possible employment of resources.

Dissenters within the world of professional economists can very broadly be categorized into two groups, namely orthodox and radical Keynesians. The orthodox Keynesians have generally been based in the National Institute for Economic and Social Research and in the 'Clare Group', chaired by Professor R. C. O. Matthews, Master of Clare College, Cambridge. It would nevertheless be fair to say that the views expressed by these two bodies reflect those of many academic economists. In March 1981 a call for economic expansion made by Sir Bryan Hopkin, chief economic adviser to the Treasury from 1974 to 1977, Professor Marcus Miller of Warwick University and Professor Reddaway from Cambridge University was supported by 360 academic economists.[8]

The orthodox Keynesians, working mostly from National Institute surveys and forecasts, argued that the government's policy was pricing British goods out of world markets and causing a recession at home. By December 1981 they were pressing for a package of measures which would expand the economy by £6,800 million. In particular they called for a reduction in the exchange rate, a cut in VAT and the abolition of the National Insurance surcharge. These steps were to be taken in conjunction with a £600 million increase in public spending, split equally between investment in nationalized industries and current spending, mainly on education. The programme was to be sustained by an incomes policy which would contain its inflationary results, co-ordinated international expansion so that the circumstances of 1974–5 would not be repeated, and foreign borrowing to head off a short-term balance of payments crisis. Subsequently the fundamentals of this strategy have remained unaltered, even though the extent of the reflation demanded may have changed.

Government ministers have never taken this programme seriously. They have argued that it would be impossible to control its inflationary results, partly because incomes policies always collapse (although wages are not supposed to cause inflation according to monetarist orthodoxy) and partly because there was no guarantee that industry would respond to higher demand. Rather, in the absence of low inflation and supply-side measures to improve industrial competitiveness, the likelihood was that economic expansion would lead to higher prices and a boom in imports. The strategy was a recipe for returning to the bad old days of 'Stop–Go'.

Radical Keynesian strategies were in general advanced by the Cambridge Economic Policy Group (CEPG), directed by Professor Wynne Godley. The CEPG based their arguments on an annual *Economic Policy Review* of developments within the British economy. Each review contained a forecast based on projections of current trends and every year the forecast became more bleak. Indeed, the CEPG had no rivals in the field of making apocalyptic pronouncements until its *Reviews* were discontinued following a cut in government financial support in 1982. Controversial though the CEPG predictions may have been, however, there can be no doubt that they were more accurate than those of any comparable group of economists. The fall in output, the collapse of investment, the growth of import penetration and the remorseless increase in unemployment all occurred broadly in line with CEPG expectations, which if anything underestimated the extent of the economic collapse of 1979–81.

The CEPG forecasts were, like those of the National Institute, based on a Keynesian model of the economy. They were different, however, in that the Cambridge model had built into it a series of assumptions founded on the performance of the British economy going back to the 1960s. In 1982 the CEPG argued (in its *Economic Policy Review* focusing on Britain):

> that over the long term British industry has suffered a

> cumulative decline in international competitiveness, manifest in falling shares of overseas markets and increasing import penetration, which is both the consequence and the cause of an unfavourable macroeconomic environment, characterised by slow growth, low profits and insufficient job opportunities. (p. 18)

A deteriorating external balance followed from declining competitiveness and, given an open economy, could only be kept under control by deflation. This had been at its most intense in postwar history after 1979 and the result had been to reinforce the downward spiral into which Britain had become locked.

The CEPG therefore agreed with the National Institute and the Clare Group: the key to improving competitiveness was expansion, leading to a rise in productivity. But the CEPG did not believe that the sustained expansion necessary to the modernization of British industry would follow from the recommendations of the orthodox Keynesians. Given the lost capacity which had resulted from government policy a reflation necessary to halt increases in unemployment would generate a massive balance of payments deficit. While it was of course true that devaluation would reduce the volume of imports, the likelihood was that to be an effective instrument of recovery it would have to be of the order of about 15 per cent each year from 1982 to 1985.[9] In consequence the rate of inflation would shoot up to over 20 per cent and in the absence of exchange controls capital would flood out of the country. This meant that an orthodox reflation would at some point self-destruct, with the presiding government forced back into contractionist measures in order either to control the external balance or to reduce inflationary pressures, since experience suggested that no incomes policy would hold if prices were allowed to race ahead of wages. The inescapable conclusion was that sustained expansion was impossible in the absence of exchange and import controls to protect the level of domestic activity. Departure from liberal practice did not cause undue anxiety to the CEPG in view of the results of adhering to it, and the imposition of tariffs round the economy was consistently recommended. In 1982 the CEPG suggested a regime whereby tariffs averaging 15 per cent were placed on imports of manufactures and services, rising to 20 per cent in the second year and 24 per cent in the third year.

The strategy of protection and expansion was of course never applied. It flew in the face of the interests and prejudices of the financial establishment and its propagandists in the newspapers. It represented a fundamental challenge to Britain's international economic orientation and was treated with contempt by the City, the government and multinational enterprise. The public debate on the CEPG proposals was of a laughably poor quality, with opponents of protectionism resorting to wild allegations ('a policy for starting to push Britons down to an Indian standard of living'; *The Economist*, 18 April 1980), preposterous analogies (imposing import controls 'will be like the man who has failed to hold down a succession of jobs and finally, in desperation, turns to the bottle'; a Trade Policy Research Centre report of November 1980), and personal abuse (the CEPG wanted to turn Britain into an East European-style society – *passim*). The Cambridge alternative was to a large extent taken up by the Labour Party and put to the electorate in 1983, but its impact was slight because of the political turmoil and confusion which surrounded it.

By 1985–6, however, there was some evidence that CEPG arguments about the state of the British economy were striking home. This was because public opinion was turning against the government and becoming more receptive to productionist strategies. The changing tide resulted to no small degree from growing popular anxiety about deteriorating public services, with the Conservatives finding themselves particularly vulnerable to charges of neglecting education and the health service. There was in addition concern about the persistence of mass unemployment, officially given as 3.25 million by the summer of 1986 with the trend rising, and the fear of inflation began to recede. The CBI started to call for more investment in the collapsing infrastructure and leading industrialists began to complain strongly about the government's neglect of manufacturing industry and its faith in the service sector.

The growing desperation of industry was powerfully articulated in the *Report of the Select Committee on Overseas Trade*. The committee had been established by the House of Lords in July 1984, with the task of investigating the causes of Britain's deficit in manufactured goods and of making recommendations. Its findings were published in July 1985. The *Report* chronicled British deindustrialization and suggested a range of measures to reverse it. These included the provision of generous export credits, lower taxes on company profits, lower rates for industry, 100 per cent investment allowances, a mechanism to provide cheap long-term finance for industry, lower interest and exchange rates, and higher public spending on training and research and development. It was pointed out that the expansion of services could never compensate for manufacturing decline because economic growth rests primarily on the health of the manufacturing sector.

This assertion derived from the fact that even in the mid 1980s over 20 per cent of the GDP is dependent upon manufacturing, whose exports account for 40 per cent of the country's overseas earnings. A fall of 1 per cent in exports of manufactured goods can be completely offset by nothing less than a 3 per cent rise in exports of services, but service industries, unlike manufacturing, do not produce goods which are tradeable in every part of the world (House of Lords, 1985, p. 42). At the same time many service industries themselves will be unable to survive the collapse of domestic manufacturing because 20 per cent of all service sector output has manufacturing industry as its customer. Tourism, of course, is an exception to this rule but it will never generate enough income to make up for the loss of manufacturing – not even if the entire country is transformed into a giant museum and leisure park. The basic argument was made to the committee by Lord Weinstock:

> what will the service industries be servicing when there is no hardware, when no wealth is actually being produced. We will be servicing, presumably, the production of wealth by others. We will supply the Changing of the Guard, we will supply the Beefeaters around the Tower of London. We will become a curiosity. I do not think that is what Britain is about; I think that is rubbish. (ibid., pp. 42–3)

In March 1986 the point was made that growth rates of between 3.0 and 3.5 per cent per annum have generally been necessary to stop unemployment from rising (Coutts *et al.*, 1986, pp. 14–19). If deindustrialization continues there can be no prospect of achieving even this modest objective because of the relationship between manufacturing and growth. Meanwhile the deterioration of the deficit in manufactured trade at the current rate, combined with the diminution of oil revenues over the next few years, is likely to leave Britain in the red to the tune of £20 billion by 1995 (1985 prices). Such a scenario assumes a growth rate of 2.5 per cent each year in non-oil output. If the government deflated the economy so that output rose by only 1.5 per cent per annum then it might be possible to keep the current account in balance. But the cost of this would be a level of unemployment over 4 million by 1995 even on present measurement techniques. In the absence of industrial modernization Britain faces a choice of futures, in the medium term at least: growing external indebtedness or continually rising unemployment and disintegrating public services.

If Britain is to avert this choice it needs a coherent industrial strategy. Such a strategy might take the form of a programme to stimulate production modelled on the Japanese postwar experience, where industrial policy is guided by the state and investment is co-ordinated by the government-owned Japan Development Bank. Public investment to stimulate output in the private sector and a British version of the Ministry of Trade and Industry (MITI) would be essential.

MITI has been crucial to the Japanese economic miracle and the establishment of an analogous agency in Britain would offer real hope of a manufacturing revival, not least because it would imply a serious attempt to end the external economic orientation of the state. What Joseph Chamberlain regarded as the 'outworn shibboleths' of free trade have never been respected in Japan. There MITI has worked continuously to build up industries in which the country had no particular comparative advantage. Since its formation MITI's objective has been the promotion of economic growth 'of a type which will also generate a substantial balance of trade surplus in manufactures' (Smith, 1986, p. 223), and in this it has succeeded triumphantly. It has encouraged steel, petrochemicals, vehicles, aircraft, industrial machinery and electronics. To this end MITI has controlled the import and use of foreign goods and technology, rationed the availability of foreign exchange to domestic firms, allocated financial assistance and subsidized, or sometimes even itself conducted, research and development programmes. Its existence has ensured a far closer co-ordination between investment, industrial development and foreign trade than has existed in Britain at any time since 1951. Just as Britain's refusal to return immediately to economic liberalism stimulated reconstruction after 1945, so Japan's repudiation of *laissez-faire* has helped it to become the world's industrial superpower. Modernization has gone hand in hand with the protection and expansion of the domestic economy.

A British government committed to similar policies would inevitably face a hard political battle with a financial establishment which now wields more power than at any time since the last war. It would need to recruit behind it a coalition of producers as popular, wide-ranging and powerful as those of 1944–5 and 1964–6. Even with this support the implementation of such a strategy would be fraught with problems, the most serious of which would be the likelihood of a capital outflow unless steps were taken to halt both the exodus of money across the foreign exchanges and the export of investment. Furthermore there is no guarantee that a Japanese-style strategy would succeed; certainly it could not in the absence of consensus between government, industry and the unions on the relationship between output, incomes, prices and dividends. But concordats at national level may require strengthening by improved industrial relations[10] if a future producers' alliance is not to collapse into overt class conflict. Clearly, sustained expansion is essential, given that the inevitable arguments between employers and workers about wage levels, conditions of employment and company policy are much more easily resolved at a growth rate of 5 per cent per annum than at one of 1 or 2 per cent. But a modernizing administration might wish to reinforce the healing effects of expansion with measures which institutionalize co-operation between management and labour at company level. A good start would be the introduction of industrial democracy, as part of an effort to remove the legacy of fear and distrust felt by each side of industry for the other after the confrontation of the 1970s. There is of course no need to emulate the specific Japanese model of company unions. What is certain, however, is that without something akin to the Japanese approach to economic policy, deindustrialization will continue.

Such a prospect is alarming. At the turn of the century Joseph Chamberlain and the radical Liberal J. A. Hobson looked ahead to the kind of society they believed Britain would become in the absence of a strategy to 'put domestic industry, rather than overseas economic interests, at the forefront of policy' (Cain, 1985, p. 20). They envisaged a future in which a parasitic community of financiers and *rentiers* lived off overseas earnings, employing 'great tame masses of retainers' in badly paid and poorly organized service trades, while millions existed without work and in poverty (ibid., pp. 1–27). Now, the need for an industrial strategy is far more urgent. In the absence of measures to reverse the trend to deindustrialization the frightening vision of Chamberlain and Hobson is increasingly likely to become the reality of life in modern Britain.

Notes: Chapter 7

1 See Keegan, 1985, p. 38. The 'real' exchange rate amplifies the 'nominal' one quoted in the markets every day by the rise in the price of British exports relative to foreign exports.
2 The real level was nearer 4 million, but this was deliberately concealed from the public by a series of 'adjustments' to the method of calculation, starting in October 1982.
3 Central Statistical Office, *United Kingdom National Accounts, 1985 Edition* (1986), Table 1.5, p. 7.
4 'Forecast for Manufacturing Cut Sharply', *Financial Times*, 21 August 1986.
5 M. Smith, 'Remembering the Election Slogan? Well, Now IT Should Read the Policy Isn't Working', *The Guardian*, 27 April 1985.
6 Neal Ascherson, 'London's New Class: the Great Cash-In', *The Observer*, 25 May 1986.
7 See 'Two-Nation Jobs Shock Revealed', *The Observer*, 4 January 1987.
8 'Economists Call for a £6,800 Million Reflation', *The Guardian*, 7 December 1981.
9 Cambridge Economic Policy Group, *Cambridge Economic Policy Review*, vol. 8, no. 1 (April 1982), p. 23.
10 For a similar view see Hodgson, 1986, pp. 331–2.

References

Contemporary Works Cited in the Text

A Better Way to Better Times: Reprint of a Statement issued by His Majesty's Government on Mr Lloyd George's Proposals (1935), (London: HMSO).

Anon. (1935), *What's Wrong with South Wales?* (London: *New Statesman*).

'Artifex' and 'Opifex' (1907), *The Causes of Decay in a British Industry* (London: Longmans, Green & Co.).

Ashley, W. (1903), *The Tariff Problem* (London: P. S. King & Son).

Ashley, W. (1914), *The War and its Economic Aspects* (Oxford: Oxford University Press).

Bacon, R. and Eltis, W. (1978), *Britain's Economic Problem: Too Few Producers*, 2nd edn (London: Macmillan).

Blackett, Sir Basil (1935), *Economic Developments in Post-War Britain* (London: *Athenaeum*).

Brooks, C. (1931), *This Tariff Question* (London: Edward Arnold).

Byng, G. (1901), *Protection: the Views of a Manufacturer* (London: Eyre & Spottiswoode).

Carter, H. (ed.) (1917), *Industrial Reconstruction: a Symposium on the Situation after the War and how to Meet it* (London: T. Fisher Unwin).

Cambridge Economic Policy Group (1975–82), *Economic Policy Review* (Cambridge: Faculty of Economics).

Cato (Michael Foot, Peter Howard and Frank Owen) (1940), *The Guilty Men* (London: Gollancz).

Coutts, K. J., Godley, W., Rowthorne, R. and Ward, T. S. (1980), 'The British economy: recent history and medium term prospects: a Cambridge bulletin on the Thatcher experiment' (Cambridge: Faculty of Economics).

Crosland, C. A. R. (1961), *The Conservative Enemy* (London: Cape).

Davenport, N. (1964), *The Split Society* (London: Gollancz).

Greenwood, A. (1914), 'Social and economic aspects of the war', in R. W. Seton-Watson, J. D. Wilson, A. E. Zimmern and A. Greenwood, *The War and Democracy* (London: Macmillan).

Hewins, W. A. S. (1929), *Apologia of an Imperialist* (London: Constable).

Hirst, F. W. (1925), *From Adam Smith to Philip Snowden: a History of Free Trade in Great Britain* (London: T. Fisher Unwin).

Hooper, F. (1903), 'The woollen and worsted industries of Yorkshire' in W. Ashley (ed.), *British Industries: a Series of General Reviews for Business Men and Students* (London: Longmans, Green & Co.).
House of Lords (1985), *Report from the Select Committee on Overseas Trade*, vol. 1 (London: HMSO).
Jeans, S. S. (1903), 'The British iron and steel industries: their condition and outlook', in W. Ashley (ed.), *British Industries: a Series of General Reviews for Business Men and Students* (London: Longmans, Green & Co.).
Jenkins, R. (1959), *The Labour Case* (London: Penguin).
Koestler, A. (ed.) (1964), *Suicide of a Nation?* (New York: Macmillan).
Liberal League (1903–5), *The Benefits of Dumping* (London: Liberal League Publications no. 69).
Macmillan, H. (1938), *The Middle Way* (London: Macmillan).
Ministry of Reconstruction (1918), *The Aims of Reconstruction*, Reconstruction Problems series no. 1 (London: HMSO).
Ministry of Reconstruction (1918), *New Fields for British Engineering*, Reconstruction Problems series no. 5 (London: HMSO).
Ministry of Reconstruction (1919), *Industrial Research*, Reconstruction Problems series no. 36 (London: HMSO).
Mond, Sir Alfred (1927), *Industry and Politics* (London: Macmillan).
Mosley, Sir Oswald (1932), *The Greater Britain* (London: BUF).
Next Five Years Group (1936), *A Summary of the Book 'The Next Five Years': An Essay in Political Agreement* (London: Macmillan).
Nossiter, B. (1978), *Britain: A Future that Works* (London: Cape).
Parliamentary Papers (1918), *Final Report of the Committee on Commercial and Industrial Policy after the War* (Cd. 9035).
Priestley, J. B. (1934, 1977), *English Journey* (London: Penguin).
Report on the reconstruction of industry prepared after a series of conferences of Plymouth and Cornish citizens who were also employers and trade unionists (1918), (Plymouth: Devon and Cornwall Association for Industrial and Commercial Reconstruction).
Sanderson Furniss, H. (ed.) (1917), *The Industrial Outlook by Various Writers* (London: Chatto & Windus).
Shadwell, A. (1905), *Industrial Inefficiency: a Comparative Study of Industrial Life in England, Germany and America* (London: Longmans, Green & Co.).
Shanks, M. (1961), *The Stagnant Society* (London: Penguin).
Singh, A. (1978), 'UK industry and the world economy: a case of deindustrialization?' *Economics Reprint* ((University of Cambridge, Department of Applied Economics), no. 25.
Stewart, A. (1916), *British and German Industrial Conditions: a comparison* (London: *Electricity*).
Thomas, H. (ed.) (1959), *The Establishment* (London: Ace Books).
Webb, S. (1901), *Twentieth-Century Britain: A Policy of National Efficiency*, Fabian Tract no. 108 (London: Fabian Society).
Webb, S. and B. (1902), *Problems of Modern Industry*, 2nd edn (London: Longmans, Green & Co.).

Webb, S. and Freeman, A. (1916), *Great Britain after the War* (London: Allen & Unwin).
Wells, H. G. (1916), *What is Coming? A Forecast of Things after the War* (London: Cassell).
Wells, W. A. (1952), *Imperial Preference: a Short Historical Sketch* (London: Empire Industries Association).

Select Bibliography

Addison, P. (1975), *The Road to 1945* (London: Quartet Books).
Aldcroft, D. H. (1968), 'Introduction: British industry and foreign competition 1875–1914', in D. H. Aldcroft (ed.), *The Development of British Industry and Foreign Competition 1875–1914* (London: Allen & Unwin).
Aldcroft, D. H. (1986), *The British Economy: the Years of Turmoil 1920–1951* (Brighton: Harvester).
Alford, B. (1981), 'New industries for old? British industry between the wars', in R. C. Floud and D. McCloskey (eds), *The Economic History of Britain since 1700*, vol. 2 (Cambridge: Cambridge University Press).
Amery, J. (1969), *The Life of Joseph Chamberlain, vols. 5 and 6* (London: Macmillan).
Anderson, P. (1987), 'The figures of descent', *New Left Review*, vol. 161, pp. 20–77.
Barnett, C. (1986), *The Audit of War* (London: Macmillan).
Best, M. H. and Humphries, J. (1986), 'The city and industrial decline', in B. Elbaum and W. Lazonick (eds), *The Decline of the British Economy* (Oxford: Oxford University Press).
Blank, S. (1973), *Industry and Government in Britain: the Federation of British Industries in Politics, 1945–65* (Farnborough: Saxon House).
Blank, S. (1977), 'Britain: the politics of foreign economic policy, the domestic economy and the problem of pluralistic stagnation', *International Organization*, no. 31, pp. 674–721.
Bonham, J. (1954), *The Middle Class Vote* (London: Faber).
Booth, A. and Pack, M. (1985), *Employment, Capital and Economic Policy: Great Britain 1918–1939* (Oxford: Blackwell).
Brittan, S. (1964), *The Treasury Under the Tories 1951–1964*, Chapter 6 (London: Penguin).
Brittan, S. (1971), *Steering the Economy: the role of the Treasury* (London: Secker & Warburg).
Brown, C. J. F. (1980), 'Industrial policy and economic planning in Japan and France', *National Institute Economic Review*, vol. 93, pp. 59–75.
Brown, G. (1971), *In My Way* (London: Gollancz).
Butler, D. and Kavanagh, D. (1984), *The British General Election of 1983* (Oxford: Oxford University Press).
Cain, P. J. (1979), 'Political economy in Edwardian England: the tariff

reform controversy', in A. O. Day (ed.), *The Edwardian Age: Conflict and Stability 1900–1914* (London: Macmillan).
Cain, P. J. (1985), 'J. A. Hobson: financial capitalism and imperialism in late Victorian and Edwardian England', in A. N. Porter and R. F. Holland (eds), *Money, Finance and Empire* (London: Frank Cass).
Cain, P.J. and Hopkins, A. G. (1987), 'Gentlemanly capitalism and British expansion overseas, ii, new imperialism, 1850–1945', *Economic History Review*, 2nd series, vol. 40, no. 1, pp. 1–26.
Cairncross, A. (1985), *Years of Recovery: British Economic Policy 1945–51* (London: Methuen).
Calder, A. (1975), *The People's War* (London: Cape).
Capie, F. (1983), *Depression and Protectionism: Britain Between the Wars* (London: Allen & Unwin).
Carpenter, L. P. (1976), 'Corporatism in Britain 1930–1945', *Journal of Contemporary History*, vol. 11, pp. 3–25.
Central Statistical Office (1986), *United Kingdom National Accounts, 1985 Edition* (London: HMSO).
Cline, P. (1982), 'Winding down the war economy: British plans for peacetime recovery 1916–1919' in K. Burk (ed.), *War and the State: the Transformation of British Government 1914–1919* (London: Allen & Unwin).
Coakley, J. and Harris, L. (1983), *The City of Capital: London's Role as a Financial Centre* (Oxford: Basil Blackwell).
Cronin, J. E. (1984), *Labour and Society in Britain, 1918–1979* (London: Batsford).
Crouzet, F. (1982), *The Victorian Economy* (London: Methuen).
Davenport-Hines, R. P. T. (1984), *Dudley Docker: the Life and Times of a Trade Warrior* (Cambridge: Cambridge University Press).
Dintinfass, M. (1984), 'The politics of producer co-operation: the FBI-TUC-NCED talks 1929–1933', in J. Turner (ed.), *Businessmen and Politics Studies of Business Activity in British Politics, 1900–1945* (London: Heinemann).
Eatwell, J. (1982), *Whatever Happened to Britain* (London: BBC Publications).
Eatwell, R. (1979), *The 1945–51 Labour Governments* (London: Batsford).
Eichengreen, B. J. (1981), *Sterling and the Tariff 1929–1932*, Princeton Studies in International Finance No. 48 (International Finance Section, Department of Economics, Princeton University).
Fay, Stephen and Young, Hugo (1978), *The Day the Pound Nearly Died* (London: *Sunday Times* Publications).
Feinstein, C. H. (1972), *National Income, Expenditure and Output of the United Kingdom, 1855–1965* (Cambridge: Cambridge University Press).
Floud, R. C. and McCloskey, D. (eds) (1981), *The Economic History of Britain since 1700*, Vol. 2 (Cambridge: Cambridge University Press).
Gamble, A. (1985), *Britain in Decline: Economic Policy, Political Strategy and the British State*, 2nd edn (London: Macmillan).
Gilbert, M. (1976), *Winston S. Churchill*, Vol. 5 (London: Macmillan).

Gospel, H. F. (1979), 'Employers' labour policy: a study of the Mond-Turner talks 1927–1933', *Business History*, vol. 21, no. 2, pp. 180–97.

Hall, P. A. (1986), 'The state and economic decline', in B. Elbaum and W. Lazonick (eds), *The Decline of the British Economy* (Oxford: Oxford University Press).

Ham, A. (1981), *Treasury Rules: Recurrent Themes in British Economic Policy* (London: Quartet).

Hancock, W. R. and Gowing, M. M. (1975), *The British War Economy*, rev. edn (London: HMSO).

Hannah, L. (1983), *The Rise of the Corporate Economy*, 2nd edn (London: Methuen).

Hare, P. (1985), *Planning the British Economy* (London: Macmillan).

Hodgson, G. (1986), 'The underlying economic crisis', in D. Coates and J. Hillard (eds), *The Economic Decline of Modern Britain* (London: Wheatsheaf).

Holdsworth, T. (1986), 'Government and industry', *Catalyst*, vol. 2, no. 1, pp. 59–68.

Holland, R. F. (1981), 'The Federation of British Industries and the international economy, 1929–39', *Economic History Review*, 2nd series, vol. 34, no. 2, pp. 287–300.

Holmes, M. (1983), *The Labour Government, 1974–79* (London: Macmillan).

Howson, S. (1975), *Domestic Monetary Management in Britain 1919–1938* (Cambridge: Cambridge University Press).

Hutchinson, Sir Herbert (1965), *Tariff Making and Industrial Reconstruction: an Account of the Work of the Import Duties Advisory Committee 1932–1939* (London: Harrap).

Ingham, G. (1984), *Capitalism Divided? The City and Industry in British Social Development* (London: Macmillan).

Jay, D. (1985), *Sterling: A Plea for Moderation* (London: Sidgwick & Jackson).

Johnson, P. B. (1968), *Land Fit for Heroes: the Planning of British Reconstruction 1916–1919* (Chicago: University of Chicago Press).

Keegan, W. (1984), *Mrs Thatcher's Economic Experiment* (London: Penguin).

Keegan, W. (1985), *Britain Without Oil* (London: Penguin).

Kirby, M. W. (1981), *The Decline of British Economic Power Since 1870* (London: Allen & Unwin).

Kynaston, D. T. A. (1983), 'The London Stock Exchange 1870–1940: an institutional history', unpublished Ph.D thesis, University of London.

Lernez, J. (1975), *Economic Planning and Politics in Britain* (London: Martin Robertson).

Leys, C. (1985), 'Thatcherism and British manufacturing', *New Left Review*, no. 151, pp. 5–25.

Longstreth, F. (1979), 'The city, industry and the state', in C. Crouch (ed.) *State and Economy in Contemporary Capitalism* (London: Croom Helm).

Macmillan, H. (1966), *Winds of Change 1914–1939* (London: Macmillan).

Marrison, A. J. (1983), 'Businessmen, industries and tariff reform in Great Britain 1903–1930', *Business History*, vol. 28, no. 1, pp. 148–78.
Marwick, A. (1965), *The Deluge: British Society and the First World War* (London: Macmillan).
Mathias, P. (1983), *The First Industrial Nation: An Economic History of Britain 1700–1914*, 2nd edn (London: Methuen).
Matthew, H. G. C. (1973), *The Liberal Imperialists: the Ideas and Politics of a Post-Gladstonian Elite* (Oxford: Oxford University Press).
Middlemas, K. (1979), *Politics in Industrial Society: the British Experience since 1911* (London: Deutsch).
Middleton, R. (1985), *Towards the Managed Economy: Keynes, the Treasury and the Fiscal Policy Debate of the 1930s* (London: Methuen).
Miliband, R. (1972), *Parliamentary Socialism: a Study in the Politics of Labour*, 2nd edn (London: Merlin).
Milward, A. S. (1965), *The New Order and the French Economy* (Oxford: Oxford University Press).
Milward, A. S. (1977), *War, Economy and Society, 1939–45* (London: Allen Lane).
Milward, A. S. (1984a), *The Effects of the Two World Wars on Britain*, 2nd edn (London: Macmillan).
Milward, A. S. (1984b), *The Reconstruction of Western Europe 1945–51* (London: Methuen).
Mitchell, J. (1963), *Crisis in Britain 1951* (London: Secker & Warburg).
Moggridge, D. E. (1969), *The Return to Gold 1925: the Formulation of Economic Policy and its Critics* (Cambridge: Cambridge University Press).
Mosley, Sir Oswald (1968), *My Life* (London: Nelson).
Nairn, T. (1973), *The Left Against Europe?* (London: Penguin).
Nairn, T. (1981), *The Break-Up of Britain*, 2nd edn (London: Verso).
Nevin, M. (1983), *The Age of Illusions* (London: Gollancz).
Newman, M. (1983), *Socialism and European Unity: the Dilemma of the Left in Britain and France* (London: Junction Books).
Newton, S. (1982) 'Britain, the dollar shortage, and European integration, 1945–50', unpublished Ph.D thesis, University of Birmingham.
Newton, S. (1984), 'The sterling crisis of 1947 and the British response to the Marshall Plan', *Economic History Review*, vol. 37, no. 3, pp. 391–408.
Newton, S. (1986), 'Operation robot and the political economy of sterling convertibility, 1951–1952', European University Institute Working Paper, no. 86/256.
Nicholson, M. (1981), 'Prologue: the proposal for a national plan', in J. Pinder (ed.), *Fifty Years of Political and Economic Planning: Looking Forward 1931–1981* (London: Heinemann).
Offer, A. (1983), 'Empire and social reform: British overseas investment and domestic politics, 1908–1914', *Historical Journal*, vol. 27, pp. 119–38.
Opie, R. (1972), 'Economic planning and growth', in W. Beckerman (ed.), *The Labour Government's Economic Record 1964–70* (London: Duckworth).

Parsons, D. W. (1986), *The Political Economy of British Regional Policy* (London: Croom Helm).
Peden, G. C. (1985), *British Economic and Social Policy: Lloyd George to Margaret Thatcher* (Oxford: Ian Allan).
Pollard, S. (1970), *The Gold Standard and Employment Policies Between the Wars* (London: Methuen).
Pollard, S. (1983), *The Development of the British Economy 1914–1980*, 3rd edn (London: Edward Arnold).
Pollard, S. (1984), *The Wasting of the British Economy*, 2nd edn (London: Croom Helm).
Pope, R. and Hoyle, B. (eds) (1985), *British Economic Performance 1880–1980* (London: Croom Helm).
Porter, D. (1978), 'Joseph Chamberlain and the origins of the tariff reform movement', *Moirae*, the Journal of the School of Politics, Philosophy and History, Ulster Polytechnic, vol. 3, pp. 1–10.
Rempel, R. (1972), *Unionists Divided: Arthur Balfour, Joseph Chamberlain and the Unionist Free Traders* (Newton Abbot: David & Charles).
Rodgers, T. (1986), 'Sir Allan Smith, the industrial group and the politics of unemployment 1919–1924', *Business History*, vol. 28, no. 1, pp. 100–23.
Rogow, A. A. and Shore, P. (1955), *The Labour Governments and British Industry 1945–51* (Oxford: Basil Blackwell).
Roskill, O. (1981), 'P. E. P. through the 1930s: the industries group', in J. Pinder (ed.), *Fifty Years of Political and Economic Planning: Looking Forward 1931–1981* (London: Heinemann).
Rowthorne, R. (1975), 'Imperialism in the 1970s – unity or rivalry?', in H. Radice (ed.), *International Firms and Modern Imperialism* (London: Penguin).
Saul, S. B. (1965), 'The export economy 1870–1914', *Yorkshire Bulletin of Economic and Social Research*, vol. 17, pp. 5–18.
Sayers, R. S. (1956), *Financial Policy* (London: HMSO).
Scally, R. J. (1975), *The Origins of the Lloyd George Coalition: the Politics of Social Imperialism* (Princeton: Princeton University Press).
Schonfield, A. (1958), *British Economic Policy Since the War* (London: Penguin).
Searle, G. R. (1971), *The Quest for National Efficiency: a Study in British Politics and Political Thought, 1899–1914* (Oxford: Blackwell).
Self, R. C. (1981), 'The Conservative Party and the politics of tariff reform, 1922–1932', unpublished Ph.D thesis, University of London.
Semmel, B. (1960), *Imperialism and Social Reform: English Social Imperial Thought 1895–1914* (London: Allen & Unwin).
Skidelsky, R. (1967), *Politicians and the Slump: the Labour Government of 1929–1931* (London: Macmillan).
Skidelsky, R. (1975), *Oswald Mosley* (London: Macmillan).
Smith, K. (1986), *The British Economic Crisis: its Past and Future*, 2nd edn (London: Penguin).
Stevenson, J. and Cook, C. (1977), *The Slump: Society and Politics During the Depression* (London: Jonathan Cape).

Stewart, M. (1978), *Politics and Economic Policy in the UK Since 1964: the Jekyll and Hyde Years* (Oxford: Pergamon Press).
Sykes, A. (1979), *Tariff Reform in British Politics 1903–1913* (Oxford: Oxford University Press).
Thane, P. (1982), *The Foundations of the Welfare State* (London: Longman).
Tomlinson, J. (1981), *Problems of British Economic Policy 1870–1945* (London: Methuen).
Turner, J. (1984), 'The politics of organized business in the First World War', in J. Turner (ed.), *Businessmen and Politics: Studies of Business Activity in British Politics, 1900–1945* (London: Heinemann).
Warwick, P. (1985) 'Did Britain change? An inquiry into the causes of national decline', *Journal of Contemporary History*, vol. 20, pp. 99–133.
Wiener, M. (1981), *English Culture and the Decline of the Industrial Spirit* (Cambridge: Cambridge University Press).
Williamson, P. (1984), 'A "Bankers' Ramp"? Financiers and the political crisis of August 1931', *English Historical Review*, vol. 99, no. 1, pp. 770–806.
Winch, D. (1983), 'Britain in the Thirties: a managed economy', in C. H. Feinstein (ed.), *The Managed Economy: Essays in British Economic Policy and Performance Since 1929* (Cambridge: Cambridge University Press).
Worswick, G. D. N. and Ady, P. H. (eds) (1952), *The British Economy 1945–1950* (Oxford: Oxford University Press).
Wrigley, C. (1982), 'The Ministry of Munitions: an innovatory department', in K. Burk (ed.), *War and the State: the Transformation of British Government 1914–1919* (London: Allen & Unwin).
Young, G. (1973), *Tourism: Blessing or Blight?* (London: Penguin).

Index

For Product Safety Concerns and Information please contact our
EU representative GPSR@taylorandfrancis.com Taylor & Francis
Verlag GmbH, Kaufingerstraße 24, 80331 München, Germany